HITLER'S ARMIES

OSPREY
PUBLISHING

HITLER'S ARMIES

A HISTORY OF THE GERMAN WAR MACHINE
1939–45

Chris McNab

First published in Great Britain in 2011 by Osprey Publishing,
This edition published in 2015 by Osprey Publishing
PO Box 883, Oxford, OX1 9PL, UK
PO Box 3985, New York, NY 10185-3985, USA

E-mail: info@ospreypublishing.com

OSPREY PUBLISHING IS PART OF BLOOMSBURY

ISBN 978 1 4728 1533 0

Page layout by Myriam Bell Design, France
Index by Sandra Shotter
Typeset in Bembo and Conduit
Originated by Blenheim Colour, UK
Printed in China through Everbest

15 16 17 18 19   10 9 8 7 6 5 4 3 2 1

Osprey Publishing is supporting the Woodland Trust, the UK's leading woodland conservation charity, by funding the dedication of trees.

www.ospreypublishing.com

Front and back cover: Parade of SS formations at the Nuremberg Rally, 1935. (akg-images)

EDITOR'S NOTE: Unless otherwise stated, all the images in this book are courtesy of Cody Images.

In the compilation of this volume we relied on the extensive Osprey library of previous military history publications. Works of particular relevance are listed in the Further Reading section.

The following will help in converting other measurements between metric and imperial:

1 mile = 1.6km
1lb = 0.45kg
1 yard = 0.9m
1ft = 0.3m
1in = 25.4mm
100fps = 30.48m/s

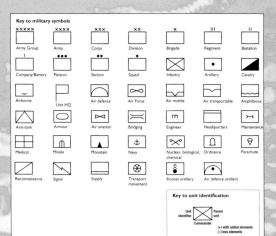

Key to military symbols

Symbol	Name	Symbol	Name	Symbol	Name	Symbol	Name
×××××	Army Group	××××	Army	×××	Corps	××	Division
×	Brigade	|||	Regiment	||	Battalion		
		Company/Battery	•••	Platoon	••	Section	•	Squad
Infantry		Artillery		Cavalry		Airborne	
Unit HQ		Air defence		Air Force		Air mobile		Air transportable		Amphibious
Anti-tank		Armour		Air aviation		Bridging		Engineer		Headquarters		Maintenance
Medical		Missile		Mountain		Navy		Nuclear, biological, chemical		Ordnance		Parachute
Reconnaissance		Signal		Supply		Transport movement		Rocket artillery		Air defence artillery	

Key to unit identification

Unit identifier — Parent unit
Commander
(+) with added elements
(–) less elements

CONTENTS

HITLER'S WEHRMACHT (LITERALLY 'DEFENSIVE POWER') WAS BORN OUT OF THE most unpromising circumstances. When the dust and arguments settled after World War I, the victorious Allies imposed a series of restrictions on Germany in the Treaty of Versailles of June 1919. Among other things, the treaty stated that by 31 March 1920, the German Army was to consist of no more than 100,000 men, of whom just 4,000 were to be officers. The treaty conditions also specified the structure and organization of this army: there were to be 21 three-battalion infantry regiments (with 21 training battalions attached), and each regiment was to have one mortar company. There were to be proportionally larger numbers of cavalry, plus seven artillery regiments of three battalions, and seven field engineer, signals, motorized and medical battalions, a total of seven divisions in all.

The German Army of 34,000 officers and nearly eight million men which had fought from 1914 to 1918 was to be reduced to insignificance, with no hope of operations larger than at corps level and, most importantly from the point of view of the vengeful French, no prospect of cross-border excursions. Furthermore, the Germans were to be prevented from forming reserves, by virtue of the restriction that men had to serve a minimum of 12 years, and officers 25 years before discharge. It was envisaged by the victorious powers that never again would Germany's armed forces be in a strong enough position to threaten the peace of Europe.

The decimation of her armed forces was not the only difficult situation Germany had to contend with. The heartfelt relief at the end of the war was almost universal but political turmoil in the wake of the conflict was keenly felt and particularly in Germany. She had removed its emperor, Kaiser Wilhelm II, at the end of the war and was struggling to find a form of government that had the power and prestige to set Germany on the way to recovery. The nation was both economically and militarily bankrupt. Although American efforts to shore up what was a much-weakened nation helped to some extent, political unrest was to continue in Germany until the mid 1930s.

This political uncertainty was compounded by the fear of her neighbours and former enemies. To the west Germany was bordered by France with an army of one million. To the east was Poland, traditionally regarded as a threat by German minds, especially with its superior force of 30 infantry divisions and ten cavalry brigades. Geographically the Danzig corridor in the east separated East Prussia – still a German territory – from the homeland, and in the Rhineland in the west the victorious Allies had insisted upon permanent demilitarization as well as occupation for 15 years. To add to this and other burdens there was also the matter of hefty reparations payment, a matter upon which the French were vehemently insistent.

On 2 April 1920, General Hans von Seeckt became de facto commander-in-chief of the remnants of the German Army, and was faced with transforming it into the

100,000-man *Reichsheer* (Imperial Army) as specified by the Treaty of Versailles. He held this role until 7 October 1926 and, despite a personal preference for cavalry, he conceived and promulgated a doctrine that was to form the basis of German operational military thought and deed until the end of World War II.

Von Seeckt had served on various staffs during the Great War, ending up as Chief of Staff of III Corps. For five months in 1919 he was Chief of the General Staff and spent much time immediately after the war evaluating operational concepts in which the machine gun, barbed wire, artillery and the tank had dominated. He realized that the *Reichsheer* (German Army) was a spent force that could not fight any future war as it had done the last.

No matter what Von Seeckt's political views were, his actions would affect the military world fundamentally. To avoid the tremendous losses incurred by the return to medieval siege tactics of 1914–18, he realized that military strategy had to be based on mobility. No doubt, like Field Marshal Haig, he had longed to loose the cavalry into the enemy's rear after a breakthrough of the frontline enemy trenches. More perceptively, however, he also saw that such breakthroughs were not easily achieved once the enemy had time to dig in and fortify. He had noted the successes of the *Sturmgruppen* (storm groups) – dedicated assault forces specializing in mobile attacks – who had made such progress in 1918. What he emphasized was that such breakthroughs had to be supplied, and then resupplied with men, weapons, food and all the other prerequisites of warfare if they were to maintain their momentum.

The essence of his teaching was that 'tactics depend upon co-operation between arms' and that the next war would be one of 'manoeuvre'.

Unlike many staff officers, Von Seeckt was well travelled and had been educated at a secondary school in Strasbourg rather than in a military school, which probably endowed him with more flexibility of mind than granted by traditional military studies. His work from 1920 to 1926 resulted in the publication of a pamphlet, *Führung und Gefecht* (Command in Battle), which emphasized the importance of movement in combat. He wanted an army that was only big enough to counter a surprise enemy attack. The real strength of this new army would lie in its mobility, which would be provided by a large contingent of cavalry, physically well-conditioned infantry and a full complement of motorized or mechanized units, machine guns and artillery. Of course, the men of the *Reichswehr* (armed forces) were already battle-hardened, experienced fighters. All he had to do was train them to exploit their mobility.

Von Seeckt's work was of such importance that from 1923 the German Army began to base its training and exercises on his published theories, and although the army had very few men to put on the ground in exercises, the basic elements of his ideas became fundamental to German strategic and tactical thinking. The emphasis was now on rapid

OVERLEAF: Mechanized forces of the German Condor Legion move through Spain during the Spanish Civil War. Germany's involvement in the Spanish conflict gave it a superb opportunity to trial tactics and technologies prior to its invasion of Poland in 1939.

reaction to new events, together with a preparedness for decisive action against the enemy. Exercises and manoeuvres from 1923 to 1926 showed how the concept of this war of movement was also becoming standard thinking in the German Army right down to section level.

Although Von Seeckt had retired by 1933 when Hitler and the *Nationalsozialistische Deutsche Arbeiterpartei* (NSDAP; National Socialist German Workers' Party) came to power, his legacy to the German Army had not been lost. Hitler was elected to the chancellorship on 30 January 1933, under the critical eye of the German president, Paul von Hindenburg. Hitler intended to enlarge the army to further his expansionist aims in Europe, and the army was naturally delighted. Senior officers believed Hitler could be controlled: nothing, however, could have been further from the truth.

Germany had been divided into *Wehrkreise* (military districts) for recruitment purposes since before World War I. Each district recruited and trained the men for the army, and within each district there were the relevant corps headquarters, barracks and training areas needed for the *Reichswehr*. On Hitler's accession he made it quite plain that the army was to expand from the original seven divisions to a total of 36 divisions in 13 corps. The army's initial reaction was one of total surprise, as they contemplated the sheer logistical problems of such voluminous expansion. However, they were delighted to be free of the restrictions imposed by the Treaty of Versailles, with the army assuming the honourable position within German society that it had enjoyed prior to 1918.

Every German male was to be liable to serve in the armed forces, even though this policy had been strictly forbidden by the Versailles Treaty. On 16 March 1935, Hitler promulgated the 'Law for the Expansion of the German Armed Forces', which reinstated conscription, and increased the army to the aimed-for 36 divisions. Then on 21 May 1935, a second law defined the duty to serve in the armed forces (or the Wehrmacht as they were now known), noting very few exceptions. Although Hitler was still establishing the power base of the NSDAP, his relationship with the army was strengthened by these laws, for it meant that at long last, the small, professional force created and trained under Von Seeckt would now have new men to train, and a much greater standing in society at home and in the military world at large.

From 2 August 1934, all German soldiers swore the following oath: 'I swear by God this holy oath: that I will always be unconditionally obedient to Adolf Hitler, Leader of the German Reich and people, Supreme Commander of the Wehrmacht, and, as a valiant soldier I am prepared to lay down my life at any time for this oath.' Hitler had, by this time, established a clear dictatorship, and the revised oath was an emphatic sign that the German armed forces were now under new management. Bolstered by a massive rearmament implemented by Hitler, the Wehrmacht expanded rapidly. Like a phoenix from the ashes, Germany's army had risen above the combined disasters of defeat in World War I and the restrictions of Versailles to be once again one of the dominant military powers on the continent. On 1 September 1939, when Germany attacked Poland, its army numbered 3,180,000 men. It eventually expanded to 9,500,000 personnel, and on 8/9 May 1945, the date of its unconditional surrender on the Western and Eastern Fronts, it still numbered 7,800,000. It was a far cry from the original 100,000-strong force that Hitler had inherited.

Hitler believed, incorrectly as events were to prove, that his political skills were matched by a unique ability as a strategic commander. His increasing influence on the Wehrmacht's conduct of World War II eventually proved to be disastrous. This book looks inside the development of Hitler's land forces from their days of victory in 1939 and 1940 to their final devastation in 1945. There is no denying that Germany produced a first-rate military organization, respected by all who fought it in combat. For the first three years of the war it was practically unassailable, and during the years of defeat it remained stubborn in the defence. What this book aims to show is how the German Army and related groups, such as the *Waffen-SS* and the Luftwaffe's *Fallschirmjäger* (paratroopers), earned their reputation, and the extent to which it was justified.

BLITZKRIEG: HITLER'S WAR MACHINE UNLEASHED, 1939–40

This column of troops wears the uniform typical of the early part of WWII. Note the soldiers may have their field caps (*Feldmütze*) rather than the *Stahlhelm* steel helmet, which hangs from their belts.

THE *BLITZKRIEG* (LIGHTNING WAR) PERIOD, FROM 1 SEPTEMBER 1939 TO 25 JUNE 1940, was ten months of almost total triumph for the Wehrmacht. With the exception of Great Britain, the German forces defeated every country that took the field against them, and for the next two years they appeared almost unassailable.

German strategy at this time combined two concepts: the traditional 'decisive manoeuvre', developed by Prussian General Von Moltke in the 1850s, and the 'armoured concept' pioneered by Heinz Guderian in the 1920s and 1930s. 'Decisive manoeuvre' used infantry to attack the enemy's line of retreat, trapping it in pockets. Guderian, however, advocated concentrations of tanks, mechanized infantry and Luftwaffe dive-bombers to punch a hole in the opposing line, and penetrate into rear areas to destroy key command centres, forcing a total collapse in enemy morale and the ability to resist. Both strategies demanded that Germany be the aggressor, a position in line with the Third Reich's xenophobic and expansionist ideology. Germany had the vital advantages of surprise and of choosing the time, place and conditions of the battles. Its opponents pinned their hopes on neutrality, diplomatic skills and static frontier defences. They were psychologically unwilling to fight, and reluctant to prepare for war.

POLAND AND THE WEST

On 26 August 1939, the Wehrmacht began a secret partial mobilization for *Fall Weiss* (Case White), the invasion of Poland, leading to full mobilization on 3 September. On 1 September, the army was finally unleashed. The invasion force, consisting of 1,512,000 men, was organized in two army groups totalling 53 divisions (37 infantry, four motorized, three mountain, three light, six Panzer), and it attacked on three fronts. Army Group North, under Generaloberst Fedor von Bock with 3rd and 4th Armies, attacked from north-east Germany and East Prussia. Army Group South, led by Generaloberst

RIGHT: An infantryman in 1934 wearing the standard field jacket and trousers of the period. Belt equipment includes ammunition pouches, each holding 15 rounds of 7.92mm ammunition for the *Gewehr* 98 in his right hand. His boots are the experimental buckled boots of 1934, which did not go into general service. 1) The German national colours, initially found on the left side of the helmet but then moved to the right when the national emblem (2) was introduced; 2) The national emblem for helmets, placed on the left side of the helmet, in white; 3) The 1916-pattern helmet; 4) The national emblem as applied to the uniform jacket; 5) Rank chevrons to the end of 1936: (i) *Oberschütze*; (ii) *Gefreiter*; (iii) *Obergefreiter*; (iv) *Oberstabsgefreiter*; 6) The shoulder board for an infantryman of the 30th Infantry Regiment; 7) Garrison cap or side hat; 8) The *Gewehr* 98, the standard issue rifle of World War I; 9) The bayonet, which was fixed below the muzzle of the rifle on a mounting post welded to the barrel: also shown is the black leather scabbard; 10) A five-round clip for the rifle; 11) The Pistole 08 or Luger; 12) Belt kit as seen from the rear; 13) The Type 24 hand grenade and (13a) pamphlets for instruction; 14) The transitional boot, with three buckles on the outside. It was soon abandoned as it was prone to let water in and was awkward in heavy undergrowth; 15) A military torch and battery. Note the coloured slides, which were interchangeable. (Adam Hook © Osprey Publishing)

Gerd von Rundstedt with 8th, 10th and 14th Armies, advanced from south-east Germany and northern Slovakia, supported by the 1st and 2nd Slovak divisions.

The Polish Army, deployed too close to the German frontier, was already being outflanked when, on 17 September, seven armies (41 divisions and equivalents) of the Soviet Red Army attacked them in the rear. Threatened on four fronts, the heavily outnumbered Polish Army officially surrendered on 27 September, and ceased all hostilities on 6 October.

Poland was the German Army's first great victory, and vindication of its tactical theories and pre-war training regimen. An eight-month 'Phoney War' followed, with much posturing by Anglo-French forces but little in the way of significant action. Nevertheless, anxious that the Allied forces might attack Germany through Norway and Denmark, Hitler decided to invade these militarily weak neutral states in a pre-emptive strike called *Unternehmen Weserübung* (Operation *Weserübung*), commanded by General der Infanterie Nikolaus von Falkenhorst. The attack against Denmark was launched on 9 April 1940. The inexperienced Danish Army, with 6,600 troops organized in two infantry divisions, its strategic position hopeless, was forced to surrender after just four hours' limited resistance.

THE FLOWER WARS

Hitler's political manoeuvrings, and Franco-British reluctance to risk war, gave the German Army five bloodless victories before September 1939. Hitler's troops annexed neighbouring territories in operations known as the *Blumenkriege*, or Flower Wars, a reference to the flowers often thrown by local ethnic Germans to welcome German forces.

On 7 March 1936, 30,000 troops from the 5th, 9th, 15th and 16th Infantry Divisions marched across the Rhine and occupied the demilitarized Saar region on the west bank. Then on 12 March 1938, 200,000 troops of the 8th Army (VII and XIII Corps, and 2nd Panzer Division) invaded Austria, annexing it and dividing it into *Wehrkreise* XVII and XVIII in April 1938, and absorbing the Austrian Army as the 44th and 45th Infantry, 4th Light and 2nd and 3rd Mountain Divisions.

The army had originally expected to deploy 39 divisions in five armies (numbers 2, 8, 10, 12, 14) for an invasion of Czechoslovakia, but following the Munich Agreement in September 1938 it occupied the Sudetenland border areas without bloodshed from 1 to 10 October 1938 with elements of the six neighbouring German corps – IV, VII, VIII, XIII, XVII, XVIII. The Sudetenland was incorporated into *Wehrkreise* IV, VII, VIII, XIII and XVII. On 15 March 1939, these units occupied the rest of Bohemia-Moravia, designated *Wehrkreis Böhmen und Mähren* in October 1942. Finally, on 23 March 1939, elements of I Corps annexed the Memel district of western Lithuania to *Wehrkreis* I.

On the same day XXI Corps, with 3rd Mountain, 69th and 163rd Infantry Divisions, disembarked in Norway, later reinforced by 2nd Mountain, 181st, 196th and 214th Infantry Divisions, with 40th Special Panzer Battalion providing token armour. They totalled some 100,000 men, and engaged six infantry divisions of the Norwegian Army (with only 25,000 of its 90,000 men mobilized), backed up by the Allied Expeditionary Force with the equivalent of two infantry divisions. Showing their growing confidence and capabilities, the German troops forced an Allied evacuation and a Norwegian surrender on 9 June 1940.

German motorbike troops bracket a staff car during the German reoccupation of the Rhineland in 1936. The staff car is the *Kraftfahrzeug* (Kfz) 15, which also served as a communications vehicle. Its long wheelbase was an impediment during cross-country manoeuvres.

FRANCE AND THE LOW COUNTRIES

Hitler had now built up momentum, and he sought to conclude his domination of Western Europe. For *Fall Gelb* (Case Yellow), the Western offensive, the German Army assembled 2,750,000 men in 91 divisions, divided among three army groups. Army Group A under Generaloberst Von Rundstedt with 4th, 12th and 16th Armies, including *Panzergruppe von Kleist* (Panzer Group Von Kleist), was to advance through Belgium into France. Army Group B, led by Generaloberst Von Bock with 6th and 18th Armies, would attack the Netherlands and Belgium, whilst Army Group C under Generaloberst Wilhelm

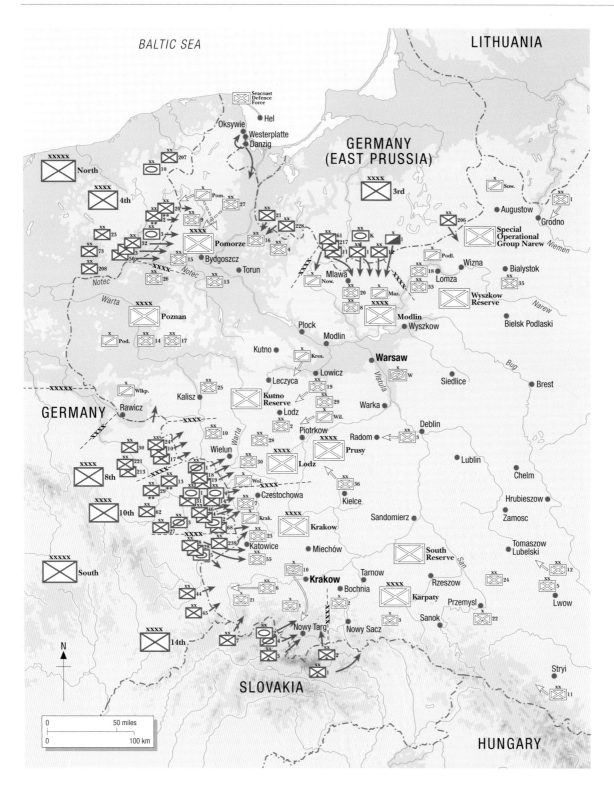

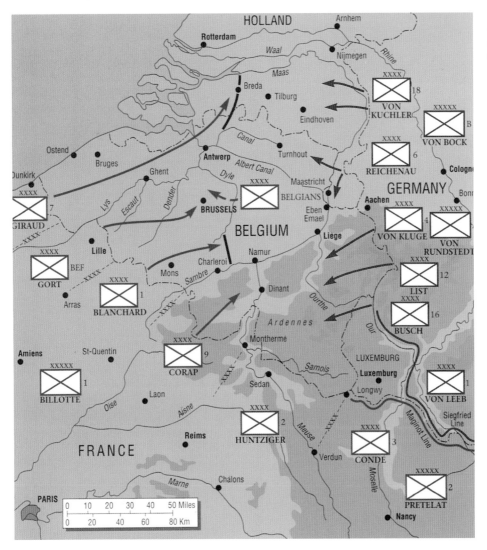

France 1940 – the opening moves as French and Belgian forces (in blue) attempt to stem the tide of the German advance.

Ritter von Leeb, with 1st and 7th Armies, would pin down French forces on the Maginot Line. These forces totalled 75 infantry divisions, including the 22nd *Luftlande* (Airborne) Division, one Luftwaffe airborne division, four motorized, one mountain, one cavalry and ten Panzer divisions, with a further 42 divisions in reserve.

The offensive began on 10 May 1940, with commandos and the *Abwehr* (the German military intelligence organization) already active in the Netherlands and Belgium. Army Group B's 18th Army, with nine divisions plus airlanding and parachute troops, attacked the neutral Netherlands, rapidly overwhelming the inexperienced Dutch Army. With 250,000 men organized in ten poorly trained infantry divisions, the Dutch put up an unexpectedly spirited defence, but surrendered on 15 May following the bombing of Rotterdam.

LEFT: The German invasion of Poland, September 1939. Routes of advance of the main German armies and formations are depicted in blue.

German troops, their helmets marked with national colours, prepare to deploy to Norway during the invasion of Scandinavia in April 1940. The ship in the background, there to provide fire support and protection from enemy naval vessels, is the heavy cruiser *Admiral Hipper*.

Luxembourg fell on 10 May to the 16th Army, the country's 82-man 'Volunteer Company' offering understandably limited resistance. The same day Army Group A, joined by 6th Army from Army Group B, began its advance through neutral Belgium, spearheaded by a daring airborne attack on Fort Eben-Emael. The 600,000-man Belgian Army, supported by British and French troops, initially fought back strongly. Its morale declined, however, as it retreated before the relentless German advance, led by the powerful Panzer Group Von Kleist's surprise outflanking attack through the supposedly impenetrable Ardennes hill country. On 28 May the Belgian Army surrendered.

On 16 May, Army Groups A and B began to advance into France. Now would be the ultimate challenge of their quality and courage. They were confronted by the 4,320,000-strong French Army, a total of 87 divisions, supported by nine British, one Czechoslovak and four Polish infantry divisions. A force of nine Panzer divisions, comprising Panzer Group Von Kleist, XV Corps and General der Panzertruppen Heinz Guderian's XIX Corps (redesignated Panzer Group Guderian on 1 June) with the *Grossdeutschland* (Greater Germany) Motorized Regiment, burst through the French 1st Army Group at Sedan, reaching the Channel coast on 22 May. Concerned that the formation containing almost all Germany's armoured troops had outrun its logistical tail and supporting infantry and was vulnerable to an Allied counterattack, Von Rundstedt ordered a halt on 23 May, allowing the Allies to evacuate 338,226 British, French and Belgian troops from Dunkirk from 27 May to 4 June.

On 5 June, Army Group B advanced along the French Channel and Atlantic coasts, stopping before Bordeaux on 22 June, while Army Group A headed through central France and Army Group C forced the Maginot Line. The French Army signed an armistice on 25 June. Eupen and Malmédy districts in Belgium were annexed and joined *Wehrkreis* VI, Luxembourg and Lorraine *Wehrkreis* XII, and Alsace *Wehrkreis* V. Northern, western and eastern France was occupied, leaving central and southern France unoccupied as a nominally independent French state under Field Marshal Pétain.

Heinz Guderian (left, in a steel helmet) here talks with Hitler during the invasion of Poland in September 1939. Guderian impressed Hitler with his theories of armoured warfare and all-arms communications, which the invasion of Poland seemed to prove effective.

THE VERDICT ON *BLITZKRIEG*

The *Blitzkrieg* period had restored the reputation of the German armed forces, but weaknesses had emerged. Success had confirmed Hitler's belief in his own genius and the corresponding inferiority of many of his professional generals. Jealousy between the *Oberkommando der Wehrmacht* (OKW; Wehrmacht High Command), and the *Oberkommando des Heeres* (OKH; Army High Command), exacerbated by the fact that Hitler controlled both, led to a division of authority. The Danish and Norwegian campaigns were controlled by OKW, and the Polish and Western campaigns by OKH. Panzer Group Kleist's classic *Blitzkrieg* tactics had proved brilliantly successful, but the infantry performance in Norway had been less decisive. The swift advances had nevertheless allowed large numbers of enemy troops to evade capture and organize themselves as guerrilla armies, a constant threat to the German occupation authorities.

THE STRUCTURE OF THE ARMY

1500hrs, 13 May 1940. The 10th Panzer Division Crosses the River Meuse near Sedan. Plan by Guderian's command, XIX Panzer Corps.

As head of state, Hitler occupied the nominal position of *Oberster Befehlshaber der Wehrmacht* (Supreme Commander of the Armed Forces), and on 4 February 1938 he took over the dominant position of *Oberbefehlshaber der Wehrmacht* (Commander of the Armed Forces), having forced his former protégé, Generalfeldmarschall Werner von Blomberg, to retire. Hitler held this post until

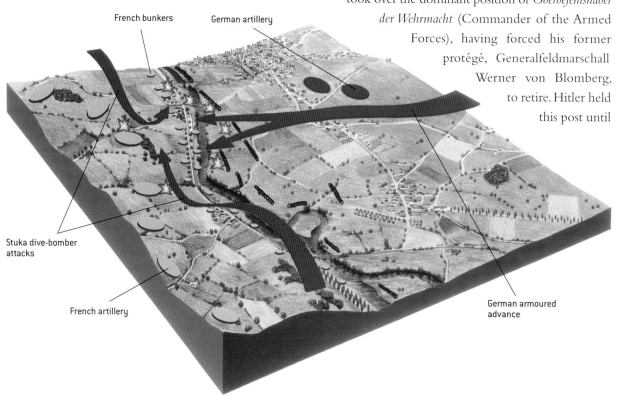

French bunkers

German artillery

Stuka dive-bomber attacks

French artillery

German armoured advance

ABOVE: Three of the great leaders of the Western Europe campaign – (from left to right) Generalmajor Heinz Guderian, Generalfeldmarschall Gerd von Rundstedt and Generaloberst Eduard Dietl. Only one published photograph shows Guderian wearing the special black vehicle uniform of the Panzer arm which he did so much to create. (Angus McBride © Osprey Publishing)

his suicide on 30 April 1945, assisted by the subservient Generaloberst (later Generalfeldmarschall) Wilhelm von Keitel as *Chef des Oberkommandos der Wehrmacht* (Chief of Staff of the Armed Forces).

The Wehrmacht was divided into three arms – the *Heer* (Army), Kriegsmarine (Navy) and Luftwaffe (Air Force). The army was by far the largest arm, averaging about 75 per cent of total Wehrmacht strength, with 2,700,000 troops in September 1939, reaching a maximum strength of about 5,500,000 in May 1945.

The *Oberbefehlshaber des Heeres* (Chief of the Army High Command) until 19 December 1941, when Hitler dismissed him and took over his post, was Generaloberst (later Generalfeldmarschall) Walther von Brauchitsch, assisted by General der Artillerie (later Generaloberst) Franz Halder as *Chef des Generalstabes des Heeres* (Chief of the Army General Staff). The *Waffen-SS*, formally established on 1 December 1939, was never technically part of the Wehrmacht, but it came under the control of the Army High Command (see Chapter 3).

In terms of the army's broadest organization structure, in 1937 the country was divided into 13 military districts, numbered I–XIII, and from 1939 these were the bases of the Replacement Army. The depots, schools and training units of a *Wehrkreis* manned and equipped initially one, and later as many as five, corps for the Field Army, keeping them supplied with a continuous stream of reinforcements. As Germany expanded its territory at its neighbours' expense, the existing districts were enlarged and six new ones formed from August 1938 to October 1942. They provided conscripts for the war effort, many of whom were not ethnic Germans or even sympathetic to the German cause.

On mobilization on 26 August 1939 prior to the outbreak of war, the army was divided into the *Feldheer* (Field Army), which went out to fight the enemy, and the *Ersatzheer* (Replacement Army), remaining in Germany in support. The Field Army constituted three types of troops. First, *Fechtende Truppen*, or combat troops, comprised staffs (armed forces and army high commands; General Staff; army group, army and corps staffs), infantry (line, motorized, light and mountain), commando and penal units, mobile troops (cavalry, armour, mechanized infantry, reconnaissance and anti-tank units), artillery, engineers, signals and field security police officials. Second, *Versorgungstruppen*, or supply troops, included transport, medical, veterinary and guard units, military police and field post officials. Third, *Sicherungstruppen* – security troops – were composed of rear-area commanders, second-line *Landeschützen* (territorial rifle) battalions and POW camps. There were also army officials (including chaplains), bandmaster officers and *Sonderführer* (specialists).

The largest wartime Field Army units had no fixed organization. There were five *Heeresgruppen* (army groups): two (North and South) for the Polish campaign, and three more (A–C) for the Western campaigns. Each army group was composed of two or

RIGHT: Ebullient crowds, no doubt carefully controlled by the Nazi propaganda machine, greet German mounted troops during the reoccupation of the Rhineland in 1936. A weak foreign response to the reoccupation served to encourage Hitler's ambitions of *Lebensraum* (living space).

three armies totalling perhaps 400,000 men. There were 14 armies, each comprising three or four corps with about 200,000 men, and, from June 1940, two reinforced armoured corps, called *Panzergruppen* or armoured groups, each one controlling three motorized corps. There were 33 corps, each with two to five infantry divisions and perhaps 60,000 men, and seven motorized corps, each with two or three armoured and motorized divisions, and one (XV) with three light divisions. One cavalry division and the four mountain divisions came directly under the control of their respective armies.

During the 1939–40 period, 143 infantry divisions were formed, their quality depending on the *Welle* (wave), to which they belonged. In addition to the 35 well-established peacetime 1st Wave divisions (1–46 series), there were divisions of elderly veterans or untrained reservists or recruits hastily assembled from occupied Poland and Czechoslovakia, as well as the nine *Ersatzdivisionen* (replacement divisions) of the 10th Wave (270–280 series). Each infantry division of 16,977 men was made up of three infantry regiments plus divisional support units: one four-battalion artillery regiment; a reconnaissance battalion,

PIONEER UNITS

The German Army collectively referred to its various engineer units as *Pioniere* (pioneers). These included *Pioniertruppen* (pioneer troops), *Bautruppen* (construction troops), *Eisenbahntruppen* (railway troops – who both built and operated railroads) and *Technische Truppen* (technical troops). The *Pioniertruppen* were what in the West would be called combat engineers. They were thought of as assault troops first and construction workers second, and were known as the *schwarz Pioniere* (black pioneers) owing to the black arm of service colour worn on uniforms. This differentiated them from the *weiss Pioniere* (white pioneers), who were combat engineer platoons assigned to infantry regiments. They were also known as the *Mädchen für Alles* (maids for all work) owing to the wide variety of jobs they undertook. The divisional pioneer battalion was the basic pioneer unit encountered in the frontlines and was considered a key unit necessary to support combat operations. On the march it reduced artificial and natural obstacles and repaired bridges. In addition, it assisted in crossing water obstacles with portable bridging, pontoon ferries, assault boats and inflatable boats. In attack they breached obstacles and supported the infantry as specialist assault troops, attacking fortified positions with demolitions, flamethrowers and smoke. In defence they constructed fortifications and shelters, erected obstacles, laid minefields, planted booby traps, cleared fields of fire, erected camouflage and maintained supply routes. In retreat they planted mines and booby traps, created hasty obstacles and destroyed bridges. It was not uncommon for pioneer battalions to be employed as ad hoc infantry, especially late in the war when divisions were forced to defend wider than normal frontages and manpower was short.

with mounted, bicycle and support squadrons; an anti-tank battalion; an engineer battalion; a signals battalion; and divisional services – up to ten motorized and horsedrawn transport columns; a medical company, a motorized field hospital and veterinary company; a military police troop and a field post office.

A pioneer squad and the rifle platoon it is supporting launch an attack on a French pillbox, 1940. The *Deckungstrupp* (covering troop), using the canal bank for cover, have opened fire on the bunker with a flamethrower and machine gun. Across the road the *Stosstrupp* (shock troop) is supported by the rest of the pioneer squad serving as the *Nebeltrupp* (smoke troop). The shock troop is contributing machine guns to the suppressive fire and the smoke troop is preparing to ignite smoke candles. Demolition men accompany the covering troop to move in from the other side of the bunker and attack the embrasures and door. From the rear, 7.5cm infantry guns and 8cm mortars commence their barrage on the woods to suppress the French company dug in there. The German concept was to keep the assault group small, make maximum use of existing cover and concealment reinforced by screening smoke, and employ heavy firepower to suppress the objective and adjacent covering positions and thus quickly overcome resistance and keep the attack's momentum rolling. (Carlos Chagas © Osprey Publishing)

An infantry regiment with 3,049 men had three infantry battalions, a 180-strong infantry gun company and a 170-strong anti-tank company. Moving further down the scale, a battalion of 860 men had three rifle companies and a 190-strong machine-gun (actually a support) company. A 201-strong *Schützenkompanie* (rifle company) had three rifle platoons, and each 50-strong *Schützenzug* (rifle platoon) was composed of a platoon staff, a light-grenade-launcher team and four rifle sections, each *Schützengruppe* (section) having ten men.

All units of a motorized division were armoured or motorized, and in early 1940 motorized divisions were reduced to two motorized regiments, giving a divisional total of 14,319 men. A *Gebirgsdivision* (mountain division) had 14,131 men with two 6,506-strong mountain regiments, plus support units and services, all with mountain operations capability.

German engineers repair the suspension of a truck. Engineer duties ranged from rear-echelon services like vehicle maintenance through to the frontline actions such as performing assault demolitions.

Turning to the tank elements of the army, a 14,373-strong *Panzerdivision* (armoured division) had an armoured brigade (two regiments of 1,700 men divided into two battalions) and a 4,409-strong motorized rifle brigade (rifle regiment and motorcycle battalion), the remaining support units and the services being armoured or motorized. A 10,000–11,000-strong *leichte* (light) division had between one and four 638-strong armoured battalions and one or two 2,295-strong motorized cavalry regiments, before reorganizing as Panzer divisions 6–9 between October 1939 and January 1940. The 16,000-strong 1st Cavalry Division had four 1,440-strong mounted regiments (each with two mounted battalions), a cavalry regiment (one mounted, one bicycle battalion) and a bicycle battalion, other support units and services being mounted or motorized.

RANKS AND RESPONSIBILITIES

The rank structure of the German Army used a system established on 6 December 1920. Officers were divided into four groups: general officers, field officers, captains and subalterns. Non-commissioned officers (NCOs), by contrast, were divided into three groups: technical NCOs, established 23 September 1937, for senior instructors in the Fortress Engineers and later the Veterinary Corps; senior NCOs, called 'sword-knot NCOs'; and junior NCOs, or 'NCOs without the sword-knot'. The *Stabsfeldwebel* rank, introduced on 14 September 1938 for NCOs re-enlisting after 12 years' service, was initially held by World War I veterans. *Hauptfeldwebel* was not a rank, but an appointment, introduced on 28 September 1938. He was the senior NCO in a company based at the company HQ and nicknamed *der Spiess* – 'the spear'. Usually an *Oberfeldwebel*, he outranked a *Stabsfeldwebel* (who could also be promoted to this appointment). Other NCOs receiving this appointment were designated *Hauptfeldwebeldiensttuer* (acting company sergeant major), but usually received rapid promotion to *Oberfeldwebel*.

The rank-class of 'men' included all privates and lance-corporals, the latter, as experienced privates, constituting a larger proportion of this rank class than would be found in other armies.

Most ranks had alternative rank titles. Some, as in the Medical Corps, differentiated specialist officers without the power of field command. Others, such as *Rittmeister* or *Oberjäger*, preserved traditional titles. Almost all officers held substantive ranks – the British system of acting ranks did not exist – so that German officers and NCOs often held higher commands than their British equivalent. It was therefore not uncommon for a *Leutnant*, for example, to be a company commander. While the first platoon of a typical rifle company was under a second *Leutnant*, the second and third were often commanded by an *Oberfeldwebel* or *Feldwebel*. Promotions to the infantry ranks of *Unteroffizier*, *Feldwebel* and *Oberfeldwebel* depended on a unit's table of organization, and were the

German operations in southern and central Norway, April 1940

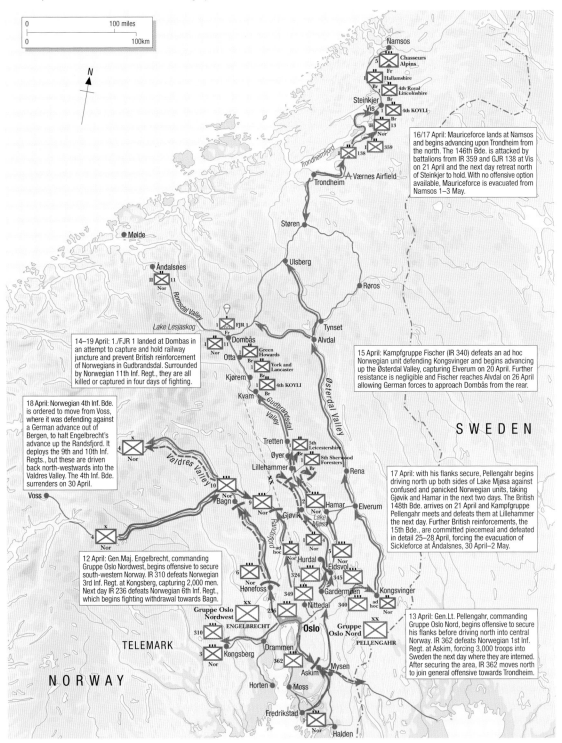

0   100 miles

0   100km

N

Namsos

Chasseurs Alpins

Fr Hallamshire

Br 4th Royal Lincolnshire

Steinkjer Vis

4th KOYLI

Trondheimfjord

138   359

Værnes Airfield

Trondheim

Støren

Ulsberg

Røros

Mølde

Åndalsnes

Romsdal Valley

Lake Lesjaskog

FJR 1

Dombås

Nor   Otta

Green Howards

York and Lancaster

Kjørem

Tynset

Alvdal

Østerdal Valley

Kvam   4th KOYLI

SWEDEN

Gudbrandsdal Valley

Tretten   5th Leicestershire

Øyer   8th Sherwood Foresters

Lillehammer

Rena

Valdres Valley

Voss

10   Nor   Bagn

9   Nor

Gjøvik

Lake Mjøsa

Hamar

Elverum

Randsfjord

Hurdal

Eidsvol

TELEMARK

6   Nor   Hønefoss

324

345

Gardermoen

Kongsvinger

349

Nittedal   340

Gruppe Oslo Nordwest   ENGELBRECHT

310

Oslo

Gruppe Oslo Nord   PELLENGAHR

NORWAY

Kongsberg

Drammen

362

Askim

Mysen

Horten   Moss

Fredrikstad

Halden

16/17 April: Mauriceforce lands at Namsos and begins advancing upon Trondheim from the north. The 146th Bde. is attacked by battalions from IR 359 and GJR 138 at Vis on 21 April and the next day retreat north of Steinkjer to hold. With no offensive option available, Mauriceforce is evacuated from Namsos 1–3 May.

14–19 April: 1./FJR 1 landed at Dombås in an attempt to capture and hold railway juncture and prevent British reinforcement of Norwegians in Gudbrandsdal. Surrounded by Norwegian 11th Inf. Regt., they are all killed or captured in four days of fighting.

15 April: Kampfgruppe Fischer (IR 340) defeats an ad hoc Norwegian unit defending Kongsvinger and begins advancing up the Østerdal Valley, capturing Elverum on 20 April. Further resistance is negligible and Fischer reaches Alvdal on 26 April allowing German forces to approach Dombås from the rear.

18 April: Norwegian 4th Inf. Bde. is ordered to move from Voss, where it was defending against a German advance out of Bergen, to halt Engelbrecht's advance up the Randsfjord. It deploys the 9th and 10th Inf. Regts., but these are driven back north-westwards into the Valdres Valley. The 4th Inf. Bde. surrenders on 30 April.

17 April: with his flanks secure, Pellengahr begins driving north up both sides of Lake Mjøsa against confused and panicked Norwegian units, taking Gjøvik and Hamar in the next two days. The British 148th Bde. arrives on 21 April and Kampfgruppe Pellengahr meets and defeats them at Lillehammer the next day. Further British reinforcements, the 15th Bde., are committed piecemeal and defeated in detail 25–28 April, forcing the evacuation of Sickleforce at Åndalsnes, 30 April–2 May.

12 April: Gen.Maj. Engelbrecht, commanding Gruppe Oslo Nordwest, begins offensive to secure south-western Norway. IR 310 defeats Norwegian 3rd Inf. Regt. at Kongsberg, capturing 2,000 men. Next day IR 236 defeats Norwegian 6th Inf. Regt., which begins fighting withdrawal towards Bagn.

13 April: Gen.Lt. Pellengahr, commanding Gruppe Oslo Nord, begins offensive to secure his flanks before driving north into central Norway. IR 362 defeats Norwegian 1st Inf. Regt. at Askim, forcing 3,000 troops into Sweden the next day where they are interned. After securing the area, IR 362 moves north to join general offensive towards Trondheim.

ABOVE: Figures from the campaigns in Western Europe. 1) A *Feldwebel* from the 36th Infantry Regiment; 2) A young Panzer crewman from the 3rd Panzer Regiment just after the conclusion of the Polish campaign; 3) A *Gefreiter* from the 12th Pioneer Battalion, active in the defence of the so-called 'Panzer Corridor' against Anglo-French counterattacks during the French campaign; 4) A Luftwaffe *Oberfeldwebel* pilot. (Darko Pavolvic © Osprey Publishing)

normal progression for a capable NCO. All other NCO and lower ranks were awarded on seniority. The rank of *Obersoldat* was held by a soldier lacking even the qualities for promotion to *Gefreiter*, while a *Stabsgefreiter* was an 'old sweat' unfitted for NCO rank.

RECRUITMENT AND TRAINING

To prepare for war, the new, much enlarged German Army needed recruits. The *Wehrkreise* were ordered to use the registration lists held by the police (listing all German nationals, their addresses and ages, as well as foreigners and Jews) to start calling up all men who had reached their 20th year. The civil and military authorities worked independently and jointly to ensure that this process was seamlessly incorporated into German life, aided by the constantly broadcast reminder that the profession of the German soldier was one of honour. Propaganda extolled the life of the soldier: increasingly civilians were trained (from childhood onwards) in military ways.

The all-pervading effect of the Nazi Party was especially felt in the newly created *Hitlerjugend* (HJ; Hitler Youth) and the *Reichsarbeitsdienst* (RAD; German Labour Service). No one of the relevant age could avoid becoming a member and both organizations (and many others with perhaps the single exception of the *Bund Deutscher Mädel* – League of German Girls,) were paramilitary in ethos. Training was based on foot drill, map reading, field craft and weapon training with small bore weapons. The RAD served as the middle stage for all German men between the HJ and the armed forces. Many men had good reason to remember their efforts on the Labour Service when they joined the army, because the experience they had already undergone prepared them both physically and mentally for army training.

Every individual who was liable to serve in the army was warned in the summer of his call-up year, receiving a letter containing the basic details of where he was to report. A second letter in September then told him when to report, and what papers he needed to bring: his membership cards and records of service in the HJ and RAD were specified as important documents.

THE TRAINING DEPOTS

RIGHT: German Army recruits run an assault course during their infantry training. Because of the emphasis on sport in the Hitler Youth, young German men tended to arrive at basic training with a decent level of fitness and a competitive attitude.

Training depots had a deserved reputation for harshness, but the aim of the training was dictated by the experiences of World War I. Most of the NCOs who were training the recruits were veterans of the trenches and knew only too well that men did not fight well if they were inexperienced at being tired, hungry, cold or wet. Rigorous training could prepare them for the realities of life on the front line. Furthermore, Von Seeckt's demands that this professional army must be mobile meant that men had to be ready at all times,

not only when they were well fed and rested. So the NCOs pushed the trainees to breaking point. Their motto was simple: *Schweiss spart Blut* – 'Sweat saves blood'.

Recruits faced 16 weeks of what was probably the most effective basic training provided by any army of the time. Basic training was designed to turn raw recruits into soldiers who would obey. However, Von Seeckt's influence was still felt, and every German soldier was also trained to act upon his own initiative if circumstances demanded it. The German Army was not inclined to Napoleon's dictum that every man has a marshal's baton in his knapsack, but rather that every man could and should act one rank (at least) higher up than his actual appointment. The recruits were constantly told that their oath was the very essence of their lives and that 'The honour of soldiers lies in their unconditional personal commitment to their people and nation, even unto death.'

Depot training was planned meticulously, with every hour of the day used to good purpose. It started by putting the men into uniform, training them in drilling together on the square, instructing them in how to wear their various uniforms, how to keep them clean, and how to stay fit and well. Further training with rifle, pistol, grenade, bayonet, submachine gun (SMG) and machine gun (MG), together with constant field exercises, combined to produce efficient soldiers.

The recruits also learned map-reading, military writing and reporting, field craft, range estimation, target description and the various aspects of the infantry land battle. They were shown films on weapons and the effect of their fire, on movement across country, anti-aircraft protection, anti-tank operations and camouflage. They were taught to dig trenches for themselves, and later for support weapons.

The result was intended to be a soldier who was capable of existing within his section in the land battle, and of fighting effectively. He was expected to be smart, respectful to seniors and a source of pride to his parents and neighbours. After 16 weeks he passed out and went on to more practical training with greater insight into the methods of all-arms warfare, based initially at company, and later at battalion and regimental levels.

THE TRAINING PROGRAMME

When recruits first arrived to muster with their regiment, they often came from the local area, and already knew some members of their battalion, perhaps even of the regiment. Nevertheless, friendship was limited to their immediate fellows in the first 16 weeks of training. They were allocated rooms on the basis of one per *Korporalschaft* (section), and they met their section commander, a *Gefreiter* whom they would learn to fear and respect when on duty.

The platoon sergeant, a *Feldwebel* with whom they would have more to do later on in their course, and their platoon commander made brief appearances, the officer to give

ABOVE: The pioneer soldier's wall locker (*Spind*) was his repository for all issue clothing and equipment as well as the few personal items permitted. It was precisely arranged, the exact arrangement varying between units, and was to be ready for inspection at any time. The helmet and backpack (1) were stowed on top. On the top shelf of the main compartment (2) were neatly stacked shirts, under-drawers, socks, nightshirts and sweater, along with the field cap. On a hanger bar (3) are the drill, field and service tunics and trousers, and greatcoat. On the main compartment's door are hung equipment items, along with a towel (4). Shoes and boots are stowed on the bottom shelf and beneath it (5). To the left of the main compartment are seven small compartments containing (from top to bottom): peaked service cap (6); bread for the day's meals, eating utensil, (plate, soup bowl, saucer, cup) (compartment has door) (7); personal items and valuables (locked door) (8); toiletries (razor, blades, shaving stick, toothbrush, toothpowder, soap, comb) (9); manuals, books, writing materials (10); cleaning materials (leather polish, shoe and cleaning brushes, cleaning cloths) (11); gas mask, mess kit and *Zeltbahn* (shelter-quarter) (12). Photos and personal letters might have been permitted to be attached inside the left compartment's door (13). (Carlos Chagas © Osprey Publishing)

them a lecture on the German Army and its place in German society. They were now officially banned from having any political affiliations whatsoever, which meant that the members of the NSDAP had to make friends (like it or not) with non-party members.

The training programme depended to an extent on the depot at which the soldiers were trained. Some depots and training areas had a reputation for extremes of discipline bordering on the sadistic; others were less intensive, but just as instructive. The room allotted to each section was theirs for 16 weeks, and so was its cleanliness. They were then issued with a range of personal uniform equipment, given a severe haircut, and finally fed at around six in the evening. After the meal they received their first ideological lecture on the German Army, its traditions and ethos, and their regiment. They were also shown how to wear their uniforms, and warned to pack up all civilian clothing for posting back home the next day. They were now soldiers, and subject to military discipline; they were also instructed on saluting in and out of doors, and reminded that respect was due to any member of the German Army senior to them – which meant almost everyone they met.

A typical training day began at 0500hrs when the men were often literally thrown out of their beds by the corporals and soldiers responsible for barracks training. The men then had to strip their beds, tidy their lockers, wash, shave and dress before breakfast. Many mornings would also include runs of increasing distance and speed before ablutions and dressing in uniform.

A breakfast of coffee and bread followed at 0645hrs, so for 15 minutes the men were relatively free to eat. Often this meal was not available, however, especially if the men were on exercise or drilling to correct the previous day's errors. Recruits learned very quickly that hunger, tiredness and personal discomfort were of little consequence, and that they had to be ready for anything at any time.

These German Army recruits wear the white uniform of the day, a severely impractical colour for any new soldier. They are seen at the rifle range, the Kar 98k rifles being held in a rack until they go to shoot. Note the gas mask – gas was still a feared possibility in the early years of the war.

The soundness of such training was proved time and again, even in the later war years, when the resilience and stamina of ordinary German soldiers was remarked on by all those who fought against them. One soldier wrote, 'In action later on, we realized time and again how valuable this training had been for us. "Sweat saves blood", that was a truism that was often confirmed later. We didn't know it yet though, so we cursed and swore at everything and everyone.'

Lectures were part of the day (and woe betide anyone who slumped in his seat, or worse, fell asleep). Topics ranged from expositions on the duties of the soldier to his comrades in arms, to the soldier and the state, and who was who in the Nazi hierarchy. Little except the very basics of battle training was included in lectures, the German method being to show men practically what they should do in the field.

Each day was divided into morning and afternoon training, and a typical morning might include a lecture and drill on the square. The afternoon might have been devoted to an hour of physical training and shooting practice. Shooting was fundamental to training and one soldier described it: 'So, it's on to the firing range, which itself is a few miles distant. There are at least a thousand men, and the firing is non-stop.' The main meal, lunch (*Mittagessen*), when it was eaten, was served at 1230hrs, giving the men another few moments of peace, although sometimes the recruits found that 'Lunch here is at eleven. You arrived late, so, it's time for drill.'

At 1330hrs, no matter what else they were doing in the afternoon, all the recruits were assembled on the square, inspected and given any notices relevant to them. This parade was taken initially by the platoon sergeants, then at a later stage of training by the company sergeant major, and later still by platoon commanders, then the company adjutant and the company commander. The men met their officers infrequently during training for the reason that they would be commanded by others in battle, and had to learn to survive at section and platoon level first, without the comforting presence of an officer.

Evenings were spent cleaning uniforms and kit, rifles, MGs, and then the room itself. The evening meal (*Abendbrot*) was taken at 1830hrs, and further activities could stretch the working day well into the dark, and later in training, throughout the night.

BARRACKS TRAINING

The German Army distinguished between barracks training and field training; field training included drill on the square, as well as field craft, weapons training, map reading and the other skills required for survival in the field. Barracks training involved personal cleanliness (which was heavily stressed), as well as weapons cleaning, and the inevitable chores of floor polishing, bed making and general household duties with which all armies concern themselves. Barracks training, however, created the bonds of friendship in sections that lasted into battle.

The recruits were issued with everything needed to perform their many duties in the appropriate dress. Needless to say, it was every man's own responsibility to keep himself and all his equipment clean and in a good state of repair. Reissues of clothing and equipment were made, but in the interim only damage due to training or exercise would warrant special replacement of any item.

Boots had to be carefully maintained, for damaged or ill-fitting boots could cause a man to drop out from the line of march, possibly with dire consequences. Certainly, foot damage caused by badly fitting boots was a serious offence.

Recruits also had to strip back their beds every morning to allow them to air. Hot, sweaty soldiers have never been renowned for their personal hygiene, especially if they are also tired, and a sweat-soaked bed needed fresh air before it was remade in the early afternoon before roll-call.

Lockers, too, were subject to the basic rule of tidiness, although the German Army at this time did not make a fetish of 'spit and polish' like some other armies. Cleanliness and tidiness were paramount, but a glass-like shine on boots, or beds squared away to the millimetre, was not demanded as a general rule.

The uniform of the day for trainees was perhaps the most awkward that could be chosen, for it was white. Once washed many times it would age to a yellow/grey colour, but it was difficult to keep clean enough for inspections. Ankle boots, belt and side hat completed the trainees' clothing. Men soon learned that they had a duty to keep themselves and their kit clean, as well as doing their allotted room-cleaning tasks.

Punishment for error was swift and effective, almost always involving physically demanding tasks that made uniforms and equipment even dirtier, thus compounding the offence. Interestingly, all such punishments were also regarded as training events, and so polishing dustbins and painting grass green were not among the prescribed sanctions. Instead, men would be made to go on a long run in full field gear, or made to practise field movements, especially crawling through muddy sumps and wading through streams and rivers. On many occasions the punishment was physically very demanding. One soldier wrote: 'I had to put on the punishment pack … which weighed nearly eighty pounds… After two hours my helmet was burning hot from the sun, and by the end I needed all my willpower to keep my knees from buckling… I learned that a good soldier does not cross the barracks square with his hands in his pockets.'

WEAPONS TRAINING

One way to show recruits the meaning of obedience was firm training in foot and rifle drill. Many hours were spent on the square during the 16 weeks of training (an average of 30 periods per week, which included muster parades and parades prior to meals).

ABOVE: The MG 08 water-cooled machine gun in the anti-aircraft role (top), and the MG 13 (bottom), also mounted to fire at a high angle against aircraft. The illustrations at bottom right show magazine filling with a filler box (upper picture) and also by hand. (Adam Hook © Osprey Publishing)

However, rifle drill in the German Army was not limited to parade handling: it also included tactical handling – loading, unloading, making safe and cleaning.

The role of the rifleman was not the same as in other European armies of the time: in the German Army the rifleman was in battle to carry out the final assault on the enemy after the machine gun had won the firefight. Other European armies regarded the rifleman as the heart of the infantry because he carried a bayonet, and regarded machine guns as support, not main weapons.

Recruits were initially issued the *Gewehr* 98 rifle, which was designed and made by the Mauser Company at Oberndorf in the Neckar Valley. Experience in World War I had shown that it was too long for practical purposes, and so it had been shortened and improved with a turned bolt, becoming the Kar 98k (the 'k' for *kurz* – short), the weapon that served throughout the period 1933–45. It was a 7.92mm calibre weapon weighing 3.89kg. The ballistics of the cartridge had also been improved, firing a bullet at a muzzle velocity of 762m/sec. The weapon had a staggered five-round magazine, barleycorn sights, and was still equipped with a cleaning/ramrod, which was to prove highly necessary in the winter in Russia. Over time, the rifle was partly superseded by semi-automatic weapons and SMGs.

One aspect of training that was common to every army (then and now) was rifle cleaning. Whether or not the weapon had been fired, it had to be carefully maintained every day. This meant wiping off any dirt from the weapon, pulling the barrel through and lightly oiling it plus the bolt, breech, magazine follower and spring, and the safety mechanism and sights.

German infantry recruits undergo rifle training, under the watchful eye of an NCO. The recruits would have to demonstrate proficient marksmanship with the rifle from all positions – prone to standing. The weapon is the 7.92mm Kar 98k, which was the standard German Army rifle throughout the war.

Every soldier also carried a bayonet on his left hip. This was sometimes of limited value, but was handy as a fighting knife (and for opening tins), and was never dispensed with. The proliferation of automatic weapons such as SMGs, machine guns and hand grenades, limited the combat use of the bayonet in World War II. SMGs were better for close-quarter fighting, although machine guns reached out so far on the battlefield that

Two German soldiers move carefully through an urban landscape, their MP 38 submachine guns at the ready. The main weakness of the MP 38 was its single-stack magazine, which held 32 9mm rounds. In its first versions, the gun was prone to accidental firing if knocked hard.

they often precluded hand-to-hand combat; the grenade was particularly effective in house-clearing work, where the bayonet imposed restrictions on the use of the rifle. Later in Russia, however, close-combat was the norm in many situations, and as long as the bayonet did not interfere with movement, it was fixed and used. The bayonet had to be cared for as much as the rifle, and so it was wiped clean with a slightly oily rag every day, and no rust was to appear at any time.

The German Army based its infantry sections on the firepower of the machine gun. The machine gun had proved its value in both defence and attack during World War I, and Von Seeckt recommended that every infantry section should consist of a machine gun to win local firefights, with a number of riflemen acting as support for the machine gun in defence, and as the assault party in the attack. This principle meant that every section now had the firepower of a platoon of riflemen (at least), and was able to lay down defensive, interdictory or suppressing fire as the situation required (more is said about section tactics below).

The first machine guns of the *Reichswehr* were extremely heavy and cumbersome.

A German machine-gunner stands guard over a bridge with his MG 34, set on a tripod to act as a medium support weapon. The MG 34 was an excellent gun, but its costly engineering processes led to it being superseded by the superlative MG 42.

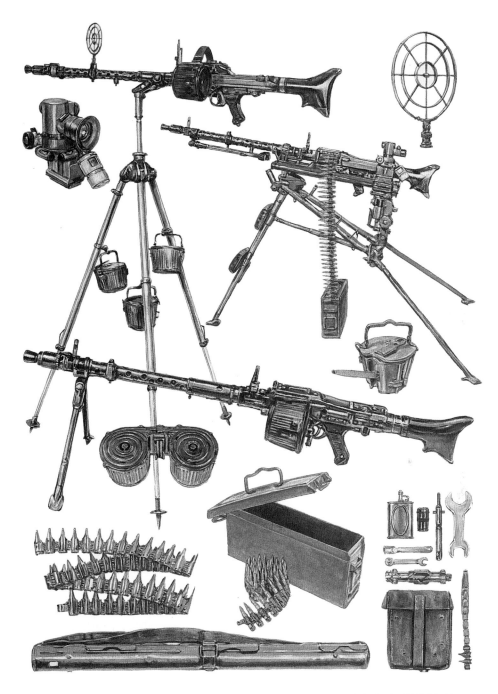

ABOVE: The MG 34, shown in various mount configurations and with component parts, including the *MG-Zieleinrichtung* (dial sight) (top right). This was used to aim via indicating stakes. The gun and sight would be aimed at one of the stakes, giving a lay on a specific bearing. A correction was then set on the sight, and the gun traversed to bring the sight back on to the original stake. The gun was now laid off on the new bearing, and after elevation had been applied, the gun could fire. (Adam Hook © Osprey Publishing)

The MG 15 (or Maxim 08) was a water-cooled gun weighing 19.28kg, and with a similarly heavy tripod. The weapon was of rifle calibre, and fired its ammunition from a fabric belt. It served well in the fixed positions of World War I, but was eventually eliminated because it was too awkward to be moved quickly. Carrying water to refill the gun's cooling water jacket was also burdensome, and if water supplies were limited the gun was prone to overheat, so the German Army went over to air-cooled weapons. Incidentally, the MG 08 and the later MG 08/15 were still on issue in 1940 to second-line divisions.

Designed around the MG 18 of World War I, the MG 13 was a lighter section weapon, bipod-mounted, air-cooled and fed by a magazine. However, it was only used as a training weapon, for the next generation of machine gun was on the drawing boards in the early 1930s: the MG 34.

The MG 34 was a belt-fed light machine gun (LMG) that was air-cooled and could be bipod- or tripod-mounted to combine many roles in one weapon. It was useful to infantry in both defence and attack, could double as an anti-aircraft local defence weapon, or could be turned into a sustained-fire medium machine gun (MMG) with no modification to the weapon itself. However, with some modification, it also served as a tank-mounted gun, for defence against enemy infantry.

The 7.92mm ammunition for the gun was supplied either by a 50-round belt or a 75-round drum. Later drums carried 150 rounds, and were issued in pairs in a carrier. The belt was a fixed-link design, and could be reloaded from cartridge boxes very quickly. Ammunition carriers for the gun both lugged two boxes of ammunition, each containing at least 294 rounds. Every gunner carried a tool and spares wallet on his belt, which contained, among other useful items, some belt starters for the gun – these allowed linked belts to be fed into the gun with the top cover closed, giving the gunner more flexibility. Linked belts could also be joined to make more cartridges available, a feature that was particularly valuable in the face of mass infantry attacks.

Each infantry section was divided into a machine-gun group and an assault (rifle) group. The machine gun was regarded as the firepower of the section, and to ensure sustained use, the group had a gunner (with the gun itself) who was supported by two ammunition carriers, one of whom carried the spare barrel (later two spare barrels) for the gun. Barrel changing was quite simple, taking only a few seconds and the use of a protective pad for holding the hot used barrel. Barrel changes were recommended after every 250 rounds of combat firing.

The MG 34 was essentially the first real general-purpose machine gun (GPMG), and it was a superb piece of engineering. Unfortunately this was its undoing, for the strict engineering processes required for its manufacture also made it prone to stoppages, as well as being very expensive to manufacture. It was eventually replaced to a large extent by the MG 42. In the early campaigns of World War II, however, the MG 34 was a valuable weapon. The rate of fire was such that in the hands of a good operator the gun could easily lay down enough fire to prevent an enemy manoeuvring close to the Germans, and in defence, could cut an attacking force to pieces.

All recruits received initial training on the weapon, but anyone who showed aptitude for the gun was given extra training in all its aspects. No doubt this was sometimes regarded as a curse by those chosen, for they now had additional duties to perform, and they had to carry the gun and its ammunition in the field. Initial training totalled 68 hours, including six hours on the range.

The recruits would also receive instruction in using hand grenades. In World War I, the German Army had probably the most effective hand grenade of the era, which became the Type 24 and was still on issue in 1935. Its long handle allowed it to be thrown far further, and with greater accuracy, than any contemporary grenade. Its effect was well known (and was later augmented with a fragmentation sleeve), and it is seen in many contemporary photographs, although the majority are posed. The weapon was so simple to use that only three hours were needed to make recruits basically proficient in its use.

In terms of handguns, the German Army's classic sidearm was the Pistole 08 (P'08 or Luger). This famous weapon was issued to officers and all machine gunners as a personal weapon, as well as to vehicle drivers, horse handlers and other personnel whose jobs precluded them from carrying a rifle. The design, by Hugo Borchardt and George Luger, was extremely interesting, but it had no special military characteristics. Like all pistols (including the later Walther P38) it was a very short-range, desperation weapon,

THE INFANTRY MORTAR

An infantry mortar was issued to every platoon. It was 5cm calibre, and fired high-explosive (HE), smoke and illumination bombs. All infantry were trained in its use, but in basic training only familiarity training was given. The role of the mortar was to give short-range area support to attacking infantry with its HE bombs, and to provide cover for movement via smoke bombs. It also fired illumination shells equipped with a delaying parachute, which were of great value during night defensive operations. Although the HE bomb was only of limited power, it had a good effect on morale, and the 5cm mortar continued in platoon use for many years. It was hampered by one particular design flaw. The first models had an extremely complex levelling mechanism (based on that used with heavier mortars), which delayed action times for the mortar team. This problem was later eradicated and the 5cm mortar served well as platoon support fire.

A German *Stielhandgranate* (stick hand grenade) is here juxtaposed with a British Mills bomb. To operate the German device, the cap was unscrewed from the wooden shaft, exposing a cord attached to the fuse. Once the cord was pulled, the grenade had either a four- or nine-second delay before it detonated.

which was carried because it was issued rather than from choice. Six hours training time was allotted to the weapon.

The Germans had observed in World War I that many weapons used in trench warfare were standard issue, and were basically too long and cumbersome to be wielded effectively in enclosed spaces such as trenches and buildings. They had therefore developed one of history's first SMGs – the MP 18 – which acted as a physically manageable 'trench broom' by firing pistol ammunition at full-auto. SMG development continued, and by 1939 the German Army had adopted the 9mm MP 38 as a section commander's weapon, and devoted some training periods to it. It was excellent at close ranges for putting a lot of fire on a target, and it was extremely simple to use, strip and clean. Furthermore, it used the standard 9mm pistol cartridge already issued for the Pistole 08 and later the P38. Ten hours training were allotted to this weapon. The MP 38 was, however, produced through expensive and slow machining processes, so was subsequently rationalized for mass production in the form of the MP 40, which went on to equip hundreds of thousands of soldiers throughout the war.

Training in rifle skills went on throughout the soldier's life in the German Army, and his marksmanship was under constant review. The training began with 'dry' aiming (no cartridge in the weapon and using tripods and an aiming disk) under the strict supervision of an NCO. Once he had learned the basics of holding and aiming his rifle properly, the soldier progressed to the training tables. Each trainee fired a few rounds from different positions from the training tables, with an NCO constantly at his side to correct faults and to improve technique.

The first shooting position was lying down with the rifle supported, then soldiers practised shooting while sitting. Trainees progressed to unsupported firing lying, kneeling, sitting and (most difficult of all) standing. Every round fired was recorded by the company clerk, and the platoon NCOs were always willing to increase the required training if necessary. The essence of the training was to make every recruit utterly familiar with his rifle and its capabilities on the range. Field firing with live ammunition came later, but only when the trainee was well versed in safety procedures and was known to be able to exercise common sense.

Throughout the 16-week training, a total of 398 instructional periods were devoted to rifle handling and drill on the square, and 234 periods on shooting, meaning that for the rifle alone, each recruit averaged 40 sessions a week. He fired more than 300 rounds on the range during this period alone. As soon as the best shots in each section were recognized, these men were instructed intensively on the MG 34, naturally in addition to their other tasks. At least five hours a week were devoted to training on the machine gun, which included loading, unloading, clearing stoppages, aiming techniques and fire plans. As the weeks went by, the machine-gun section and the rifle section were slowly integrated into their battle sections.

German soldiers were also instructed in the classroom on the basic technical aspects of ballistics, learning about the components of their rifle and the cartridge it fired. They learnt about which type of cartridge they were firing, and what its purpose was.

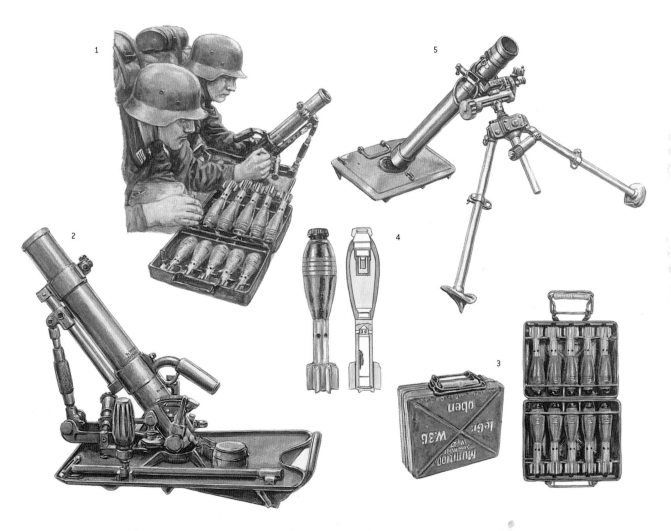

ABOVE: 1) The 5cm mortar and a two-man team; 2) The 5cm mortar; 3) Mortar bomb case and contents; 4) Section of an HE 5cm mortar bomb, weighing 800g with TNT filling; 5) The 8cm infantry mortar, a much more effective weapon, firing a 3.5kg round out to 1,200m. (Adam Hook © Osprey Publishing)

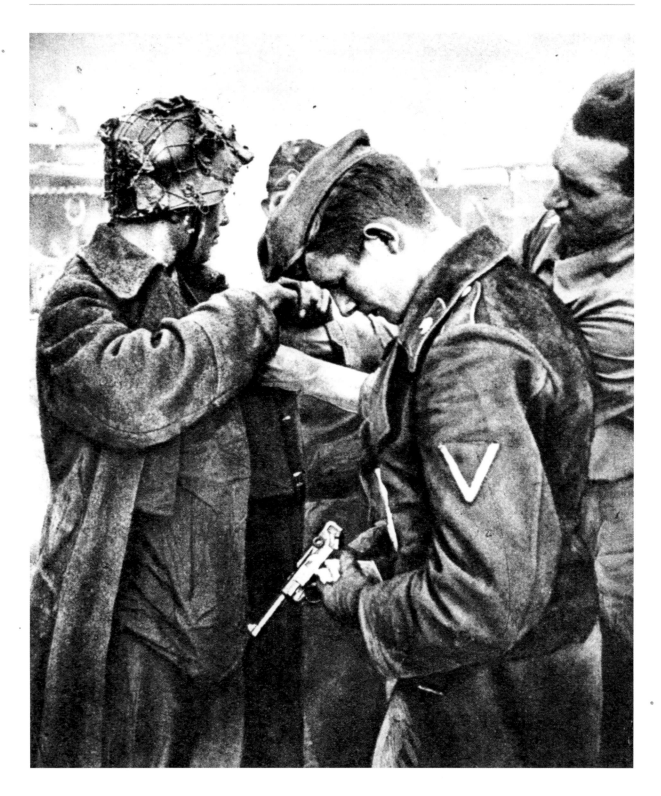

The German Army used a standard 7.92mm rimless rifle and machine-gun cartridge, which had a variety of bullets. The basic infantry cartridge was the sS cartridge, a simple lead-cored, fully jacketed round. It also had the SmK round, which was cored with steel beneath a lead tip, again fully jacketed. A third type of round was the SmKL'spur, a cored tracer round whose trajectory was similar to that of standard ammunition. This was particularly important in night firing, as it followed the same trajectory as the invisible non-tracer rounds that were also being fired. A fourth type was the incendiary bullet, which was filled with phosphorus. Further ballistics training went into some detail about mortar and artillery shells.

OTHER TRAINING

Once the basics of self-organization were instilled into the recruits, they were able to go on to more advanced aspects of their training. Each individual German infantryman, for example, had to be able to use a map. This was a reflection of the basic concept that every soldier had to be able to do the job of his superior. He was trained in the use of the compass and square, and was able to give eight-figure grid references, to assess dead ground from a map (by drawing a section), and learnt how to orient his map and navigate with it. Troops also had to be able to recognize and name land forms, and to evaluate the cover that terrain might afford them in attack and defence. They were taught to do this partly by map reading and partly by practical exercise. The recruit had to be able to work out the best route for crossing country both in attack and defence. He could get some help from the map, but frequent practical exercises drove home the lesson that cover was essential when moving.

The skill of range estimation was also important, for although at battalion level the machine-gun company had a portable range-finder, it was vital for every soldier to be able to estimate range so that effective fire orders could be given. The aforementioned lectures in ballistics helped infantrymen to judge distances accurately, so that the effective 'beaten zone' of bullets at the end of their trajectory was where it needed to be – on top of the enemy.

All infantry were also given basic instruction in issuing fire orders to mortar teams at battalion level and above, and to the regimental artillery. When the artillery observation officer was not on site, any infantry unit could call for fire from the regimental guns, in addition to fixed 'SOS' fire tasks. The co-operation between infantry in the line and mortars and artillery was good at all times, meaning that fire support was usually effective and timely. Those who showed a particular aptitude with a specific heavy weapon could expect further training with it, and might be transferred to the relevant platoon when capable of carrying out the duties required to fight with the weapon.

LEFT: A German *Gefreiter* (the rank is indicated by the single chevron on the sleeve) inspects his Luger P'08 pistol. The Luger was a toggle-locked recoil-operated 9mm handgun, developed before World War I but seeing official military service until 1945.

ABOVE: 1) An anti-tank section in training hitch their 3.7cm PaK (35/36 L/45) to a light tractor (SdKfz 10); **2)** A shell for the 3.7cm PaK. This armour-piercing tracer shell weighed 1.5kg complete; **3)** The gun in action. The gun commander is observing through binoculars (a), the gun layer (b) is to the left of the breech, the loader (c) to the right. Behind them is the ammunition carrier (d). (Adam Hook © Osprey Publishing)

In the new German Army, infantry/armour co-operation had become an essential element of training during the 1930s. The men were introduced to mock tanks during their 16 weeks' training, until such time as the real thing was available. Very few of the infantry regiments were given any in-depth familiarization with the new weapon, however, as the Panzer divisions were expected to work on their own, with the infantry coming up behind to consolidate the tanks' territorial gains. Not enough thought or effort had gone into motorizing the infantry, and the German Army began to suffer as the war went on; tanks unprotected by infantry are vulnerable to anti-tank weapons, and infantry on their own cannot break through well-defended frontlines.

TACTICAL FIELD TRAINING

Tactical field training was at the heart of all German infantry skills. German soldiers learned to be aggressive above all else, and were drilled in vigorous movement both before the attack and during it. In defence they had an equally belligerent attitude towards the enemy. Training began once every man in the section was conversant with the use of the rifle and the LMG. The emphasis was always upon learning by practice, and only a few classroom periods were devoted to the infantryman's battle skills. These skills were considered by all instructors to be best acquired in the field, not at a desk.

Field training was designed to be as realistic as possible, and a German officer commented that 'We have considerable losses in battle training, but this is unavoidable', because 'machine guns fire ball ammunition over the heads of attacking troops, with a very small safety margin, and mortars support the infantry to within 50 yards of the objective'.

Every soldier was trained almost incessantly by his NCOs in how to move across country. A primary aim was to ensure that men got into battle without being killed

MACHINE-GUN COMPANY

The Order of Battle (OrBat) of the German infantry regiment had support elements at each level. The machine-gun company in each battalion had four pairs of heavy machine guns (HMGs) and six medium mortars. The HMGs in 1939–42 were MG 34s with tripod mounts and dial sighting systems, enabling them to undertake indirect-fire tasks. By using map plotting and aiming stakes, the machine guns could be aligned with a primary, long-range and unseen target onto which fire could be directed as required. Further targets could then be plotted at will and recorded on a master plot by the section or company commander. All the gunners had to do was lay out guide stakes for pre-planned fire tasks, and simply aim the dial sight at them, adjusting elevation and deflection as necessary.

The main task for the HMGs was shooting in an attack. Individual section guns were on the move during infantry attacks, and the Germans reasoned that more machine-gun support constantly firing on the *Schwerpunkt* (the main attack point where maximum effort was concentrated for penetration of the frontline) of the attack would be of great value. This led to the formation of machine-gun companies, tasked with firing over the heads of, or through gaps in, the attacking infantry. Training for heavy machine gunners was particularly detailed, giving the individual gun commanders and the gunners exact safety margins for overhead and flank firing to avoid hitting German troops.

A high standard of map-reading skills was expected of all machine gunners in the company, but they were also expected to reconnoitre the land and, if possible, the targets before laying their guns. In an attack they would stay in their chosen position until the attack had succeeded, and then move to new, already selected, positions where they would plan their new defensive fire tasks (if staying put) or reconnoitre their next offensive fire plan.

The six mortars of the machine-gun companies were 81mm calibre, firing a 3.66kg bomb to ranges of 540–2,400m, with a rate of fire of ten to 12 rounds per minute. The mortar fired HE bombs and smoke – the former bombs were particularly effective when concentrated on enemy positions and soft-skinned vehicles in the attack, and were murderous in their effect on concentrated infantry during enemy movements and attacks.

before they could contribute to the combat. The section tactics for moving across country (see below) were only taught after each man knew how to move himself, whether in open country, woods and trees, or in a built-up area.

Tactical exercises filled half the training time. Within six weeks new recruits were taking part in field manoeuvres that involved units as large as a division, and that included all arms. The Germans profited from the lessons of World War I, when they found that half-trained troops accomplished less and sustained greater losses.

Communications were central to German combined-arms tactics, which relied on good co-ordination between all combat elements and commanders to work effectively. Here we see two men of a *Waffen-SS* signals units operating a Torn.Fu.b1 field radio, which weighed about 20kg.

The soldier in the field had to be capable of organizing himself to survive and to fight. Many hours were spent both on tactical training in field craft, and in survival on the battlefield. Not every meal could be guaranteed to come up to the front in a steaming food container. Sometimes, often frequently, the men had to cook for themselves. The *Esbit* personal cooker could be used to heat both food and water for coffee. Unless troops were trained in the careful use of cooking fires, they would invite retribution from artillery or aircraft for their folly. Hence recruits were taught to dig trenches for their fires and to make sure that the flames were fully extinguished before nightfall to avoid observation by the enemy from either ground or air. They were also taught how to use their *Zeltbahn* shelter quarter to make a waterproof coverall for themselves, and how to erect a weather shelter. Such skills were particularly important in periods of rain or cold, as troops soon lose morale and fighting spirit if they cannot keep dry and relatively warm.

There was also practical training in the use of camouflage. The matter of camouflage had been brought up time and again in the 1920s by the inspectors of exercises conducted by the *Reichswehr*, and even Von Seeckt had noted his disapproval of the somewhat casual attitude taken by the army in matters of personal camouflage. The German Army was not much better at camouflage a decade later, and even in the early part of the war it was a failing noted by many observers and participants. Things really only improved when they lost their air dominance in Russia in 1942.

The German Army prided itself on the ability of its men to march long distances with full loads. In training, distances and loads were increased during the first 16 weeks until by week 13 they were expected to march 28km in full battle order and with battle ammunition issues, which added a significant 9kg to their load. As they made this march they were also expected to exercise security measures front and rear and to the flank, and to carry out forward reconnaissance. Such training would stand them in good stead in the years to come. Needless to say, the route march was also used as yet another form of punishment for mistakes made in training.

SQUAD TACTICS

The *Gruppe* (squad) was the basic root formation of the German Army, and understanding how it fought is vital for comprehending the tactical process of larger formations. The basic aggressive squad tactics of the German Army were devised as solutions to the problem of how to advance by means of fire and movement, and dislodge the enemy from his position. At the same time, the squad had to minimize casualties, while maintaining unit effectiveness and control.

The German squad was enjoined to remain well concealed unless active in the *Feuerkampf* (firefight) or advancing to contact, but never to hesitate on the battlefield,

OVERLEAF: A German infantry column moves through Poland in 1939. As this photograph indicates, the *Heer* was a long way from full mechanization during the early years of the war, and would never fully attain such a goal. Horsepower and footpower remained the dominant forms of transportation.

and hence become easy targets. The machine-gun team and the rifles were not separate entities, but part and parcel of the squad, even though the men would generally be firing at will. Victory was likely to go to the side achieving the most concentrated rapid fire on target. Usually troops were instructed to hold their fire until 600m or closer. Even then only large targets would be fired upon; individual enemy soldiers would not normally be shot at until within 400m.

When moving on the battlefield, the German squad had two main formations. Advancing in the *Reihe* or loose single-file formation, the squad leader took the lead, followed by the machine gunner and his assistants; these were followed by the riflemen, with the assistant squad leader bringing up the rear. The *Reihe* was highly practical for moving along tracks, presented a small target from the front, and it allowed the squad leader to implement quick decisions, directing the squad as needed. In some circumstances the machine gun could be deployed forward while the remainder of men were held back. In all instances, the men were to take advantage of terrain, keeping behind contours and cover, and rushing across exposed areas when alternatives were lacking. As Wilhelm Necker later observed in *The German Army of Today* (1943), the loose formation was important to 'avoid losses', and 'clustering' around the machine gun was to be avoided, but 'connection' had to be maintained.

From the *Reihe* the squad could easily be deployed into the *Schützenkette* or skirmish line. With the machine gun deploying on the spot, the riflemen could come up to the right, left or both sides, bringing their weapons to bear. The result was a ragged line with the men about five paces apart, taking whatever cover was available. The advance to contact was in bounds from one visible objective to another, with a new objective specified as soon as the leaders had reached the first. Where resistance was serious, the advance became fully fledged fire-and-manoeuvre, either with a whole squad taking part, or a machine-gun team down and firing while others advanced. However, instructions cautioned squad commanders not to open fire with the machine gun until forced to do so by the ground and enemy fire; Weber's 1938 *Unterrichtsbuch für Soldaten* (Instruction Book for Soldiers) stated that in the assault the machine gun was to open fire 'as late as possible'. The objective of the firefight was not simply destruction of the enemy, but *Niederkampfen* – to beat down, silence or neutralize them, thus ensuring the success of close assault.

As described in the British 1941 manual *German Infantry in Action: Minor Tactics* (based on close observation of German combat methods during 1940), the final phases of aggressive squad action that were observed were the firefight; the advance; the actual assault; and the occupation of a position:

The Firefight The section is the fire unit. When fire has to be opened, the section commander usually opens fire with the LMG only. He directs its fire. When good fire effect is possible and when plenty of cover exists, the riflemen take part early in the firefight. The majority of riflemen should be in the front line and taking part in the firefight at the latest when the assault is about to be made. They usually fire independently, unless the section commander decides to concentrate the whole of their firepower on to one target.

The Advance The section works its way forward in a loose formation. Within the section the LMG usually forms the spearhead of the attack. The longer the riflemen follow the LMG in narrow, deep formation, the longer will the machine guns in the rear be able to shoot past the section.

The Assault The section commander takes any opportunity that presents itself to carry out an assault and does not wait for orders to do so. He rushes the whole section forward into the assault, leading the way himself. Before and during the assault the enemy must be engaged by all weapons at the maximum rate of fire. The LMG No.1 takes part in the assault, firing on the move. With a cheer, the section attempts to break the enemy's resistance, using hand grenades, machine pistols, rifles, pistols and entrenching tools. After the assault the section must reorganize quickly.

Occupation of a position When occupying a position the riflemen group themselves in twos and threes around the LMG in such a way that they are within voice control of the section commander.

The 1941 German infantry manual *Ausbildungsvorschrift für die Infanterie* (Training Provisions for the Infantry) adds significant additional information on the assault phase, first noting that it is 'self-confidence' in overcoming the enemy that makes the soldier successful in close combat. The LMG assault posture is specified as with the hand around the pistol grip, with the weapon couched under the right arm and held close to the body. The left hand clutches the feet of the bipod, so as to hold the muzzle down on firing, or ready to set up the weapon on arrival at the position. Riflemen are also enjoined to indulge in assault firing, the best method being to cant the rifle on to its left hand side at the hip, with bayonet fixed, and to let fly at just 5–10m range. The soldier then wades in, able to use both arms to full effect in any ensuing hand-to-hand fighting with bayonet and butt.

Although grenades were best thrown from behind cover, they could also be used on the move. The soldier was instructed to grasp his rifle in the left hand and the grenade in the right, using the fingers of the hand holding the rifle to pull the fuse cord at the opportune moment. In circumstances where showers of grenades were needed the order '*Handgranaten!*' from the squad leader would prompt the men to throw.

On the defensive, German squad tactics stressed the importance of integration with larger plans, and the principles of posts scattered in depth. The individual squad was expected to dig-in on a frontage of 30 or 40m, this being the maximum that a squad

A post-action photograph of some of the *Fallschirmjäger* (paratroopers) who participated in the victorious airborne attack on the Eben Emael fortress in Belgium, on 10–11 May 1940. The man in the centre is gripping the muzzle of an MG 34 machine gun, for which the ammunition is draped around his neck.

leader could effectively oversee in a defending battle. Major landmarks such as single trees or crests were best shunned, as they were too attractive to enemy fire. When digging positions, one member of the squad was to stand sentry, preventing surprise from ground or air. Gaps between squads might be left, although covered by fire. Key to the defence was the location of the machine gun, which would be given several alternative positions, perhaps 50 or more metres apart, identified from the outset. It would cover longer range targets, while the riflemen – who might well be held further back – were concerned mainly with sweeping the terrain at close and very close range.

The usual deployment would see the men of the squad in pairs in foxholes, trenches or ditches, posted close enough to communicate with their partner. These little sub-section nests would be slightly separated, echeloned, or at different levels, thus decreasing the effect of enemy fire. In the event that an enemy attack did not materialize immediately, the second phase of construction would see the digging of trenches behind the main line in which much of the squad could be kept back under cover until needed. Good camouflage was complemented by the avoidance of any obvious movement to attract enemy observation.

The defensive firefight was initiated by the machine gun at effective range, riflemen remaining concealed until the enemy assault, at which point all were to open fire regardless of cover. Hand grenades falling on the position were to be dealt with either by the men diving away into cover, or by picking up the grenade and throwing it back. The latter was obviously a particularly dangerous game, and the soldier playing it ran the risk of losing an arm, a foot or his life.

Some squads would be detailed to act as *Vorposten* (outposts) beyond the main line. Acting as defensive 'door bells', they might also contain observers and listening posts. Such details were given advance orders as to what to do in specific eventualities, for example when to fall back on the main line. The job of the *Vorposten* was made slightly more secure by pre-planned artillery support, numerous dummy positions to distract attention and identified safe routes away from the front. According to the 1943 British publication *Regimental Officer's Handbook of the German Army*, advanced posts were commonly within range of close support weapons such as mortars and infantry guns, and were thus to be found within about 2,000m of a main position.

According to Weber's *Unterrichtsbuch*, the ideal *Schützenloch* (rifle pit) for a standing soldier was an excavation about 1.4m deep. It was shaped with a slight lip to provide an elbow rest, and a deep sump hole at the base to give some drainage. A small niche provided a handy ammunition store. The infantryman would peg his folded *Zeltbahn* to the rear of the hole in such a way that it could be pulled over the aperture to provide both concealment and protection against the elements.

A more elaborate *MG-Stellung* (machine-gun nest) could be dug in the field by two men, working to enlarge a hole while concealed by a camouflage net. The resulting position was about four times the size of a rifle pit, and was ideally provided with a flooring of brushwood or other means of keeping the floor well drained. Holes dug horizontally into the face of the excavation nearest to the enemy provided the crew with a sheltering *Fuchsloch* (foxhole), a munition store and an *MG-Unterschlupf* – literally a 'machine-gun refuge' – a lined oblong cavity in which the gun could be stowed during bombardment or heavy rain. The somewhat simpler advice of the *Ausbildungsvorschrift* could be summed up in relatively few words: 'deep and narrow' was best against artillery and aircraft. (More about German defensive tactics is described in Chapter 4.)

An example of the efficiency of German small-unit tactics in 1939–40 comes from the German crossing the River Meuse, during the assault into France in May 1940. On 13 May, German forces were attempting a forcible crossing of the river under heavy French resistance directed from a chain of bunkers and strong points. It was the men of the assault engineers who initially succeeded, as an account by Feldwebel Rubarth records. Rubarth had a group of 11 engineers. Putting four into each of two rubber dinghies, each intended to carry three men, he crossed the river under intense fire.

An aerial photograph of the 7th Panzer Division on the move through France, 1940. The photograph neatly illustrates some of the key components of combined-arms *Blitzkrieg* – aerial reconnaissance and radio communications; tanks as the main striking force; mechanized troop deployment; and vehicular logistics.

During the crossing he ordered his driver, Gefreiter Podszus, to engage the slits of the nearest bunker with a machine gun, using another man's shoulder to steady the aim. As soon as the dingy reached the bank, Rubarth succeeded in silencing this bunker and led his men into dead ground to the rear of the next bunker. This time he used an explosive charge, which ripped out the rear wall. Soon the French defenders surrendered. 'Thus encouraged we flung ourselves at two further field-works we had spotted some 100 metres half left of us.' The first was attacked by Gefreiter Brautigam; Rubarth, with his *Feldwebel* and two of the *Gefreite*, took the second one, and the first line of bunkers had been broken. Rubarth then reached the railway embankment about a hundred metres from the river. Here he came again under heavy fire and with his ammunition exhausted decided to move back for reinforcements and ammunition, but the crossings had again been halted by heavy fire. The French meanwhile launched an attack, and Brautigam was killed and two corporals wounded before Rubarth's little party could beat them back. Soon, however, some of the riflemen and some engineers succeeded in getting over the river and Rubarth advanced again to open a gap in the second line of bunkers. By nightfall, with the riflemen of 86th Regiment, Rubarth finally reached his objective on the high ground above Wadelincourt. Of his group of 11, he lost six dead and three wounded on that one day. He was immediately awarded the *Ritterkreuz* (Iron Cross) and a *Leutnant's* commission.

What we see here are high levels of co-ordination, personal courage and a unified commitment to achieve a tactical goal, all reasons why the German Army excelled in the early campaigns of the war.

PLATOON TACTICS

Looking beyond the squad, the German infantry *Zug* (Platoon) saw considerable change over time. Under the organization pertaining from 1940 to the end of 1943, the *Zug* had four sections, a headquarters and a three-man 5cm light mortar section – a total of 49 personnel at full strength. Under the later 1944 organization this was drastically reduced to a three-section model; so, even at maximum strength, the German platoon of the latter stages of the war was just 33 strong, with one officer and three NCOs (or four NCOs) and 29 other ranks. Nevertheless, their firepower was fearsome, with four LMGs, seven SMGs and 22 rifles. Although Volksgrenadier platoons had an establishment of only three LMGs from late 1944, Panzergrenadier platoons had many more, the full LMG establishment of the armoured infantry platoon being nine.

German officers were taught that inactivity and delay were greater crimes than the wrong choice of action. In specific cases where two solutions to a tactical problem offered equally good prospects of success, 'then the more aggressive of the two must be chosen'. Commonly, the German platoon advanced in an 'arrowhead' formation, although both column and line (with sections forward and back, similar to the US model) were also used. It was up to the platoon commander to state the deployment areas and objective, to decide the formation, and to detail the sections to their tasks. Attacks would be carried out in bounds, with platoon commanders identifying weak spots in the enemy defence and deciding exactly where the blow would fall. Thereafter, according to *German Infantry in Action*:

> If the first assault is successful, even if penetration is made only on a narrow front, the attack must be pressed forward into the depth of the enemy position. At this moment the personal example of the platoon commander, who must concentrate on maintaining the momentum of the attack, is of great importance. Immediate pursuit at places where the enemy resistance weakens is therefore required. Premature movement to a flank before the enemy position has been completely penetrated is wrong. The flanks of attacking sections must be protected

ABOVE: *Fallschirmjäger* deploy for the epic assault on Eben Emael in Belgium, 1940. One man has a folding assault ladder. Some of the fortress walls were over 4m high, and the ladders had been specially made to exactly the right length. Another man has a Model 40 flamethrower, a weapon that weighed 21.32kg, and could fire ten one-second bursts to a range of about 25m. (Velimir Vuksic © Osprey Publishing)

by troops in the rear. It is the duty of reserves following up the attack to destroy any centres of resistance which remain.

The description here suggests a vigorous, violent but intelligent movement. Indeed, the strengths of German squad and platoon tactics became apparent in the 1939 and 1940 campaigns, when less well-trained European forces were outmanoeuvred or out-fought by the German teams. Of course, there were larger elements in the initial German success story, not least the Wehrmacht's armoured formations, to which we now turn our attention.

FORCE DISPARITIES

To judge the power of the German Army at the beginning of the war, it is enlightening to compare it to the forces of the first enemy it faced – Poland. German superiority was in no small measure due to the enormous economic disparity between the two countries. Although Poland devoted a significant share of its gross national product to the armed forces, its defence expenditure was dwarfed by Germany's. In the period 1935–39, Germany had defence budgets totalling about $24 billion; 30 times greater than Poland's expenditure of $760 million during the same period. The differences were most noticeable in the technical branches of the service, such as the air force and navy.

In terms of peacetime strength, the German Army was more than three times the size of the Polish; about 600,000 men compared to about 210,000. The mobilization potential of Germany was also considerably greater, with an active force of 51 divisions and a wartime

German engineer troops practice amphibious assault tactics, developing skills that would prove useful on the waterways of Poland, Western Europe and the Soviet Union. Note the use of camouflaging foliage at the front and rear of this vessel.

force of 102 divisions. Poland was able to muster only 30 divisions, though theoretically another 15 reserve divisions could eventually be deployed in a protracted conflict.

The Wehrmacht committed its best divisions to the Polish campaign and left units with reduced training and equipment facing the French. In total, the two army groups deployed the following divisions – 37 infantry, one mountain, four motorized infantry, four light and six Panzer, plus a cavalry brigade and a variety of border units, gendarme and other paramilitary formations. For the invasion of Poland, Army Group North had a total of 630,000 personnel earmarked, with a further 886,000 allocated to the more powerful Army Group South.

As of 1 September, the Polish Army had deployed 23 regular infantry divisions, three reserve infantry divisions, eight cavalry brigades, three mountain brigades, and one motorized brigade, as well as some border troops and other paramilitary formations. In terms of combat power, the Wehrmacht fielded the equivalent of 559 infantry battalions against 376 on the Polish side. This was a force ratio of 1.5:1 in the German favour overall, though if assessing the force ratios only along the major avenues of attack, the Wehrmacht enjoyed a 2.3:1 advantage. In field artillery, the Wehrmacht deployed 5,805 guns compared with Poland's 2,065 for a force advantage of 2.8:1 overall and 4.4:1 along the main avenues of attack. The disparities were greatest in armoured forces, with the Wehrmacht deploying 2,511 tanks to Poland's 615, for an advantage of 4.1:1 overall and 8.2:1 along the main avenues of attack. Moreover, these numerical comparisons underestimate the German strength advantages, since many Polish formations were only partially mobilized, while German units were on war footing at the outset of the campaign.

The most obvious qualitative inequality between the two forces was in the greater mechanization of the Wehrmacht. Germany had formed six Panzer divisions and four light divisions, starting in 1935, while Poland fielded only a single mechanized brigade. The German Army in World War I had been slow to adopt tanks, but the role of Allied tank formations in the 1918 defeat convinced many German officers of the need to embrace this new technology. During Von Seeckt's reforms of the *Reichswehr* in the 1920s, therefore, extensive experimentation was carried out with mechanized formations, even though Germany was not allowed tanks under the terms of the Versailles Treaty. The project was continued by Von Seeckt's successors, Heinz Guderian in particular, and during the 1932 manoeuvres, a motorized cavalry corps was deployed. Even the infantry experimented with motorized reconnaissance. When German remilitarization under Hitler began in 1933, therefore, the groundwork had already been established for further mechanization.

In contrast to many other armies, the Wehrmacht committed none of its tank strength to separate battalions for close infantry support. Instead, armoured advocates like Guderian insisted that the Panzers should be concentrated into divisions with their own combat mission. Guderian argued that these formations had the power to overcome enemy infantry defences on their own by shock and firepower. Once the enemy's main line of resistance had been penetrated, their mobility would allow them rapidly to exploit the penetration by either enveloping the enemy from the rear in a pincer movement with neighbouring Panzer units, or racing deep into enemy territory to attack key command and supply nodes. These views were criticized by some older German generals, but they won the personal approval of Adolf Hitler.

In fact, the experience of fighting in Poland provided some harsh lessons in the limits of Panzer use. On 1 September 1939, a most dramatic encounter between Polish cavalry and German Panzers took place when the Wolynian Cavalry Brigade confronted the 4th Panzer Division near the small village of Mokra. Polish defences at Mokra hinged on the two principal types of anti-tank weapons: anti-tank rifles and the Bofors 37mm anti-tank gun. During the afternoon fighting around the village, the German Panzer companies managed to break through the forward Polish defences, and a few infiltrated as far as the railway line running behind the village. The Wolynian Cavalry Brigade was supported by Armoured Train 53 *Smialy*, and the Panzers were taken under fire at close range, with several German tanks being knocked out. These trains had two artillery cars, each armed with two turreted guns and several machine guns. They also had an assault company of infantry in a special armoured car, and a few tankettes on special flat-cars that could disembark for scouting or attack.

Despite making repeated attacks throughout the day, the 4th Panzer Division could not dislodge the cavalry. For in 1939, *Blitzkrieg* was still in its infancy, and the German

The 25th Panzer Regiment advances across the French countryside on 5 June 1940. The vehicle on the right and in the background is the SdKfz 222, an armoured car that entered Wehrmacht service in 1938 and became the German Army's standard reconnaissance vehicle.

Motorcycle-mounted troops of the 1st Cavalry Division, seen here in Poland in 1939. The motorbikes themselves are BMW R75s, which were powered by 750cc flat twin engines and gained a deserved reputation for reliability under adverse conditions.

assault demonstrated the need for further refinement of Panzer division tactics, particularly in the area of Panzer/infantry coordination against a prepared defence. In the future, the Wehrmacht would rely on their infantry divisions to effect the breakthrough, and use the superior mobility of the Panzer divisions to exploit the breakthrough, as the 4th Panzer Division would demonstrate a few days later in the race for Warsaw.

Having suffered a bloody nose at Mokra, the 4th Panzer Division crunched through the battered Polish lines during the following two days. With the brittle Polish defences cracked wide open, the 4th Panzer Division was able to take advantage of its mobility to carry out one of the most successful Panzer missions of the campaign, exploiting its breakthrough and racing to Warsaw. Reaching the outskirts of Warsaw a week after the start of the campaign, the 4th Panzer Division pushed into the Ochota suburbs in the south-western approaches to the city.

Yet there were still lessons to be learnt. The ensuing battle highlighted the problems with operating mechanized forces in urban areas. By the time the 4th Panzer Division reached Ochota, the Poles had managed to scrape up a number of units to defend the capital. Lacking dedicated anti-tank weapons, the Poles deployed 75mm field guns to cover key street intersections. The German Panzers of 1939 were not the impregnable steel fortresses of later years, and were vulnerable to nearly any weapon heavier than a light machine gun. They could be blown open by a 75mm field gun, and a confrontation between a Panzer blindly stumbling through unfamiliar streets and a well-placed field gun behind a barricade had predictable results. Many Panzers were lost. The solution was to use infantry to locate and eliminate the field guns. But the early Panzer divisions had too few infantry for such a mission, especially when faced with Polish infantry blockaded in houses and behind barricades. Furthermore, the 4th Panzer Division had advanced so quickly that German infantry divisions were days behind. Tank/infantry co-operation in urban environments was also extremely difficult as the infantry had no way to communicate with the tanks, lacking a radio link except at battalion level. The experiences of tank use in Warsaw would convince German Panzer commanders that urban battles were better left to the infantry, a lesson that still resonates with contemporary armour officers.

Combat lessons aside, the Panzer divisions were part of a broader effort to adopt combined arms tactics and they were actually mixed formations of tanks, motorized infantry and motorized artillery. The power of a Panzer division came from its ability to exploit the virtues of all three arms of service to accomplish the mission. One of the Panzer division's least appreciated advantages was its extensive deployment of radios. Guderian was a signals officer and realized the need for radios to co-ordinate fast-moving mobile formations. The radios were a critical ingredient in combined arms operations, since they gave the various formations the ability to

This photograph of the 7th Panzer Division in France in 1940 shows the high percentage of light tanks present in the campaign. Such armour had become largely obsolete by the end of the year, and were removed from service by the end of 1942.

STRUCTURE OF A PANZER DIVISION

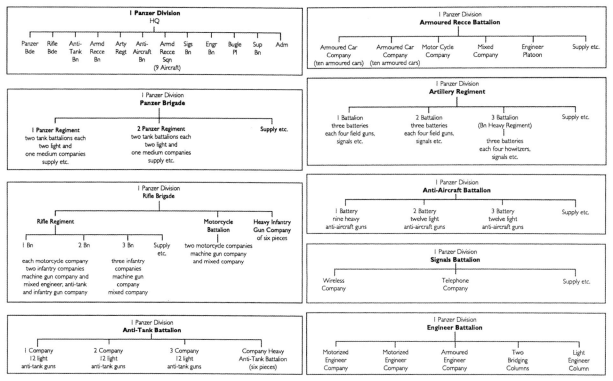

communicate with each other and synchronize their actions. No other European army had so successfully integrated radio into their command and control structure. The Germans deployed radios in a large percentage of their tanks, and unit commanders travelled in a type of radio-equipped tank called a *Befehlspanzer* (command Panzer). Most of the 215 *Befehlspanzer* in service in 1939 were a turretless type based on the *Panzerkampfwagen* (PzKpfw) I chassis, but 38 were the more capable *Panzerbefehlswagen* (PzBefWg) III on the medium-tank chassis.

The light divisions, which were an attempt to mechanize the German cavalry, were more controversial than the Panzer divisions as some generals, including Gerd von Rundstedt, felt that horse cavalry divisions would still be needed if operating in Eastern Europe, due to the poor roads. Hitler had an aversion to horses, however, and settled the matter in favour of the French model of dragoons with a small armoured element. The resulting divisions were intended to function in the traditional cavalry role of strategic reconnaissance and flank security. Compared with the Panzer divisions, they had fewer tanks and more motorized infantry.

German tanks in 1939 were not particularly impressive in terms of either firepower or armour compared with models used later in the war. The majority were light tanks, including the machine-gun armed PzKpfw I and the slightly larger PzKpfw II, which made up three-quarters of the force. While the PzKpfw I is sometimes dismissed as a training tank, this was certainly not the case. Like most armies of the 1930s, the Germans felt that a machine-gun armament would be adequate for most missions. Tank-versus-tank fighting was almost unheard of until World War II. Previously, the main mission of tanks was seen as defeating enemy infantry. The fighting during the Spanish Civil War (1936–39) made it clear that more attention had to be paid to the enemy tank threat. In Spain, the Condor Legion's PzKpfw Is stood little chance against Soviet T-26 tanks armed with 45mm guns, and the Nationalists preferred to use captured T-26s rather than the weakly armed German tanks. There were 1,445 PzKpfw I tanks in service in September 1939. The PzKpfw II was a better design, and its 20mm gun could penetrate the armour of any Polish tank of the period. Nevertheless, such a weapon was of little use in suppressing enemy anti-tank guns or troops in field fortifications. PzKpfw IIs were almost as numerous as the PzKpfw I, with 1,223 in service in September 1939.

The light tanks were supported by small numbers of medium tanks. The PzKpfw III was a new medium tank armed with a 3.7cm gun. While it would become the mainstay of the Panzer force in the years of victory in 1940–42, there were only 98 in service in 1939, with a dozen in each Panzer division. The larger PzKpfw IV was intended to

The PzKpfw III Ausf. F, seen here with a Panzer division during the campaign in France, was mostly armed with 3.7cm cannon, although 100 of the 435 produced took the more powerful 5cm gun.

PREVIOUS PAGE: Members of
the Nazi and Wehrmacht high
command inspect a massed
formation of PzKpfw I light tanks
at the Nuremberg parade ground
prior to the beginning of World
War II. Such vehicles were little
more than lightly armoured
machine-gun carriers, but they
demonstrated Germany's tactical
innovation and freedom from the
Versailles Treaty.

provide fire support for the light tanks and was armed with a short-barrelled 7.5cm gun; there were 211 in service in 1939, normally six per regiment. In total, these medium types made up only about 10 per cent of the Panzer force in 1939. Germany also benefited from the absorption of the Czech tank force, which was used in two of the light divisions. A total of 196 PzKpfw 35(t) and 78 PzKpfw 38(t) were in service in 1939, representing about 8 per cent of the Panzer force. Of the 3,466 tanks available on 1 September 1939, 2,626 were committed to the Polish campaign.

Germany also had a significant force of armoured cars, including 718 light armoured cars such as the SdKfz 221, 222 and 223, and 307 heavy armoured cars such as the SdKfz 231 and 232. Armoured cars were used in the reconnaissance regiments of the light, motorized infantry and Panzer divisions.

Anti-tank defence in both armies was similar. The German Army used the 3.7cm PaK 36 (*Panzerabwehr Kanone*; armour defence gun) anti-tank gun, while Polish infantry used the licence-manufactured Swedish Bofors 37mm anti-tank gun. In the Polish case, they were deployed in platoons at battalion level for a total of 27 per division. In the German case, they were deployed in companies at regimental level with 12 guns each. The German infantry divisions had slightly more anti-tank guns than comparable Polish divisions, as they also had a separate anti-tank unit at divisional level in addition to the three companies at regimental level. Both the German and Polish armies deployed anti-tank rifles for company defence. The German Army used the *Panzerbusche* (PzB) 38/39, while the Poles used the wz. 35 anti-tank rifle. The two weapons had similar performance; each was able to penetrate about 30mm of armour at 100m, which was more than adequate against the poorly armoured tanks of the period (see Chapters 2 and 4 for more on anti-tank weaponry).

The divisional firepower disparity was greatest in artillery. Even though the total number of tubes was only slightly greater in the German case (68 versus 48), the actual salvo power was about double that of the Polish divisional artillery. The Wehrmacht relied on the 105mm leFH 18 as its principal field gun, which was a more modern and powerful weapon than the Polish 75mm field guns based on the French M.1897 and rechambered Russian Mod. 02/26. For heavy firepower, the Germans used the modern sFH 18 while the Poles used a mixed bag of Skoda Mod. 14/19 100mm howitzers, 105mm Mod. 29 Schneider guns and 155mm Schneider Mod. 17 howitzers. In addition, German infantry divisions had 20 75mm and 150mm infantry guns for direct support, for which the Poles had no equivalents.

The German firepower advantage was not only in the number and calibre of tubes, but also in ammunition supply and fire control. Due to greater use of radios, German artillery fire control was a generation beyond that of the Poles, who still relied on World War I techniques. In addition, the greater motorization of the German forces

meant that the Wehrmacht divisions had more ammunition on hand, and could replenish the gun batteries in a more timely fashion. A German division carried with it some 230 tonnes of artillery ammunition, an impossible amount for the Poles due to a lack of trucks. Although much has been made of the damage caused by Stuka attacks, it was in fact the German artillery that had the most devastating effect on the Polish infantry during the fighting. The effect was even greater at corps and army level, with the Wehrmacht having advantages in both the number and quality of heavy-calibre weapons.

Although both sides relied on horses as their principal means of transport and supply, the Wehrmacht infantry divisions were more heavily motorized than the Polish units (although motorization was far from total). The Wehrmacht infantry division had 5,375 horses, 938 motor vehicles and 530 motorcycles compared with 6,937 horses and only 76 motor vehicles per Polish division. The difference reflected the greater wealth of the German economy, which before the war had about 1.4 million motor vehicles compared with only about 33,000 in Poland.

In terms of command-and-control, the German divisions had a motorized radio company in addition to a field-telephone company while the Poles relied almost

An 8.8cm Flak gun in action in Poland in 1939. Used as both an anti-aircraft and an anti-tank weapon, the '88' became a critical component of German Army artillery, not least because of the volume produced – more than 18,000 guns (all variants).

exclusively on field telephones. In a war of manoeuvre, the new means of communication were a vital ingredient in German victory; they not only enhanced the tactical advantages of the Wehrmacht in areas such as artillery firepower, but also made it possible to exploit aerial reconnaissance to manoeuvre German formations rapidly and to synchronize the activities of neighbouring German units faster than the Poles could react.

TRAINED TO WIN

While the German Army enjoyed a clear superiority in numbers of armoured vehicles over the Poles, the same did not apply in its campaign in the West in 1940. The combined Allied forces could bring about 3,000 tanks to bear against roughly 2,500 deployed by the Germans. And yet, the German Panzers were still triumphant. This was partly due to the very nature of *Blitzkrieg* tactics — many Allied armoured formations were simply outmanoeuvred on the battlefield. There were also deficiencies in Allied tactics, command structures and technologies. French tanks were 'lobbed out' among the infantry division, some 1,500 to 1,700 of them; while about 700–800 were given to other formations. Regarding technology, four-fifths of French tanks had no radio. Yet arguably most important of all was that Allied tank crew training and doctrine was vastly inferior to that of the German Panzer troops.

On receiving his call-up notice and reporting for duty, the prospective Panzer soldier underwent the basic military training common to all German soldiers. Even for tank crews, basic infantry training was essential. If a vehicle was knocked out or disabled, the crew would have to fend for themselves, and in the event, many of them did so admirably. Photographs show a surprisingly large number of Panzer soldiers wearing the Close Combat Clasp, awarded for hand-to-hand fighting.

A PzKpfw 38(t) light tank moves alongside an infantry force during the invasion of France. This tank was really only suited to light reconnaissance and support duties, its main armament consisting of an inadequate 3.7cm Skoda gun, while its armour (at least in the early types) had a maximum depth of just 25mm.

On completion of his basic infantry training, the recruit commenced specialist Panzer training. From the beginning, Guderian had favoured highly structured training. First the individual would receive his own training, then the various crew members would come together and exercise as a team. Trained crews would take part in unit level exercises and finally the units themselves would be involved in large-scale manoeuvres.

Guderian had immersed himself in studying tank tactics during the 1920s, and in 1931, having been given command of 3rd Mechanized Battalion in Berlin, he set about putting his theories into practice. His transport unit made dummy hardboard superstructures that were fitted over the bodies of light cars to give the appearance of a tank. As a result, by the time the first Panzer Mk Is rolled off the production lines, training of tank crews, at least in tactical exercises, was already under way.

Finally, in November 1933, Panzer training proper began, with the establishment of a new training school, the *Panzertruppen-Schule* (Panzer Troop School) at Wunsdorf-Zossen. The school was eventually split to form two new schools: Panzer School 1 at Bergen, which specialized in training tank and anti-tank personnel; and Panzer School 2 at Potsdam-Krampnitz, where Panzergrenadiers and Panzer reconnaissance troops were trained. Later on in the war, in addition to basic tank training, specialization courses were run for Panther crews at Erlangen training grounds and Tiger crews at Paderborn training grounds. For most of the war, NCO training for tank crews was carried out by the *Feld-Unteroffizier-Schule* near Warsaw in occupied Poland.

A PzKpfw 38(t) is transported to the battlefront on a German armoured train. The rail network was the lifeline of German Army logistics during World War II. Armoured trains were introduced into the Wehrmacht following encounters with Polish equivalents in 1939, and they were mounted with an assortment of field and anti-aircraft guns.

Officer candidate training was the responsibility of the *Fahnenjunker-Schule der Panzertruppen* (Cadet School for Panzer Troops) at Gross-Glienicke near Berlin, and specific courses were run at Panzer training establishments at Gross-Glienicke, Ohrdruf and Wischau. Advanced officer candidate training was also carried out at Gross-Glienicke and Wischau by the *Oberfähnrich-Schule der Panzertruppe* (Officer Cadet School for Panzer Troops). Tank commanders were selected from the best of the trained tank crews, and in turn the *Zugführer* (platoon leader) would be selected from the best of the commanders.

At the outbreak of the Spanish Civil War, Germany dispatched a number of its PzKpfw Is to support the Nationalist cause. Although the German personnel who accompanied the tanks were intended to train Spanish crews for the tanks rather than crew them themselves, once the training had been completed, the German crews were also permitted to go into action. Thus the *Panzerwaffe* (Panzer Arm), in the years leading up to the outbreak of World War II, had the priceless opportunity to test themselves, their tactics and their vehicles in action. They learned many valuable lessons in the process.

In September 1937, the first large-scale tank training manoeuvres were held around Neustrelitz in front of a high-ranking audience, which included the Italian dictator Mussolini. By the outbreak of war, it was clear to the Germans that their Mk I and Mk II Panzers were hopelessly under-gunned, the former having only machine guns and the latter only a 2cm cannon. Nevertheless, these vehicles would form the backbone of the *Panzerwaffe* during the attack on Poland.

It soon became clear that in many ways, the Panzer crew closely resembled the crew of a U-boat in that it was a small team, each dependent on his crewmates, fighting within an enclosed steel environment. As with the U-boats, it was essential that each Panzer crewman had a working knowledge of the skills required for each job within the crew, in case one of his comrades was killed or injured. The loss of any one crewman (typically, medium tanks would have a crew of five) could seriously impair or even totally negate the tank's fighting ability if a colleague could not step in and fill the breach.

Initial driver training was given using cut-down examples of the PzKpfw I or II with the turret and superstructure removed. As well as the army's own instructors, considerable use was made of the facilities of the *Nationalsozialistisches Kraftfahrkorps* (NSKK; National Socialist Motor Corps), the Party's own motor formation. Many period photographs show tanks on training exercises with the letters NSKK stencilled on the front glacis plate. Of course, prior to Germany's open rearmament, the country was prohibited from having tanks by the Treaty of Versailles, so the first Mk Is were designated as small tractors. But whether tanks or tractors, the important thing was that the trainee had the opportunity to learn the art of driving a tracked vehicle, something quite different to controlling a wheeled conveyance.

Gunnery training was undertaken at the ranges at Putlos on the Baltic. As the *Panzerwaffe* grew, so did the number of designated training schools and training areas. Many such sites, for example the Sennelager training area, are still in use today as Panzer training grounds.

The most important part of Panzer training, apart from the technical training on how to operate the vehicle itself, was on how to use the tank as an efficient fighting weapon. The *Panzerwaffe* was particularly adept at collecting tactical lessons from frontline experience and distributing it through the training schools. This gave the training conditions realism and pressure, which meant that the experience of real combat was less shocking for the Panzer crews. Panzer forces also enjoyed an extremely high *esprit de corps* and unit pride, which gave them high levels of integration and motivation on the battlefield.

A German Army *Leutnant* consults his orders just prior to the assault on Warsaw in September 1939. These soldiers wear the army uniform issued from 1936, which included a single-breasted five-button tunic, with two hip and two breast pockets.

ARMOURED DEVELOPMENTS

The German Army drew to the end of 1940 basking in the glow of battlefield success. Its Panzer arm, much like the Luftwaffe, had acquired particular distinction, and it grew rapidly in the year before Operation *Barbarossa*. Eleven new Panzer divisions were formed in 1940. The strength of the *Waffen-SS* Panzer and Panzergrenadier wing was also growing. A more detailed study of the *Waffen-SS* is made in Chapter 3, but in the long run the elite divisions of the *Waffen-SS* gained the greatest fame, or notoriety, as Panzer divisions.

The *Leibstandarte SS Adolf Hitler*, for example, was the premier unit of the SS, and it had its origins in Hitler's personal bodyguard. By the outbreak of war in 1939, it had reached the status of a motorized infantry regiment and served in this capacity in the Polish campaign. It went on to achieve divisional size in November 1942, and it converted to Panzer division status in October 1943. The *Leibstandarte* recruited throughout Germany and only the highest quality candidates were accepted. Hitler is said to have insisted, 'My *Leibstandarte* will accept no one who is not the best that Germany can offer!' Recruits had to be at least 1.86m tall, of the highest possible standards of physical fitness, of traceable Aryan ancestry (back to 1800 for other ranks and 1750 for officers), no criminal record and even his physical features had to match Himmler's standards for Nordic appearance. Recruits signed on for four years in the ranks, extending to 12 years for NCOs and 25 for officers.

During the war a total of seven *Waffen-SS* divisions were either established as, or converted to, Panzer division status. It has often been suggested that *Waffen-SS* divisions were given unfair priority in re-equipping with the latest, improved versions of various armoured vehicles. There is, however, little evidence to support this theory, as elite army units such as *Grossdeutschland* (see feature box) were also equipped with the best tanks available. It is more likely that the best vehicles were given first to those units that would make best use of them, i.e. those that were the most aggressive and daring in the attack and most tenacious in defence, and the *Waffen-SS* Panzer divisions certainly qualified on both counts.

It should be noted that the Luftwaffe was also fielding significant ground forces in the form of *Fallschirmjäger* (paratroopers) and air landing troops, of which more will be discussed in the next chapter. In terms of armoured forces, the head of the Luftwaffe, Reichsmarschall Hermann Göring, was also watering the seeds of his own armoured formation, the Fallschirmpanzer Division *Hermann Göring*.

The origins of this massive formation lay with an obscure pre-war Prussian police detachment (at the time, Hermann Göring was Prussian Minister of the Interior). It was upgraded to a regiment in 1935 and transferred to the Luftwaffe in October of that year. The regiment was largely uninvolved in the Polish and Scandinavian campaigns, but acquitted itself well in the battle for France. It was subsequently enlarged again, this time to brigade size in July 1942, and within just three months it had increased in size again to divisional status. Panzer Regiment *Hermann Göring* was formed in April 1943 and shortly thereafter the division itself was accorded Panzer division status. By the end of the war, further expansion had seen the creation of *Fallschirmpanzer* corps, consisting of the 1st Fallschirm Panzer Division *Hermann Göring* and the 2nd Fallschirm Panzergrenadier Division *Hermann Göring*.

SERVICE AND FIELD UNIFORMS

The German Army had a particularly distinctive form of uniform, both practical and visually professional. All dates connected with the introduction of new uniforms, equipment and insignia give the date of the Army Order. However, as in all armies, there was a delay (ranging from a few weeks to as much as two years) in new items reaching individual units, especially frontline units, remote garrisons or the Replacement Army. Furthermore, individual soldiers, especially senior officers, often preferred to retain obsolete items if they were of sentimental value, or of better quality than the replacement. They gave the owner an air of individuality and marked him as an experienced 'old sweat'. An army order of 10 July 1942 decreed that all obsolete clothing could continue to be worn for the duration of the war.

The most visible symbol of the Wehrmacht was the breast eagle, the *Hoheitsabzeichen*, or 'Sovereignty Badge', worn by all ranks above the right breast pocket of most uniform items, and identifying the wearer as fit to bear arms. The army version, introduced on 17 February 1934, with effect from 1 May 1934, depicted an eagle with straight, outstretched wings grasping a circled swastika. Most other uniformed organizations, including the *Waffen-SS*, introduced various styles of eagle badges, but were obliged to wear them on the left upper arm, since the right breast was reserved for the Wehrmacht and, curiously enough, the *NS-Fliegerkorps* (NSFK; National Socialist Flying Corps).

The various uniform items of the new army uniform began to appear following publication of the Dress Regulations of 8 April 1935, and by the end of the year the main uniform styles were established. The basic uniform colour was a greenish-grey, introduced on 2 July 1929 and given the traditional but inaccurate title of *feldgrau*, 'field grey' (originally designating a plain mid-grey introduced on 23 February 1910). Facings were in a bluish dark-green 'facing-cloth', finely woven to give an appearance of a thin felt, introduced on 29 June 1935, and the same material was usually used for branch colour patches and pipings. *Reichswehr* uniform items, in M1929 *feldgrau* but with a darker greenish-grey facing-cloth, should have been withdrawn by 1937, but were still occasionally encountered in the 1939/40 period.

The Regulations of April 1935 prescribed ten orders of dress in peacetime for officers, two ceremonial uniforms and a parade uniform for formal occasions; a walking-out and reporting uniform for semi-formal occasions; service, undress and guard uniforms for training and barracks duties; the field uniform for combat; and sports dress (omitted in this study). NCOs and other ranks had nine, omitting the ceremonial uniforms and adding a fatigue uniform for work duties in barracks or in the field. Some uniform items were manufactured in different versions for officers and other ranks, while others were standard items worn by all ranks.

OVERLEAF: The fruits of victory. Mounted German troops take part in a victory parade through Paris in 1940, the Arc de Triomphe clearly visible in the background. A full 80 per cent of German transportation was provided by horses, at a significant cost to mobility and to the beasts themselves.

A PzKpfw III hides in the shade of the Ardennes in 1940, prior to the invasion of France. The German deployment through the heavily forested Ardennes region – which the French had believed to be impassable for armour – demonstrated Werhmacht mobility at its best.

LEFT: A military policeman, 1940. The shoulder straps and collar patches have orange-red *Waffenfarbe* branch of service colour for the military police and on his left sleeve are both the *Gendarmerie* eagle, again in orange-red embroidery, and the cuff title '*Feldgendarmerie*'. In addition, only when on duty, a special gorget plate or *Ringkragen* was worn on a chain around the neck. (Velimir Vuksic © Osprey Publishing)

OFFICERS' FIELD CAPS

The M1934 officers' 'old-style' field cap, introduced on 24 March 1934, became the M1935 peaked cap with the addition of a bluish dark-green cap band on 10 September 1935, and the omission of the metal crown stiffener, chincords and buttons. The visor was made of soft black patent leather and, from 30 October 1935, the eagle, cockade and wreath were of bright aluminium thread on a bluish dark-green backing. The visorless flapped M1938 officers' 'new-style' field cap, introduced 6 December 1938, was made of *feldgrau* cloth, piped along the crown and the front of the flap with 3mm aluminium thread cord. The narrow aluminium cord national cockade was enclosed by a branch colour chevron, point up, in facing-cloth, with a machine-woven or hand-embroidered bright aluminium thread eagle on a bluish dark-green backing above. From 24 October 1939, general officers wore gold thread crown and flap piping and a gold artificial silk chevron.

New regulations were issued on 28 December 1939 to cover the wartime period and the earlier strict observance of regulations eased. The types of uniforms were simplified. Service uniform could be worn on most formal and semi-formal occasions, but, inevitably, the field uniform became the most common uniform encountered in the front line and rear areas. Furthermore, Replacement Army units were often issued captured Austrian, Czech, Dutch, French and even British uniform items, dyed and remodelled to conform to German patterns.

For officers, service uniform consisted of the officers' peaked cap, M1933 field tunic with ribbons, M1935 field greatcoat, leather belt, breeches and riding-boots, grey suede gloves, standard pistol and holster. The officers' field tunic was introduced on 5 May 1933, replacing the M1920 *Reichswehr* service tunic. It was manufactured from superior quality *feldgrau* cloth with five matt-grey painted pebbled buttons, four patch pockets, turn-back cuffs and a *feldgrau* cloth collar, replaced by *feldgrau* facing-cloth on 26 July 1934 and by bluish dark-green facing-cloth in March 1936. All insignia was field quality: the breast eagle was in matt aluminium thread on a bluish dark-green facing-cloth backing; the bluish dark-green facing-cloth collar patches had two matt aluminium 'Guards' braids', each with a branch colour silk-embroidered centre cord. Many general officers retained the M1920 or M1928 service tunic with field-quality insignia and no front piping. The officers' field greatcoat was like the dress greatcoat, but with field-quality shoulder-boards and the back seam left open.

In the field, all army officers except platoon leaders wore the standard M1935 steel helmet, officers' field tunic, with the field greatcoat if ordered, brown belt, breeches and riding-boots and grey suede gloves. Personal field equipment was usually limited to the P'08 Luger or P38 Walther pistol in a smooth leather holster – general officers and field officers favoured the smaller Walther 7.65mm PPK – and 6x30 black binoculars in a smooth black or tan leather or bakelite case carried on the right front hip. Behind the front line the M1934 or M1938 field caps replaced the helmet.

In the field the shape and colour of the helmet was often camouflaged by daubing it with mud, or tying on chicken-wire or the straps of the M1931 bread-bag and securing foliage to them. On 21 March 1940 the conspicuous national shield was removed and the helmet surface roughened and repainted from matt *feldgrau* to matt slate-grey.

From 31 October 1939, all officers below general officer rank in combat units were ordered to wear the M1935 other ranks' field tunic, trousers and marching boots with the black leather belt and officers' field-quality shoulder-boards. Many officers, however, continued to wear their former uniforms or modified the other ranks' tunic by adding officers' roll-back cuffs, collar-patches and the sharper-pointed, higher officers' collars.

Subalterns acting as infantry platoon leaders wore the standard riflemen's field equipment, adding the brown or black leather M1935 dispatch case on the left front hip, with binoculars, compass and signal-whistle. Riflemen's field equipment consisted of the standard smooth or grained black leather M1939 infantry support Y-straps with aluminium fittings (introduced on 18 April 1939), supporting two sets of three black leather ammunition pouches for the rifle. The bayonet in a black scabbard with the black leather cavalry bayonet-frog (introduced on 25 January 1939) and entrenching-tool were worn on the left back hip. On the right back hip were the M1931 *feldgrau* canvas bread-bag and M1931 brown felt-covered canteen and black painted aluminium cup. Webbing supported the M1931 mess-kit and M1931 camouflage shelter-quarter on the upper back, and on the lower back the M1930 or M1938 gas mask in the distinctive *feldgrau*-painted cylindrical corrugated metal canister. The dark greenish-brown gas cape hung on the chest from a thin brown leather strap and a field flashlight was usually carried on the left shoulder. By September 1939 most officers had the MP 38 submachine gun, for which two olive-green canvas M1938 magazine pouches were issued to replace the black leather ammunition pouches.

The service uniform for technical and senior NCOs consisted of the peaked cap, M1933 field tunic with ribbons, M1935 field greatcoat, trousers and marching-boots, black belt with pistol and holster and grey suede gloves. Junior NCOs wore the helmet instead of the M1935 other ranks' field cap instead of the service cap, and Y-straps, ammunition pouches and a bayonet instead of the pistol and holster. Junior NCOs also wore grey suede gloves. The other ranks' field greatcoat, introduced on 10 September 1935, was identical to the officers' version but was of lesser quality and the insignia was other ranks' field quality.

The M1935 other ranks' field cap, also introduced on 10 September 1935, resembled the later M1938 officers' field cap, and was developed from the M1934 cap of 24 March

ABOVE: Mountain troops were naturally of value for the Norwegian campaign of 1940. Here we see (from left to right) a mountain trooper, a mountain troop *Unteroffizier* and a *Gebirgsjäger Unteroffizier*. Items of Luftwaffe paratrooper dress are mixed in with standard army uniform. (Stephen Andrew © Osprey Publishing)

ABOVE: Typical equipment and weaponry carried by a pioneer platoon commander in 1940. The equipment includes wire cutters, minefield marker flags, issue march compass and case, Walther signal pistol and cartridges and officer's map case. (Adam Hook © Osprey Publishing)

1934. It was made of *feldgrau* cloth with a *feldgrau* flap, and the eagle and swastika and national cockade was embroidered in white cotton on a *feldgrau* backing from 30 October 1935, and on a bluish dark-green backing from 19 June 1937. Embroidery changed to silver-grey on 5 February 1939, and on 4 June 1940 to mouse-grey on *feldgrau* backing. The cockade was enclosed by a 4mm woollen branch colour chevron, point-up. The field uniform consisted of the helmet or field cap, field tunic with ribbons, field greatcoat if ordered, plain trousers and marching boots. All NCOs had grey suede gloves.

TANK CREW UNIFORMS

The M1934 black uniform was closely associated with the Panzer branch, but initially only tank crews were authorized to wear it. Later, units of other branches in Panzer divisions were allowed to wear this prestigious uniform: signals battalions from 2 April 1937, artillery regiments from mid 1938, armoured reconnaissance battalions in March 1940, and on 10 May 1940 armoured engineer battalions. However, unauthorized personnel, such as general officers, staff officers and members of unit staffs such as doctors, paymasters and company sergeant-majors, unofficially adopted the uniform. The colour, the distinctive double-breasted jacket and the collar patch skulls were intended to evoke the prestige of the Imperial German Cavalry.

The black uniform, introduced on 12 November 1934, could be worn on all occasions except ceremonial. It consisted of the standard M1934 padded beret, later replaced by the M1940 field cap; a dark-grey tricot pullover shirt and black tie; the M1934 field jacket; M1934 field trousers and black lace-up shoes. The padded beret was made of thick felt or red rubber sponge covered in black wool. From 30 October 1935 officers wore an eagle and swastika in bright aluminium bullion on the front of the beret, other ranks the badge in matt silver-grey machine-woven cotton thread above a white cotton thread, later matt silver-grey machine-woven cotton thread, cockade and wreath, all insignia on a black backing. The beret proved too cumbersome in armoured vehicles, and on 27 March 1940 it began to be replaced by the M1940 officers' black field cap and the M1940 other ranks' black field cap. These caps were identical to the M1938 and M1934 *feldgrau* versions, but were in black cloth, with the eagle and cockade on a black cloth backing. Many officers and NCOs also favoured the *feldgrau* officers' M1935 peaked cap, M1934 peaked field cap or M1938 field cap, or other ranks' M1935 peaked cap or M1934 field cap.

The black wool double-breasted hip-length Panzer field jacket had a wide collar, with a 2mm branch colour facing-cloth piping, and wide lapels. The fly-front was closed by four large black horn or plastic buttons, with three smaller buttons left exposed above. Officers wore a matt aluminium thread breast-eagle, other ranks a white cotton, later a matt silver-grey, machine-woven cotton thread breast-eagle, all on a black cloth backing. All ranks wore standard black cloth collar-patches with branch colour piping and a bright aluminium stamped skull. All ranks wore field-quality shoulder and sleeve rank insignia, with black cloth replacing the bluish dark-green facing-cloth for NCOs and men. NCOs did not wear bright aluminium yarn braid collar braid. The M1934 plain black trousers tapered at the bottom to give a bloused effect, and buttoned and tied at the ankle.

In the field, all ranks wore a leather belt with a pistol and holster.

Hitler's armed forces had served him with distinction in the battles of 1939–40. They seemed to vindicate all the tactical innovations and technical investments of the pre-war period. As we have seen in this chapter, the German Army went into war superbly trained and generally well equipped. Yet from 1941 the war would expand on a huge scale, and the pressures on the Wehrmacht's capabilities and professionalism would dramatically increase.

NORTH AFRICA AND THE BALKANS, 1940–43

GERMAN MILITARY INVOLVEMENT IN NORTH AFRICA WAS BROUGHT ABOUT AS a gesture of support by Hitler for his incompetent Italian ally Mussolini. The Italians, eager to share in Hitler's continuing military success, had invaded Egypt from their colony in Libya in September 1940, outnumbering the meagre British forces by some five to one. The Italian 10th Army advanced from Cyrenaica (north-east Libya) into Egypt, only to be forced back into Tripolitania (north-west Libya) by the first offensive from the British imperial garrison. Hitler, sensing trouble, decided to send a small expeditionary force to bolster Italian forces by blocking the Allied advance and prevent an Italian collapse in Libya.

The contingent that disembarked at Tripoli on 14 February 1941 became the 5th Light Division four days later. It constituted the first unit of the infamous *Deutsches Afrika Korps* (DAK; German Africa Corp) under Generalleutnant Erwin Rommel.

The actual state of the German unpreparedness for the war in the Western Desert is hard to fathom; uniforms were the only desert item actually available, and vehicles arrived in Libya still painted in the European standard dark grey. Rommel, albeit a successful Panzer division commander during the campaign against France, had no experience as a corps commander or of the desert. Units were mostly equipped for the European

The DAK divisional headquarters staff study maps around an SdKfz 250/3 command vehicle, which was equipped with a FuG12 radio and was designed to provide radio command to armoured and motorized forces. A large tarpaulin covers the rod aerial.

DAK TITLES

The *Deutsches Afrika Korps* title is often used, incorrectly, as shorthand for all German forces in North Africa. Actually, the DAK itself went through several incarnations and expansions. On 1 September 1941 the DAK — eventually comprising 15th, 21st Panzer, 90th Africa and 164th Light (*leichte*) Africa Divisions, and one to three Italian corps — became Panzergruppe Afrika (Panzer Group Africa); then on 30 January 1942, *Panzerarmee Afrika* (Panzer Army Africa); on 1 October 1942 the *Deutsch–Italienische Panzerarmee* (German–Italian Panzer Army); and on 22 February 1943 the 1st Italian Army under the Italian general Giovanni Messe. On 14 November 1942, the *Stab Nehring* (HQ Nehring), which on 19 November was redesignated LXXX Corps and on 8 December, 5. *Panzerarmee* (5th Panzer Army), was formed for operations in Tunisia with three German divisions. Combining with the 1st Italian Army, it formed Army Group Africa on 22 February 1943.

theatre, and would soon prove unsuitable for North Africa, not to mention the absolute lack of any kind of acclimatization to an unfamiliar and harsh environment. Yet, thanks both to Rommel's initiative and to the British diversion in Greece, on 23 March 1941 Rommel launched his first offensive with 5th Light Division and three Italian divisions, storming El Agheila and advancing through Cyrenaica, before halting on 27 May at Halfaya ('Hellfire') Pass, just inside Egypt.

It was a strong start, but there now began to establish a see-saw pattern of victory and defeat that characterized war in North Africa. On 18 November, the British 8th Army commenced its second offensive into Cyrenaica, forcing Rommel back into Tripolitania where he halted at El Agheila on 31 December. There, on 21 January 1942, Rommel counterattacked, penetrating 400km into Egypt before stopping at El Alamein.

Despite the Axis successes, the action in North Africa was wearing German forces down, and long, vulnerable supply lines became a serious issue. In July 1942 the hard-pressed Rommel received reinforcements, when the Crete Fortress Division was flown in and reformed on 15 August as a mechanized unit. Yet such strengthening was not sufficient for what would follow. On 23 October 1942, a total of 230,000 Allied troops advanced from El Alamein, forcing back Rommel's 100,000 men (by now four German and ten Italian divisions). The German–Italian Panzer Army retreated through Libya, eventually halting on the Mareth Line, 160km inside Tunisia, on 15 February 1943. On 19 February, Rommel displayed his old brilliance by routing US Army forces at the Kassarine Pass before handing over command to Generaloberst Hans-Jürgen von Arnim and returning to Germany.

Worse was now to come for German forces in North Africa. On 8 November 1942, an Anglo-American expeditionary force landed in Morocco and Algeria. They had advanced to within 80km of Tunis when, in late November, the 10th Panzer Division reached Tunis as part of LXXXX Corps (later 5th Panzer Army).

It broke out of the Tunis bridgehead in November 1942, and by February 1943 had established a 60km-deep defensive line around Tunis. Then, in late March 1943, the 999th Africa Division arrived. Originally formed as a brigade on 6 October 1942 and expanded to a division on 2 February 1943, this unique formation, with all its sub-units carrying the 'black number' 999, was composed of disciplinary troops led by regular officers and NCOs. The last-minute bolstering was not enough, and on 20 March the British Eighth Army broke through at the Mareth Line, and on 12 May Von Arnim surrendered in Tunis.

GENERAL CHANGES IN THE GERMAN ARMY

On 31 July 1940, Hitler began to prepare for the invasion of the Soviet Union, Operation *Barbarossa*. Now the theatre of combat dictated the quality of army divisions that were used: those in North Africa were generally makeshift units, reflecting the low priority of that theatre; the forces committed to Operation *Marita* – the invasion of Yugoslavia and Greece in April 1941, another German rescue of the Italians – were frontline divisions earmarked for *Barbarossa*. They were replaced by second-line units

Reconnaissance troops of the 10th Panzer Division are here deployed in an SdKfz 250 – one of the German Army's most versatile light armoured vehicles – in Tunisia in 1942.

An idealized propaganda photograph of an *Afrika Korps* soldier socializing with the locals in North Africa. He wears the pith helmet made from compressed cork, which although appearing suitably 'tropical' was actually fairly unpopular with the troops, who preferred light field caps.

with limited mobility and combat potential, first-line units making limited appearances in the Balkans until August 1943 and the arrival of the formidable 2nd Panzer Army.

The period of the North African war, therefore, was a complicated time for the German Army, which had to cope with multiple demands and structural changes. Mountain corps were formed after September 1940 and motorized corps were redesignated Panzer corps after June 1942.

ERWIN ROMMEL

Born in 1891, Erwin Rommel would go on to become one of the greatest military innovators and commanders of the 20th century. He entered the army as an officer cadet in 1910, and subsequently saw action as a troop commander during World War I, winning the *Pour la Mérite* for his leadership during the battle of Isonzo. During the inter-war years he rose through the ranks steadily, and became an acknowledged expert in infantry tactics – his book *Infanterie greift an* (Infantry Attacks), published in 1937, became a standard tactical manual and brought him to the attention of Hitler.

In World War II, Rommel made his mark during the 1940 French campaign, showing a bold and daring (and often controversial) handling of the 7th Panzer Division. His early victories leading the DAK in North Africa gave him the nickname 'Desert Fox', but the arduous campaign took a toll on his physical and mental health, and he was evacuated from the theatre in March 1943. Later in the year he commanded Army Group B in northern Italy, and was then sent to France in November to build up the Atlantic Wall defences. He became an army group commander in France, but had serious disagreements with his superior, Von Rundstedt, over defensive deployments. He was in the thick of fighting following the Normandy landings of June 1944, and on 17 July was seriously wounded when his staff car was strafed by an enemy fighter. Back in Germany, he was then implicated in the July bomb plot against Hitler (he had been approached by the plotters, but had rejected their goal). On 14 October, at his home, Nazi officials gave him a choice – suicide but protection for his family and a state funeral, or arrest, trial and execution, plus persecution for his family. He took the proffered cyanide pill, and was later buried with full military honours.

First-line infantry divisions generally retained their 1939 organization until 1942, although often adding a reinforcement battalion. On 13 April 1941, '700-series' infantry divisions – only 8,000 men strong – were formed from second-line troops for occupation duties. They consisted of two infantry regiments (which lacked heavy equipment), an artillery battalion, reconnaissance, engineer and signals companies and minimal logistical support. On 1 April 1943 these divisions, along with light infantry divisions (formed in December 1940 for combat in hilly terrain) and selected reserve divisions, were reorganized as *Jäger* (rifle) divisions with younger personnel and M1939 infantry organization, but with only two rifle regiments. From 1942 territorial rifle units were gradually redesignated security units, and in a questionable attempt to raise morale, all infantry regiments were redesignated grenadier regiments on 15 October 1942. Back in March 1940, anti-tank assault-gun batteries were formed, and on 10 August 1940 they were grouped into battalions, each with 31 self-propelled guns. Army anti-aircraft battalions were introduced in February 1941, with three batteries of 8.8cm anti-aircraft guns also serving as anti-tank guns. Armoured and mechanized forces also underwent changes, explained in detail in the next chapter, yet throughout such widespread changes, the German Army continued to function superbly in combat if kept well-supplied (an increasingly big 'if', particularly from late 1941). For those troops operating in North Africa, however, the theatre provided a very different range of challenges than experienced in Europe.

LIFE ON CAMPAIGN

Terrain and climate were crucial factors in the life of *Afrika Korps* soldiers, as they were for all forces fighting in North Africa. The aspect of desert life that most affected the men was undoubtedly the harsh climate, with temperatures sometimes rising up to 75°C (the average stood at about 50°C) during the summer months. Physical fitness was a basic prerequisite for service in the region, for which men aged under 35 were best suited. Even so, the intense heat would often have a paralyzing effect on the unaccustomed soldier, further aggravating any disease caused by poor diet and hygiene. During rest and lull periods, to avoid the heat of the noon hours, three hours of rest without any physical activity were allowed. It was at this time of the day that cold rations were served, while hot rations were given during the cold nights (when temperatures fell below 0°C).

The extremes of temperature soldiers encountered within a single 24-hour period were aggravating. Hans von Luck, serving in 1942 with a motorized infantry battalion of the 21st Panzer Division, recalled how they used to wear the greatcoat (necessary during the night) and thick scarves until well into the morning. Slowly, the heat would make its way through them, and at that point they had to be taken off. Gradually, during the day, the heat would become more and more unbearable. The popular image of soldiers frying bacon and eggs on the heated armoured plating of a Panzer, as shown by propaganda newsreels, seems to have been subject to quite a debate. Von Luck wrote that it did really happen, and that he did it himself; others revealed that it was some kind of a trick for propaganda purposes, with the armour plating having been heated using an oxy-hydrogen flame. The truth can probably be discerned from a simple remark from the history of the 5th Panzer Regiment: watching the newsreel, its veterans could only think how hard it had been to get hold of a few eggs, not to mention bacon.

Obtaining drinkable water was an issue in North Africa. As early as March–April 1941, the DAK had set up a system based on combat units carrying a four days' water supply, while many water supply units existed both to find and to transport water. These included the *schwere* (heavy) and *leichte Kompanie für Wasserversorgung* (Water Supply Company, the latter with 28 vehicles), the *Kompanie für Wasserdestillation* (Water Distillation Company, some 200 strong with 105 vehicles) and the *Filterkolonne* and the *Wasserkolonne* (Filter and

Water Columns), the latter capable of carrying 60 tonnes of water. The use of those large and resistant canisters that, pressed into British service, became known as 'jerrycans', also proved particularly valuable.

Washing was permitted using non-drinkable water only, which was itself scarce — all too often it was salty sea water. During battle or combat operations, it was strictly prohibited to wash at all, which resulted in a great number of vermin and caused uniforms and underwear to deteriorate accordingly. It also seems that there were never

Tanks and motorized infantry from the 15th Panzer Division attack towards Alam Halfa Ridge on 1 September 1942. Rommel's last attempt to break through the Eighth Army's lines at El Alamein and drive on towards the Nile Delta was delayed by the strength and depth of British minefields. When his *Afrika Korps* finally emerged from the eastern limit of the obstacles, he was forced to try to swing his armour around the western end of the Alam Halfa Ridge to make up for lost time. Yet his Panzers and Panzergrenadiers were lured onto a mass of hull-down tanks and concealed anti-tank guns, and suffered heavy losses in a storm of fire. The offensive eventually failed on account of severe casualties and fuel shortages. (Howard Gerrard © Osprey Publishing)

serious shortages of drinkable water, even though some scarcity was experienced. During combat operations the daily ration issued was supposedly 4–5 litres per man, but in reality it was closer to 3 litres. This ration was, however, only issued to the field kitchens for cooking and for making tea and coffee. Individual soldiers would get a daily ration of three quarters of a litre, in the form of either water, tea or coffee, enough to fill their own canteen and intended to last for the entire day. This explains why some took care to acquire an extra canteen.

A striking propaganda image of *Afrika Korps* soldiers marking their claims with the German flag. Although the swastika flies on the flag, the war in North Africa was largely conducted without the ideological unpinnings of the conflict on the Eastern Front.

Sand and ever-present dust added further strain on men and equipment. Sandstorms, raised by the *ghibli*, the desert wind, were amongst the most annoying and dangerous problems; when the *ghibli* blew from the south it could raise the temperature beyond 50°C, and fill the air with such volumes of sand that the only available protection (goggles, scarves, etc.) was quite useless. The sand could also cause skin complaints, painful and watery eyes and stomach problems (sand would unavoidably get into food and be ingested). When the problems of sand combined with extreme heat, swarms of flies and the disconsolate monotony of a featureless desert, it is unsurprising that the German Army in North Africa often struggled to maintain morale and motivation.

Food was another sore point; on paper this was to be supplied by the Italians, who proved eventually unable to deliver any foodstuff with a high nutritional value, such as ham, eggs, butter and evaporated milk. Large quantities of food therefore had to be supplied directly from Germany. Ease of transportation took precedence over type of food. Therefore in 1941 the soldiers of the DAK received large amounts of pulses, canned meat and sausages, while only once a week did they get rice, semolina, barley, porridge oats and other farinaceous food. Until August 1941 there was no butter at all, and later on it would have been available only occasionally, along with other fresh items like fish, vegetables (only dried ones were available), fruit and potatoes. Eventually, some items had to be entirely replaced; in the place of butter soldiers got pilchard oil that, while a delicacy in Europe, was nauseating when served in temperatures of about 50°C. Canned meat made of fat, cartilage and sinews was also supplied in large quantities by the Italians and eaten cold. Cans bore the letters 'AM' for *Amministrazione Militare* (Military Administration), but were soon given the less formal nickname of 'Alter Mann' (old man) or 'Asinus Mussolini' (Mussolini's ass). Tuna, cheese, liver sausage and pork were also part of the very monotonous diet of the German soldiers. Attempts to make the food more palatable failed owing to the inadequacy of available freezing facilities.

Bread was another early problem, since until summer 1941 there was only a single bakery company in North Africa, which was unable to supply all the German troops.

A German tank unit bivouaced in the desert. This image illustrates the harsh nature of the North African theatre, the landscape offering little protection from tropical sunlight and a pervasive, grinding dust.

Moreover, German bakeries, designed to use wood as fuel (which was quite scarce in the area), had to be modified to use coal, which turned into another supply requirement. Long-life bread had to be supplied directly from Germany for several months, though by spring 1942 bakery companies were able to work at full capacity in spite of the constant lack of water. However, there were successful experiments in making bread using sea water which helped, but nonetheless, by November 1942 bread rations were curtailed from 375g of fresh bread a day to 250g, and this of the long-life variety.

The diet of German soldiers in North Africa hardly altered day after day, week after week and month after month. Indeed, a change would occur only when stocks of British food were captured, which were much-welcome booty. Strange as it may sound today, Italian food was seldom welcome, especially when German soldiers ate it in the Italian messes; these were strictly divided by rank, with officers receiving macaroni with tomato sauce, olive oil and meat; NCOs had macaroni with tomato and olive oil; and enlisted men receiving only macaroni with tomato. Trade with the local Arabs could provide only a few additional eggs or a melon, and at very high prices. Vitamins were acquired only by eating lemons and drinking lemonade, and these were at least supplied in large quantities, while it was only seldom that marmalades or jams (mainly supplied by the Italians) were available, if at all. In addition, the actual quantity of food available was often inadequate, and there were times (such as the period between June and August 1941 and July and August 1942) when inadequate supplies, widespread theft and the difficulties supply convoys faced in reaching frontline units resulted in hunger amongst the troops.

This photograph of a German Panzer advance in March 1942 clearly illustrates how dust acted as a visible marker of vehicular movement in the desert. The Western Desert was an extremely exposed landscape for German vehicles and bases. Allied fighter-bombers would sit at altitude looking for dust trails, a good indicator of enemy movement.

The terrain and climate, with the intense heat and the sand, together with inadequate uniforms and nutrition, all contributed to the spread of disease and sickness. This was not a real problem during the early months, but after the summer and autumn of 1941 the number of cases grew to serious proportions.

In the autumn of 1941, thorough research into North Africa theatre health issues was carried out, concluding that diet was to a greater or lesser extent responsible for the problems. Legumes and pork (in particular bacon, lard and sausages) affected the already exhausted intestines of the soldiers, who were in large part suffering from dysentery and jaundice. After a few weeks of service in North Africa, soldiers were generally found to have suffered from a loss of about 10 per cent of their weight. Diet was not the only source of disease, however. The wearing of woollen belly bands (waist bands intended to protect the belly), necessary to withstand the harsh extremes of climate during night and day, was not compulsory until later during the campaign, a fact that also contributed to the spread of intestinal diseases.

Insects, in particular the plague of flies and mosquitoes, also played their part in spreading illnesses; other than aiding epidemics, the constant presence of these swarms became a heavy burden for soldiers who had to fight against them constantly, particularly while eating. They were not easily dealt with, as they attacked every part of the body, including the mouth, nose and eyes. A dentist's surgery in Derna eventually found a solution to the problem by obtaining a chameleon to keep the flies away. One measure that had to be undertaken to prevent the spreading of infections transmitted by flies was the use of boxed latrines, with a rudimentary anti-insect wick, though hardly any kind of prevention was possible for frontline troops, especially during combat.

Another problem faced by the DAK was the lack of medical units and facilities in the early stages of the North African campaign. As much as 70 per cent of the medical equipment for the 5th Light Division (later the 21st Panzer Division), for example, was sunk en route to Africa and only dressings and first-aid items could be brought in by air. It was only following the arrival of the 15th Panzer Division in February 1941 that a complete dressing station with ambulances and a field hospital was available. The 90th Light Division would arrive later, itself lacking any medical unit at all.

The overall situation would improve in early 1942, thanks largely to acquired experience and an improved supply situation. Problems were still encountered concerning the evacuation of the sick and wounded to rear areas, and from there to Europe, owing to British interdiction of the German supply lines. Once brought back

OVERLEAF: Here we see a PzKpfw I Ausf. B pass a burnt-out truck. The tank featured improvements to the chassis and drive system compared to the Ausf. A, although by the end of the first year of the Western Desert campaign they were being phased out of service.

LEFT: Two *Afrika Korps* pioneer soldiers and an *Obergefreiter* in the artillery. The pioneers clearly show the German Army belt order, including the long magazine pouches for the MP 40, while the artilleryman is dressed for night guard duty in the tropical greatcoat of heavy brown wool. (Ron Volstad © Osprey Publishing)

to Tripoli, these soldiers would take the same route as the replacements, but going in the opposite direction; they would be embarked in a transport plane that took them to Italy (Greece later in the year), and from there back to Germany.

One of the (often overlooked) strains imposed on the soldiers of the *Afrika Korps* was the lack of leaves of absence; such was quite a heavy burden given the fact that, even during lull or rest periods, there were hardly any distractions available. Leave was granted only at the end of June 1941, and even then it was very limited; only two soldiers per unit (generally a company) were granted a leave of three weeks (a longer period than average, because of desert service) after four months of service in North Africa, which was calculated as starting from the day after they sailed from Italy. This state of affairs did not last for long, and soon leave was prohibited because of the situation at the front. In the 21st Panzer Division periods of leave were granted again on 20 September 1942, after prohibition had been enforced on 20 May, but only those who had served for more than a year in North Africa were granted a period of leave back to Germany. Limited transport facilities were available, so personnel were transported by air, with the sick and the wounded being granted priority. This heavily curtailed the number of those who could actually spend their leave as intended.

WEAPONS AND EQUIPMENT

German lack of preparedness to fight a war in the desert influenced the DAK's weapons and equipment. Infantry in North Africa had the same armament as all other German infantry units, but sand and dust caused many problems with weapons maintenance. Automatic weapons like the MP 38/40 and the MG 34 were the most affected, with the latter in particular experiencing troubles with its cartridge belt feed (the MG 42 was less affected). Extreme care was required and, apart from using muzzle covers, soldiers had to wrap every bolt and moving part in cloth and had to pay much attention to the use of lubricating oil (only a very thin coat of oil had to be put on moving pieces). Lack of training and practice in handling and maintaining the weapons caused certainly as many problems, if not more, than the climate.

In 1941 the DAK was unfortunate in having three different infantry units organizations, each one possessing a different strength and weaponry. The 5th Light Division's two *Maschinengewehre Bataillone* (machine-gun battalions) were particularly strong with their 46 light and heavy machine guns, nine PzB anti-tank rifles, 15 light and heavy mortars and 6–15 37mm Pak 35/36 anti-tank guns. The 15th Panzer Division's Rifle Brigade had a larger amount of firepower that included 366 light and heavy machine guns, 75 light and heavy mortars, 15 37mm Pak 35/36 plus six 50mm Pak 38, and 22 light and heavy *Infanteriegeschützen* (IG; Infantry Support Guns).

ABOVE: *Afrika Korps* unit insignia: 1) Special tropical version of the army collar patch; 2) The breast eagle pattern for the army tropical tunic; 3) The breast eagle pattern for the naval tropical tunic; 4) The Luftwaffe tropical breast eagle; 5a) The special arm badge for *Sonderverband* 200; 5b) The original silvered breast badge; 6) The silk woven arm shield for members of the *Deutsche-Arabische Lehr-Abteilung* (German Arab Training Battalion); 7a–d) National colours shields and helmet badges; 8) Tropical version of the mountain troop arm badge; 9) Tropical version of the SS cap insignia. (Ron Volstad © Osprey Publishing)

A DAK gun crew open fire with a 10.5cm le FH 18 cannon. Designed by Rheinmetall in 1929/30 the le FH 18 was in service from 1935, and could deliver a 14.81kg high-explosive shell to a maximum range of about 10,675m. Its main drawback was its bulk and weight, which made it slow to deploy by horsepower.

The divisional reorganization of September 1941 gave a better balance of firepower, with the 21st Panzer Division's infantry units now fielding 132 light and 64 heavy machine guns, 11 PzB, 27 light and 18 heavy mortars, nine Pak 35/36 and 19 Pak 38 plus four light and two heavy IGs. A comparison with the 15th Panzer Division (it had 187 light and 78 heavy MGs, 11 PzB, 36 light and 24 heavy mortars, 12 Pak 35/36 and ten Pak 38, plus six light and two heavy IGs) shows the latter was still stronger, though the difference was no longer as great. On paper at least, *Afrika Division zbV* (*zur besonderen Verwendung* – 'for special utilization') – the formation that eventually became the 90th Light Infantry Division – had superior infantry firepower, with 333 light and 84 heavy MGs, 148 PzB, and 42 light and 42 heavy mortars. One should keep in mind, however, that this was its only firepower, since the division lacked artillery and any of the support units enjoyed by the two Panzer divisions. Minor organizational changes introduced in September 1941 apart, in the same period a new weapon made its appearance: the tapered-bore heavy 28/20mm *schwere Panzerbüchse* 41, a light (despite the '*schwere*' adjective) anti-tank gun capable of piercing 52mm of 30-degree inclined armour at 500m.

In 1942 there were many further changes in infantry unit organization and firepower. First, 'light' weapons – in particular mortars, light anti-tank rifles and infantry guns – were deemed unsuitable for North African warfare, either because their lightweight projectiles were not capable of piercing enemy armour or because they had not much effect on the ground (sandy ground actually reduced the effect of explosive shells). Second, infantry units were reorganized to emphasize both their firepower and their anti-tank capabilities. Machine-gun and heavy companies were disbanded and absorbed into the new rifle (*Schützen*) – from late July Panzergrenadier – companies, four of which now formed a battalion. The established weapon allowance of the new regiment was quite impressive considering that its allocation of light MGs was now almost twice that of the old *Schützen* regiment, while the number of HMGs had only been reduced by two. Also the new regiment possessed more mortars (39 rather than 30, all heavy), and its anti-tank capabilities had been improved with its 39 PzB (mostly PzB 41) and 42 Pak 38. The new organization was introduced on 1 April 1942. More or less at the same time, DAK units began to receive examples of the new MG 42 for evaluation, which proved to be a very effective weapon in North Africa.

ORDER OF DRESS

By 1940 the German Army, later followed by other branches, had developed a desert uniform and desert equipment for its troops. It was designed at the Tropical Institute of Hamburg, and eventually saw widespread use even outside North Africa, the area where it was first intended for use. This explains how it was possible to dress and equip DAK units quickly in early 1941, even though the first units of 5th Light Division set out for North Africa still dressed in their European *feldgrau* uniform, which they exchanged with their desert one only once en route to Tripoli (apparently the Italians were concerned about having these men going around in their shorts).

In a way, the German desert uniform was quite innovative and introduced certain unique peculiarities in German Army field dress. Its elements included the *Tropenhelm* pith helmet made of compressed cork (Dutch ones were also issued), the olive cotton cloth *Feldmütze* (field cap) and the olive canvas material peaked *Einheitsfeldmütze* (unit field cap). The European steel helmet was retained, eventually being camouflaged in a sandy colour.

The uniform, also made of olive lightweight cotton material, consisted of a jacket or blouse (*Feldbluse*) that was open at the collar and cut in the same style as the European *feldgrau* jacket, and of three different kinds of trousers all with a built-in cloth belt: *lange Hosen* (long trousers), *Stiefelhosen* (desert breeches), not intended for mounted personnel, and worn with high boots, and *kurze Hosen* (shorts) cut high at the thighs. There was only one version of the desert shirt, in lightweight olive cotton, with four buttons (it could be worn with a necktie), long sleeves, two breast pockets and loops for shoulder straps. A double-breasted greatcoat, made of dark-brown woollen cloth and cut in the same style as the *feldgrau* one, was issued for warmth on the cold desert nights. The only variation was

AFRIKAKORPS CUFF TITLES

A peculiar insignia of the *Afrika Korps* were the 'Afrikakorps' and 'Afrika' cuff titles. The former was introduced on 18 July 1941 and could be worn by all personnel on the right forearm of their jacket and greatcoat; it was awarded after two months' service in North Africa or a shorter period for those who were wounded. Here was a unique case in the German Army of a unit cuff title being shared by all the members of a corps and Panzer army; generally these were reserved for smaller units. It was only later in the war that the *Grossdeutschland* cuff title would share the same role, and only following the reorganization of the unit as a corps. The 'Afrika' cuff title was introduced on 15 January 1943 in order to replace the 'Afrikakorps' one, and it was no longer intended to mark the distinction of belonging to a unit but rather as a campaign decoration. It was awarded to those who had served for six months in North Africa, or a shorter period for those who were wounded or had fallen sick.

the desert version of the motorcyclists' coat, intended to protect men from rain, made of heavy olive cotton twill material. Leather greatcoats, used only by generals and high-ranking officers, also saw use. Footwear included desert high boots with leather soles and toecaps and knee-high olive green laced canvas, and the short ankle boots (*Schnürschuhe*, or laced shoes), made of the same stuff and cut in the same design. *Afrika Korps* soldiers would often modify the former into the latter by cutting off the knee-high canvas.

Equipment consisted of a mixture of desert items, which were of the same style as the European ones, and those already in use with the European *feldgrau* uniform. The desert belt gives a practical example of the changes introduced to the normal equipment; the use of leather, unsuitable in arid climates, was avoided and it was replaced by canvas and webbing of a brown olive, reed-green, sand, tan or light-brown colour; metal components were also painted in olive. Thus the desert belt was made of webbed fabric about 4.5cm wide, with the normal buckle already in use with the *feldgrau* uniform attached. A belt with a round buckle was also issued, for use by officers, who often would rather use the simple frame 'two-hook' brown leather belt of the *feldgrau* uniform.

The basic equipment infantry soldiers carried included support suspenders (or 'Y' straps), also made of canvas or webbing, to which the desert version of the harness (or assault pack) could be attached. Riflemen had brown leather ammunition pouches for the *Karabiner* 98k,

LEFT: From left to right, an *Unteroffizier* of the Panzer troops, an *Obergefreiter* of the infantry and a Panzer *Feldwebel*. The junior NCO in the centre is wearing freshly issued tropical kit, including the unpopular pith helmet. The *Feldwebel* is in full tropical service dress, whereas the *Unteroffizier* wears the more practical shirtsleeve order and tropical shorts. (Ron Volstad © Osprey Publishing)

while for the MP 38/40 machine pistol a desert version of the three-magazine pouch was issued. Bayonet web frogs were also made either of leather or olive-coloured webbing, with all frogs in the desert having a securing strap. Desert versions of the bread bag, the rucksack and the hand-grenade bag were also made, whilst only details (like the use of canvas and webbing or of olive-coloured fabrics) were changed for the entrenching tool, the canteen and the cup. No changes, other than the addition of sand-coloured paint, were made to the mess kit and the gas-mask canister. The camouflaged *Zeltbahn* (shelter quarters) used in Europe saw also widespread use in North Africa.

Some personal items specifically made for use in desert areas became quite common amongst DAK soldiers. These included scarves used to protect oneself from sand, olive-coloured sweaters (though the European grey ones were also used), gloves and a wide variety of sun and dust goggles, which were very popular. It is worth noting that the use of canvas and webbing does not necessarily denote items produced specifically for use in the desert, since these also saw much use later in the war. Indeed, the hasty redeployment of units to North Africa during the summer of 1942, and later in Tunisia, saw widespread use of the European *feldgrau* uniform items. One of the most interesting matters relating to the German desert uniforms is the lack of any difference between ranks; the basic uniform was intended for use by officers, NCOs and enlisted men without distinction.

Only minor variations were introduced to the desert uniforms of the *Afrika Korps* from the German Army staff and the manufacturers. After 1942 a new jacket was introduced without the pleated breast and side pockets, while the new shirt no longer had loops for the shoulder straps. Also, both the *Feldmütze* and the *Einheitsfeldmütze* lost the inverted 'V' soutache or branch of service colour worn above the national cockade, while retaining the silver lining for officers. The normal practice saw a more relaxed attitude toward uniforms and dressing than might have been envisaged; the use of Italian (particularly the much sought-after *Sahariana* jacket) and of British pieces of uniform became quite common, in the latter case especially after the capture of large stocks at Tobruk in June 1942 (British shorts were longer and more comfortable than the German ones). All through the campaign in North Africa there was a certain slackening in the dress attitude of DAK soldiers, which brought some rebukes from the corps and Rommel's own command. Soon items like the pith helmet were discarded by frontline troops, though it was still used to some extent by those serving in rear areas and by vehicle crews.

The German desert uniform, developed on the basis of the knowledge and experiences gained in the German colonies in eastern Africa before and during World War I, soon revealed some inadequacies. The jacket, for example, was too tight and uncomfortable to wear, and was therefore very unpopular, while the material used for uniforms and caps bleached very fast and eventually became quite visible on the ground (the same effect was observed with new uniforms, though in this case because their colour was too dark).

LEFT: Two SdKfz 231 communications vehicles on the move, clearly displaying their top-mounted radio antennae. A shortage of communications vehicles often hampered the mobile command-and-control capabilities of the Africa Corps.

The situation worsened with time and experience; uniforms washed in sea water shrank, not to mention the fact that the fabric they were made of (which was overly heavy) offered little if any protection against the rocky terrain or the sand. It was also inadequate against the cold nights and hot days. In 1942 the desert breeches were no longer in use, while those who could happily exchanged their German shorts (which were too short and worn only during periods of rest or in the rear areas) with British

Panzerwaffe tactics, North Africa, c.1942. The *Panzerwaffe* face a defended enemy position in this illustration, and so the target is first 'softened up' by bombardment both from artillery and by dive-bombing attacks from Ju 87 Stukas. The tanks carry out a classic 'pincer' movement whilst continuing the bombardment of the target area, eventually completing the encirclement of the enemy-held area before moving on to the next objective. The attack would begin whilst the aerial and artillery bombardment was still underway. As the bombardment goes on, Panzergrenadiers in their SdKfz 251 armoured half-tracks make a three-pronged attack, hitting the enemy frontline defences and their flanks before they have time to fully recover from the effects of the explosions. (Velimir Vuksic © Osprey Publishing)

ones. Even the popular and appreciated *Einheitsfeldmütze* (field cap) had its shortcomings and some alterations were required, namely a leather perspiration band. The greatcoat proved useful against the cold at night, but it was too short and hampered movement. Only the laced shoes turned out to be a good and suitable solution (several variants were

ABOVE: Various *Afrika Korps* uniform insignia. Numbers 1–6 illustrate different patterns of DAK cuff titles and bands, while 7–10 show tropical shoulder straps for the Luftwaffe, Kriegsmarine and SS respectively. (Ron Volstad © Osprey Publishing)

produced up to 1942), and unsurprisingly, as previously noted, soldiers would cut off the top portion of the high boots, turning them into laced shoes.

In contrast to uniform, equipment (particularly for infantrymen) proved adequate and suitable. The reason for this was that, because it was modelled on that in use with the European *feldgrau* uniform, men were already accustomed to it, and the use of canvas or webbing proved to be a good choice (it was also adopted later in the war). There were only a few remarks of criticism, which were about the bakelite components of certain items, such as the canteen's cup, which were too fragile. It is interesting to note that both the Luftwaffe and the SS would develop desert uniforms, or parts of uniform, for their own men, which proved better both in their cut (the SS one was made like the Italian *Sahariana*) and in the fabric used, though it must be added that their actual use was quite limited in comparison with the DAK uniform.

In terms of tank crew uniforms, the M1934 black uniform was impractical for North Africa, so crews wore the standard M1940 tropical uniform. However, all members of the three Panzer regiments – 5th, 7th and 8th, including attached administrative officials (and Assault Gun Battery 287) – pinned aluminium skulls detached from black collar-patches to the lapels of their tropical field tunics. The M1940 standard tropical tank-crew field cap (effectively the M1940 tropical peaked field cap without the peak) was the same design as the M1934 2nd pattern *feldgrau* other ranks' field cap. Made of light-olive cotton twill it had the same insignia – eagle and swastika, cockade and, until 8 September 1942, a pink (for Panzer troops) branch colour facing-cloth chevron, with aluminium cord piping for officers. This cap was a substitute for the pith-helmet, which was unsuitable for the confines of an armoured vehicle, but it was superseded by the tropical peaked field cap. Some armoured personnel retained the black continental tank crews' M1940 officers' or other ranks' field cap, against regulations.

PANZERS IN NORTH AFRICA

The experience of the DAK proves that, in the Western Desert, the tank was the master of the battlefield. When they were sent to North Africa, both the 5th and 8th Panzer Regiments were in the middle of a reorganization process that only the latter had actually completed. This included a re-equipment with the new 5cm Kwk-armed tanks and the transition to new tables of organization, issued on 1 February 1941. According to these, each Panzer battalion was composed of an HQ, two light and one medium Panzer companies, plus a Panzer squadron grouping together all available spare tanks. *Stabskompanien* (HQ Company) included a *Nachrichtenzug* (communications platoon – two Panzer *Befehlswagen* and a PzKpfw III) and a light Panzer platoon with five PzKpfw II (the 5th Panzer Regiment had an extra light Panzer platoon per battalion and one with the regimental HQ). Light Panzer companies were composed of a *Kompanietrupp* (company troop – two PzKpfw III), a light Panzer platoon and three light platoons, each with five PzKpfw III. Medium Panzer companies included a company troop (two PzKpfw IV), a light Panzer platoon and three platoons, each with four PzKpfw IV. Regimental paper strength, therefore, consisted of six Panzer *Befehlswagen*, 45 PzKpfw II (60 with 5th Panzer Regiment), 71 PzKpfw III and 28 PzKpfw IV.

In 1941 the German tank inventory in North Africa included every type of tank then available, from the light PzKpfw I to the 'heavy' PzKpfw IV. With its weight of 5.4 tonnes and two MG 34s, the PzKpfw I Ausf. A (the variant sent to North Africa) was rather more of a tankette than a tank. Built in 1934–36, they were already obsolete in 1939 and also suffered from engine breakdowns and overheating that made them extremely unreliable. Nevertheless, they saw frontline service in the Western Desert, before they were removed from action (either because they became unserviceable or because they were used to provide spare parts for the *Panzerjäger* I) in the autumn of 1941. Another light tank was the PzKpfw II Ausf. C, largely used by the 5th and 6th Panzer Regiments. Lightweight and poorly armoured, it was armed with a 20mm Kwk 30 L/55 and a single MG 34. Produced until April 1940, it was obsolete as well and almost useless against enemy tanks and infantry; it was soon relegated to reconnaissance roles, though its poor speed (40km/h on a good road) made it unsuitable for this role as well.

The workhorse of the Panzer divisions in North Africa was the PzKpfw III, the principal German main battle tank in 1940–42. Actual delivery of the earlier models PzKpfw III Ausf. E/F to North Africa is not certain; but what is known, however, is that every PzKpfw III sent to North Africa was retrofitted and armed with the new 50mm Kwk 38 L/42 gun. The most common variant used in 1941 was the PzKpfw III Ausf. G, mounting the 5cm as a standard gun since July 1940. Its 'tropicalized' version, designated *Trop* (short for *Tropen*, tropical), mounted special ventilation and air/oil-filtering systems to protect the engine and gearbox from sand and dust. It had a limited weight (about 20 tonnes) and a good speed (40km/h), though it was poorly armoured, with a frontal protection of only 30mm non-face hardened steel, 37mm on the gun mantlet.

The PzKpfw III's 'big brother' was the PzKpfw IV, considered then a 'heavy' tank designed to provide support with its short 75mm Kwk 37 L/24. Forty PzKpfw IV Ausf. D and Es were sent to North Africa in 1941 with both the 5th and 8th Panzer Regiments. The Ausf. E had, in most cases, 20–30mm extra hull armour and a standard storage bin. Armour on both variants was 30mm on the front hull and up to 35mm on the gun mantlet.

In spite of the adoption of tropical ventilators and filters, German tanks suffered from both the heat and sand. The crews naturally endured much more than their vehicles, especially during combat, when hatches had to be closed and, with an inside temperature

VOLSTAD 91

ABOVE: Vehicle formation signs of the major units serving in North Africa. These were generally painted in white or yellow on the front glacis plate and rear hull of tanks, and on the front and rear fenders of soft-skinned vehicles. (Ron Volstad © Osprey Publishing)

of 45°C, the ventilating systems had to be shut off due to fuel shortages. On the other hand, gun optical equipment proved excellent, since it functioned well even in the high temperatures and at night.

The Panzers' poor armour and their guns' limited armour-piercing capabilities caused a great deal of problems. Using the standard *Panzergranate* 39 (PzGr 39) armour-piercing shell, the 5cm Kwk 38 could penetrate 54mm of homogeneous armour plate at 100m, 46mm at 500m and 36mm at 1,000m. The use of the tungsten-core PzGr 40, even more effective at close range, improved the performance as follows: 96, 58 and 42mm. The 7.5cm Kwk 37 was only capable of penetrating 70–100mm at 100m, though by using *Sprenggranate* (explosive shells) it could damage British tanks at greater distances.

Early British Cruiser tanks were not much of a problem for Panzers in 1941, but the Matilda and Valentine infantry tanks, as well as the Crusader and American-produced Grant, proved formidable opponents, especially given the scarce availability of PzGr 40 shells and the Kwk 38's overall poor performance. Their deficient armour made most of the Panzers extremely vulnerable to British anti-tank and tank guns, even at long distances (the British 2-pdr was capable of penetrating 40mm of 30-degree homogeneous armour at 800m).

A column of PzKpfw II tanks stops for a break during operations in the Western Desert. This variety of Panzer was effectively obsolete by 1941, and it was easy prey for heavier Allied armour. It found some future utility, however, as a reconnaissance vehicle and even a flame-throwing tank.

In December 1941, the first PzKpfw III Ausf. H arrived in North Africa, followed by the early production PzKpfw III Ausf. J and PzKpfw IV Ausf. F (the new PzKpfw II Ausf. F also arrived at the same time). Though their armament remained unchanged, their armour protection was now increased. The PzKpfw II Ausf. F's frontal armour was now 30–35mm, the PzKpfw III Ausf. H had a 30mm armour plate added to its 30mm standard plate while the Ausf. J had a standard 50mm frontal armour plate, like the PzKpfw IV Ausf. F. This increased armour neutralized the British 2-pdr gun and the adoption of wider 400mm tracks as standard (already tested with the PzKpfw III Ausf. G) made the vehicles much more mobile over soft terrain.

From early 1942, modern Panzers became available to the DAK, models really suited to tank-versus-tank combat. The first to arrive was the late-production PzKpfw III Ausf. J, similar to the earlier production models but armed with the long-barrelled 5cm Kwk 39 L/60 capable of penetrating 67–130mm at 100m, 57–72mm at 500m and 44–38mm at 1,000m. Used in combat for the first time at Gazala, it was available in relatively large quantities only from August 1942, and could deal on equal terms with both the Valentine and the Grant. The new long-barrelled 7.5cm Kwk 40 L/43 (capable of penetrating as much as 72mm of armour plate at 1,500m) could fight on equal terms even with the American-built Sherman. It was used to retrofit the old PzKpfw IV Ausf. F variant that, converted as such, became known as the PzKpfw IV Ausf. F2. The first examples arrived in North Africa in June 1942, but it remained a rare beast until late summer. Both the long-barrelled PzKpfw III and IV were known as *Spezial* (special), a name the British adopted as well.

In spite of the excellent job done by tank recovery teams and engineers, losses due to either mechanical breakdown or combat as well as supply problems greatly reduced the number of available Panzers. As a consequence, the reorganization implemented in September 1941 saw a reduction in the established numbers of PzKpfw IV, now set at ten per battalion with only two platoons per each medium Panzer company. Otherwise, the rest of a Panzer regiment's established strength remained unchanged. This organization and weapons' allocation, however, proved unsuitable for the large armour-versus-armour battles that characterized the war in the Western Desert and was therefore changed again. The established tank strength introduced in April 1942 for both the 5th and 8th Panzer Regiments, which saw minor changes until mid May, marked a definitive increase in both the availability and quality of Panzers. Light companies' light platoons were transformed into ordinary Panzer platoons and equipped with PzKpfw IIIs, thus increasing the total number of medium tanks in a regiment from 71 to 135. This increase had also been made possible by the decision to bring to three the number of light companies in a Panzer battalion, a policy that was effectively carried out in early 1942. In the meantime, the number of PzKpfw IIs fell from 45 to 29, two of which were used to equip the Panzer

LEFT: A PzKpfw III crosses a Tunisian bridge. Note how the vehicles put plenty of distance between them – it was not uncommon for heavy tanks to crush bridges, so it was best to move across one at a time.

battalion's pioneer platoon. Only the number of PzKpfw IVs remained below authorized strengths, since DAK's Panzer divisions only had 11 per medium company rather than 14. The overall marked increase in tank strengths, as well as the new models available, played a major role in DAK's victories in the spring and summer of 1942.

ANTI-TANK WEAPONS

Despite all their emphasis on mobile armoured warfare, the Wehrmacht entered the war with marginal anti-tank capabilities. The army was so oriented toward aggressiveness that anything smacking of defence was viewed slightly with disfavour. *Panzerabwehr* (armour defence) units were redesignated *Panzerjäger* (armour hunter) on 1 April 1940, to play down their defensive nature. Anti-tank guns were increasingly mounted on tracked chassis to improve mobility.

The principal anti-tank gun in the early years of the war was the Rheinmetall–Borsig 3.7cm PaK 35/36. Nine guns were allotted to the three-platoon regimental anti-tank company and 27 to the divisional anti-tank battalion. Copied by many countries, the PaK 35/36 was an excellent weapon in the mid 1930s, but by 1940 it was obsolescent – as acknowledged by its army nickname of *Türklopfer* (doorknocker). Operated by a six-man crew, it originally fired an armour-piercing round that could penetrate 29mm of 30-degree homogeneous armour plate at 500m. In the early 1940s its limited armour-piercing capabilities rendered it virtually useless, unless used against lightly armoured vehicles. The introduction of the *Panzergranate* 40 (PzGr 40; Armour-Piercing Shell Model 40) and eventually the development, in early 1942, of the muzzle-loaded *Stielgranate* 41 (Stick Grenade 41) brought no real improvement, since the PaK 35/36's effectiveness was still limited to 100m.

On the other hand, the 5cm PaK 38, fielded in late 1940, was a superb weapon, though not very effective against heavy armour. Weighing less than a tonne and just 1.1m metres high, it was sturdy, reliable, easy to handle and not easy to detect. It was superior to the British 2-pdr because of its greater armour-piercing capabilities. At 100m it could punch through 69mm of 30-degree homogeneous armour plate (130mm using the PzGr 40), which became 59–72mm at 500m and 48–38mm at 1,000m. Able to deal with much of the British armour in the Western Desert, it remained the German standard anti-tank gun until late 1942 along with the 76.2mm PaK 36(r), mainly used by the 90th Light Division's units.

Before the 5th Light Division left for Tripoli, the OKH ordered its 39th *Panzerjäger* Battalion exchange its new 5cm PaK 38 for the old 37mm PaK 35/36, though it was eventually left with a single PaK 38-armed platoon per company. In early 1941, both Panzer divisions only had a limited anti-tank capability, partly mitigated by the presence of the 605th *Panzerjäger* Battalion's self-propelled anti-tank guns. However, soon both the 33rd and 39th *Panzerjäger* Battalions began to exchange their old PaK 35/36s with the PaK 38. Between May and September 1941 the number of PaK 38s in each *Panzerjäger* battalion increased from nine to 12, and, by 20 September, both had handed all of their PaK 35/36s, to other units, though the 33rd Battalion was still not up to full strength.

A further scaling up of the PaK 38 resulted in the 7.5cm PaK 40, also fielded in late 1940. This became the main divisional anti-tank gun, but some were assigned to regimental anti-tank companies as well. Heavy to manhandle, it nonetheless proved to be an effective weapon. It could knock out most tanks, penetrating 105mm at 450m with standard armour-piercing ammunition, and 115mm with PzGr 40. Many captured Soviet 76.2mm FS-22 guns were also rechambered for German 7.5cm and further modified for anti-tank use as the 7.62cm PaK 36(r). The 3.7cm, 5cm, and 7.5cm were all provided with HE rounds.

From 1941 the Germans made limited use of two Gerlich-type tapered or 'squeeze' bore guns, the 2.8cm (tapering to 2cm) and 4.2cm (actually 4.5cm, tapering to 2.94cm). The 2.8cm sPzB 41 was a small, wheeled weapon meant to replace 7.92mm anti-tank rifles, and the 4.2cm PaK 41 was mounted on a 3.7cm carriage. These guns used a special projectile that was 'squeezed' down to a smaller calibre when fired in order to achieve a higher velocity. Guns and ammunition were expensive to produce – the rounds required scarce tungsten carbide cores – and production ceased in 1942. Penetration was good, however: the 2.8cm achieved 60mm at 400m, and the 4.2cm, 75mm at 450m. Nevertheless, their usefulness was limited by their lack of HE rounds.

The Germans had small numbers of anti-tank rifles in service in 1939, the *Panzerbüchse* (PzB) 38 and 39. Only 1,600 examples of the complex and expensive PzB 38 were produced, but 39,232 of the PzB 39 were made. Both models were 7.92mm calibre, taking a necked-down 94mm-long World War I 13.2mm anti-tank rifle cartridge, capable of penetrating 30mm at 100m. The bullet was too small to do much interior damage; a larger round would ricochet around and hit different crewmen, but the little rifle bullet would usually stop when it hit the first man. The early rounds had a tiny tear gas pellet, but this was too small to be effective. Later ammunition had a carbide core – something learned from the Poles. Both rifles were single-shot and bipod-mounted. The PzB 38 weighed 15.99kg and the PzB 39 12.43kg, so they were onerous weapons to lug around. Several other 7.92mm anti-tank rifles saw limited use, along with numerous captured weapons including Soviet types, and various Swedish-made 20mm rifles such as the Solothurn s18-1100. A rifle company had a seven-man anti-tank section with three weapons; one might be attached to each platoon, but it was preferred to keep them grouped for concentrated fire.

Recognizing that these weapons were outdated, in 1943 the Germans modified the PzB 39 into the *Granatbüchse* 39 (GrB 39; Grenade Throwing Model 39) anti-tank grenade rifle, shortening the barrel by 600mm and attaching a grenade discharger cup. Capable of firing any German anti-tank grenade, it was still heavy at 10.5kg, and its range of 150m was not much further than that of the same grenades from a standard rifle. The *Gewehrgranate zur Panzerbekämpfung* 40 (GG/P40; Rifle Grenade for Anti-armour Combat Model 1940) used a spigot-type launcher. The grenade, copied by the United States, was ineffective even though the Germans used a base-detonating fuse; it lacked stand-off distance. It was withdrawn in 1942 and replaced by a 30mm cup discharger system. The first *Gewehr Panzergranate* (rifle armour grenade) was a 30mm shaped charge with 20 to 30mm of penetration and an effective range of 50–100m. By 1942 a 40mm over-calibre grenade was introduced, capable of penetrating 50mm at up to 150m. Almost 24 million 30mm and 40mm grenades were produced. The 46mm and 61mm versions were introduced in late 1942 and late 1943 respectively, with an effective range of 80–100m. The 46mm penetrated 70–90mm, and the 61mm pierced 100–120mm.

While a few anti-tank hand grenades saw limited use, the principal German hand anti-tank weapon was the magnetic hollow-charge 3kg *Hafthohlladung* (Haft-Hl 3; tank breaker). This brutal *Panzerknacker* (armour-cracker) was adopted in November 1942. It was of truncated cone shape, with a handle holding the fuse, and three pairs of magnets around the base that allowed it to be attached to a tank, fortress gun cupola, pillbox doors or shutters. Early models had a friction-ignited 4.5-second delay fuse, which sometimes did not allow time for the attacker to seek cover; a 7.5-second fuse was introduced in May 1943. The charge could penetrate up to 140mm of armour or 500mm of concrete. Some 553,900 were made in 1942–44; the *Hafthohlladung* was declared obsolete in May 1944, to be replaced by the *Panzerfaust* (armour fist; see Chapter 4), although existing stocks remained in use.

Discussion of German anti-tank and anti-aircraft weapons in North Africa often centres around the dreaded 8.8cm Flak gun that, in spite of its fame, was actually not widely used in the theatre. No more than 30–40 could ever be deployed at the same time: the 135th Flak Regiment had 36 of them in May and 39 in August 1942. Much of its fame actually derives from the lack of suitable purpose-built anti-tank weapons in 1941.

In the early war years, not much attention had been paid to self-propelled anti-tank guns. The development of the 4.7cm PaK (t) L/43 (sfl) auf PzKpfw I Ausf. B appears to have been a belated attempt to make better use of the otherwise obsolete PzKpfw I chassis. With only 202 produced from March 1940 to February 1941, it was armed with a Czech-produced anti-tank gun capable of penetrating 54mm of 30-degree armour plate at 100m (100mm with the PzGr 40), which became 48/59mm at 500m and 41mm at 1,000m (the PzGr 40 was no longer effective at this range). Used to equip 605th *Panzerjäger* Battalion, whose 1941 establishment was of 27 vehicles, it was not the best solution but the only one available.

Battlefield experience soon suggested a number of improvements. An ingenious and impromptu solution was found by combining the chassis of an obsolete tank and a powerful anti-tank gun, in this case the Soviet 76.2mm gun, which the Germans had captured en masse (along with ammunition) during the first months of their advance into the Soviet Union. Mounted on the chassis of the PzKpfw 38(t) it created the *Panzerjäger* 38(t) für 7.62cm PaK 36(r) (SdKfz 139), also known as Marder III, the first of a long and successful series of self-propelled anti-tank guns. Produced between April and October 1942, the *Panzerjäger* 38(t) was perhaps the most powerful anti-tank weapon ever used by the DAK. Although the vehicle was rather heavy and high (about 11 tonnes and 2.5m high), it was well armoured (50mm on hull and superstructure) and was armed with a very powerful weapon capable of penetrating 98mm of 30-degree homogeneous armour plate at 100m (135mm using the PzGr 40), 90/116mm at 500m, 82/94mm at 1,000m, 73/75mm at 1,500m and 65/58mm at 2,000m – enough to make it a real 'tankbuster' in the desert.

A StuG III in Tunisia heads to the front bearing a force of Panzergrenadiers. The regiments formerly known as *Schützen* (rifle) regiments were renamed 'Panzergrenadiers' in July 1942, and their title reflects the concept of motorized infantry so central to *Blitzkrieg*.

Availability was, however, the real problem since only 66 were sent to North Africa between July 1942 and May 1943. The gap was filled thanks to the development of another ad hoc solution. In mid October 1941, the OKH ordered the fast development of a more powerful self-propelled anti-tank gun for the DAK using the Soviet 76.2mm PaK 36(r). A suitable solution was found by mounting the gun on a Büssing-NAG BN9 5-tonne half-tracked vehicle, producing the 7.62cm FK 36(r), otherwise known a 'Diana'. A rather clumsy vehicle about 3m high, the first six examples were sent to North

ABOVE: Three figures from the Tunisian campaign of January–May 1943. From left to right: a *Waffenoberfeldwebel* of the 200th Panzergrenadier Regiment at Kasserine Pass in February 1943; a *Feldwebel* of the 756th Mountain Regiment at Longstop Hill, also in February 1943; and a *Schütze* of the 961st Africa Rifle Regiment at Fondouk, March 1943. All wear the tropical field uniform, with minor variations. (Stephen Andrew © Osprey Publishing)

Africa in January 1942, followed by three others in February (only nine were produced in total). Seven examples of the 'Diana' were used at Gazala with good results (on 28 May one of them stopped the 4th Armoured Brigade at El Adem), but their number was soon reduced. By mid June 1942, before the 605th *Panzerjäger* Battalion was withdrawn to Bardia for rest and refitting, only two 'Dianas' were left, though apparently three were still available in August.

To understand fully how important these lesser-known weapons were in comparison with the famous 8.8cm it is worth considering that on 21 October 1942 the 15th Panzer Division only had eight 8.8cm Flak guns, but 72 5cm PaK 38s and 16 7.62cm self-propelled *Panzerjäger* 38(t)s.

VEHICLES AND OTHER AFVS

For a motorized corps like the DAK, the availability and efficiency of motor vehicles was a crucial factor. Established allotment of motor vehicles for a late 1941 Panzer division numbered about 3,500–4,000. Most of them, about 90 per cent of the total, were non-combat wheeled vehicles used to transport men and supplies.

The 21st Panzer Division's vehicle establishment in late December 1941, for example, included almost 1,000 motorcycles (of which more than 700 were combination), still largely used by combat units in spite of their unsuitability for desert warfare. On the other hand the division had about 1,000 cars, a figure including about 450 small staff cars like the *Kübelwagen* (Kfz 1 to 4 models), about 350 medium staff cars (Kfz 12, 17), about 15 heavy staff cars (Kfz 21 and 23) and more than 150 off-road light trucks for personnel transport, like the *Krupp Protze* (Kfz 69, 70 and 81), as well as 52 Kfz 31 ambulances.

The greatest part of the division's 1,700 lorries, mainly used by the artillery, service and supply units, was made up of medium lorries, including four-wheel drives like the Opel 'Blitz'. Being an armoured division it also had a large allocation of half-tracked vehicles, only some of which were attached to combat units.

As a matter of fact, only a small fraction of DAK's infantry was mounted in armoured personnel carriers, known as *gepanzert Mannschafts Transport Wagen* (MTW). In December 1941, for example, the 21st Panzer Division had only had ten armoured SdKfz 251 troop carriers, while all other half-tracked vehicles were used in other roles. The SdKfz 251/6 was a command vehicle, 251/7 a pioneer vehicle and the SdKfz 253 a light armoured observation vehicle. Most half-tracks were simply tractors mainly used to pull artillery. There was actually a larger allocation of wheeled combat vehicles than wheeled armoured vehicles, including 64 *Panzerspähwagen* (armoured cars) mainly used by the *Aufklärungs Abteilung* 3 (3rd Reconnaissance Battalion).

Vehicles were always a problem for the DAK, first because of their shortage and also because of the many problems they faced in the desert. The OKH was behind one of these problems since, without caring to check whether the Italians used diesel-fuelled vehicles or not (they actually did, with great success), it decided to avoid problems caused by having vehicles using two different types of fuel and initially only sent petrol-fuelled vehicles to North Africa, thus limiting their number and quality. The result was that many two-wheel drive vehicles were used by the DAK, either derived from civilian models or even civilian models pressed into military service, and they were particularly unsuited to the desert. To have an idea of the proportion, in summer 1941 out of 1,000 lorries used by the 15th Panzer Division, only 45 were four-wheel drive. In the same period, the 21st Panzer Division's *Nachschubkolonne* (supply convoy) only had 74 lorries suitable for desert terrain.

The strain imposed by the lack of paved roads and by sand, dust and heat had impressive effects on German vehicles that, as opposed to British ones, had not been designed for tropical use. The sturdy *Kübelwagen* was much loved and proved an extremely useful and reliable vehicle, especially when equipped with the large, over-sized aircraft tyres, yet – in spite of the special filters adopted – its engine only had a lifetime of 12,000–14,000km (5,000km before the adoption of special filters), that is about one-fifth of its normal lifetime (60,000–70,000km). In comparison, a tank needed a new engine every 3,500km, which was about half of its normal lifetime (7,000–8,000km). Springs also suffered heavily, in particular those of the Kfz 17, which proved extremely prone to breaking. As a consequence, many vehicles were soon out of service, thus limiting actual availability: in August 1941 the 21st Panzer Division's supply columns only had 191 serviceable lorries out of an established strength of 315; the other 124 were under repair. In January 1942, the division lacked 2,459 vehicles (625 motorcycles, 565 cars,

831 lorries, 151 tractors and 287 Armoured Fighting Vehicles [AFVs]) out of an established strength of 3,528; more than 70 per cent were unserviceable.

Lack of half-tracked armoured vehicles was also a major problem, especially in 1942. Even the few issued to infantry units were withdrawn and used as command and communication vehicles. Some of them were also modified by having a French-built 25mm Hotchkiss anti-tank gun mounted to improve the anti-tank capabilities of those units. Generally speaking, it is no exaggeration to say that the DAK relied heavily on

ABOVE: From left to right, a *Major* in the 33rd Reconnaissance Battalion, and an *Oberstleutnant* and *Generalmajor* of the infantry. Note the difference in footwear between the high lace-up canvas and leather boots, and the standard German jackboot. (Ron Volstad © Osprey Publishing)

captured British vehicles, always used in large quantities. In the summer of 1942 about half of the DAK's vehicle inventory was made up of captured vehicles, and without them Rommel would have had great difficulty in carrying his offensive into Egypt.

COMMAND, CONTROL, COMMUNICATIONS AND INTELLIGENCE (C3I)

An efficient C3I complex is of foremost importance in mobile warfare, especially in difficult terrain like the Western Desert. To master the battlefield both sides needed a practical command system, an adequate control of their own units, a workable communications net and a good view of the other side of the hill, which implies an efficient intelligence service. Most of the German C3I systems in North Africa were similar to those used in Europe, yet some particular aspects need to be highlighted.

The German approach to command was based on what is (incorrectly) called *Auftragstaktik* (mission tactics). It was actually a system based on the 'mission command' principle that saw senior commanders giving their subordinates only an objective to attain. They then left them the choice of how to attain it, which they had to do using their own initiative and knowledge of both the terrain and of their own unit. Such a system was in open contrast to the one called 'top-down command', ruled by rigid and detailed orders specifying both the objective and the way to attain it – a method widely used by British forces in North Africa. Though apparently superior, the 'mission command' principle was a two-edged sword since it required good, if not excellent, field commanders and a workable control system. Without an adequate control system, flexibility, which is one of the main advantages of the system, could easily turn the battlefield into chaos. This is the reason staff work was so important, and it is no exaggeration to say that the German staff in North Africa were excellent.

Rommel had his own particular approach to the 'mission command' principle, one that actually enhanced another principle emphasized by German doctrine: commanders were to lead from the front. This was the only way a commander could properly evaluate the situation on the battlefield and acquire a good knowledge of both the terrain and his enemy, which enabled him to react swiftly to any unexpected event. A commander facing a superior enemy could choose a different approach into battle, while a commander facing a weak enemy could take full advantage of success obtained on the battlefield. In a word: flexibility, something in which German commanders excelled and to which many of their successes can be ascribed.

An interesting feature specifically aimed at helping commanders lead their units from the front was the development of the *Befehls Staffel* (Command Detachment), clearly a consequence of the experiences in North Africa during Operation *Crusader*, when

RIGHT: A German radio unit sets up its communications from a *Funk-Kraftwagen* (radio car). As well as being responsible for radio transmissions, signals units would also spend much of their time intercepting and deciphering Allied radio traffic.

DAK's HQ was overrun by British troops. The use of an advanced and a rear command echelon was a common practice with German HQs. The commander, along with the operations and intelligence officers, spearheaded his units while administrative and supply-concerned parts of the staff moved in the rear. The innovation introduced by Rommel was the creation of a small, highly mobile and well-armed support unit specifically designated to escort the advanced echelon with the purpose of protecting it against enemy actions, including air attack.

In spite of this improvement, only introduced in April 1942, DAK's officers paid a heavy price for their 'lead from the front' principle. Between 18 November 1941 and 20 February 1942, the 21st Panzer Division had 47 officers killed, 61 wounded and 40 missing. (It is worth noting that officers represented 10 per cent of all killed, but only 4 per cent of all wounded and 2 per cent of all missing.) Figures for the period 21 May–20 September 1942 are similar, with 57 officers killed (7.5 per cent of all killed), 214 wounded (7.4 per cent, but 59 of them lightly) and 17 missing (2.4 per cent). The pattern was repeated across the other divisions. Losses suffered by the 90th Light Africa Division between November 1941 and 31 March 1942 included 27 officers dead (7.6 per cent of the total), 27 wounded (3.6 per cent) and 86 missing (2.3 per cent). Between 20 October and 21 November 1942, the 15th Panzer Division had 13 officers killed (7 per cent), 28 wounded (5.8 per cent) and 29 missing (3 per cent).

Most noticeably, those figures also included high-ranking officers. Generalleutnant Ludwig Crüwell, who succeeded Rommel as DAK's CO on 15 August 1941, was shot down and captured during a reconnaissance flight on 29 May 1942. His successor, General der Panzertruppe Walther K. Nehring, was wounded at Tobruk on 31 August 1942. DAK's command was next held for a brief period by Generalmajor Von Vaerst and then, from 17 September 1942, by General der Panzertruppe Wilhelm von Thoma, who was captured at El Alamein on 4 November. Casualties were even higher amongst divisional commanders: Generalmajor Johann von Ravenstein, the successor of Generalmajor Johannes Streich, the 5th Light Division's first commander, was captured on 29 November 1941. The most famous commander of the 21st Panzer Division, Generalmajor Georg von Bismarck (who succeeded Generalleutnant Karl Böttcher), was first wounded on 17 July 1942 and, back with the division some days later, was eventually killed in action on 31 August 1942. Generalmajor Heinz von Randow, who became CO on 18 September, was killed on 21 December 1942.

The record of the 15th Panzer Division is not much different: its first CO, Generalmajor Heinrich von Prittwitz und Gaffron, was killed on 10 April 1941 and his successor, Oberst (then Generalmajor) Hans-Karl von Esebeck, was wounded on 25 July 1941. Generalmajor Walter Neumann-Silkow, who took over from him, was himself wounded on 6 December 1941, as was Generalleutnant Gustav von Vaerst on 26 May

1942 at Gazala. Generalmajor Heinz von Randow, CO from 8 July, temporarily had better luck, since he was transferred on 17 September 1942, like Generalleutnant Gustav von Vaerst who, back with the division, went on sick leave on 11 November. The 90th Light Africa Division's first commander, Generalmajor Max Sümmermann, was killed on 10 December 1941, while Generalmajor Ulrich Kleeman, CO from 21 June 1942, was wounded on 8 September 1942.

Casualty rates amongst lower units were similar. Between November 1941 and September 1942, 90th Light Division's 361st Panzergrenadier Regiment had three different commanders; one of them was killed and another severely wounded. In the

A column of tanks, half-tracks and transport vehicles of the 10th Panzer Division advance into the valley approaching El Guettar, Tunisia on 23 March 1943. The subsequent battle with US forces brought a German defeat, not least because US artillery took a heavy toll on both troops and men. By the end of the day, the 10th Panzer Division was down to 26 serviceable tanks. (Michael Welply © Osprey Publishing)

same period, the 2nd Battalion of the same regiment had four commanders; one of them was wounded while two others were replaced because of sickness. The worst record belongs to the 7th Company: three out of nine of its commanders (temporary ones included) were killed, while two others were missing in action.

CONTROL

Staff officers' work was certainly safer than that of their commanders, though no less important. Apart from maintaining their units in working order, they had to assure that commanders maintained control of their units and therefore mastery of the battlefields. This required handling a continuous stream of reports from both the subordinate units and their own intelligence, whose evaluation was designed to produce a (more or less accurate) overall view of the actual situation on the battlefield. Their commanders used it to prepare their own plans, and eventually to issue their orders. A peculiar problem encountered in North Africa was the difficulty in assuring tight control of large units operating in a featureless terrain like the Western Desert. Formations often broke down or took a different route and, especially in 1941, untrained officers proved unable to establish their own position accurately. As a consequence, staff officers could not produce an accurate view of the situation, and commanders had problems in issuing their orders. Improved training was one solution and the use of small, purpose-built units was another.

Actually the German Army made extensive use of the *Kampfgruppe* (battlegroup), ad hoc formations that offered many advantages, amongst them ease of control. North Africa was no exception, and battlegroups were widely used on many occasions. A closer look at their different typologies reveals how they too were ruled by the principle of flexibility. The simplest battlegroup was the one formed out of a single unit, either supported by other minor units or not. In May–June 1942, during the Gazala battles, the 90th Light Division formed several battlegroups simply by having its battalions redesignated after their commanders' names (e.g., the 900th Pioneer Battalion was known as *Kampfgruppe Kube* after its commander, Hauptmann Kube). In some other cases, single battalions or regiments would form a battlegroup along with minor support units; on 5 January 1942 *Kampfgruppe Ballerstedt* (named after Oberstleutnant Ballerstedt) was formed using *Kradschützen Bataillon* 15 (15th Motorcyle Battalion) and a series of support units, including a company from the 33rd *Panzerjäger* Battalion, a platoon from 1st Battalion, 33rd Flak Battalion, a company from the 33rd Panzer Pioneer Battalion, a battery from 2nd Battalion, 33rd Artillery Regiment and a signal detachment.

Other battlegroups were more complex, since they were formed from a variety of units, often for specific combat purposes. In late March 1942, the 15th Panzer Division created two different battlegroups to man a portion of the German defensive line facing

El Agheila; these included the *Aufklärungsverband Eleba* (Reconnaissance Formation Eleba) and *Kampfgruppe Geissler*. Both encompassed a mixture of HQ, infantry, anti-tank, armoured, artillery and communications units.

Although the use of such mixed battlegroups created balanced units capable of reproducing a kind of miniature Panzer division, it is interesting to note that this was not the most preferred solution. Rather, the choice fell in most cases upon a battlegroup composed of a single, reinforced sub-unit, which, if required, could always co-operate with other battlegroups from the same division. That system worked within a single division when it was broken down into multiple battlegroups, each one just little more than a single sub-unit. On 21 November 1941, during Operation *Crusader*, the 15th Panzer Division broke down into three battlegroups before moving to Bir Chatria following three different paths. Each battlegroup had a peculiar composition and a determined role though, when needed, they could co-operate supporting each other. Battlegroup A, built around the 8th Panzer Regiment and reinforced by two artillery battalions, was led by the divisional

German tanks lie wrecked in Tunisia. The North African theatre brought German forces into first contact with the US Army, and despite early victories at places such as the Kasserine Pass, Rommel's troops could not resist the material might of the United States.

HQs and had its own communications. While this acted as a spearhead, Battlegroup B, built around the 115th Rifle Regiment, was the main support unit, though it could also fight alone as well. Battlegroup C, built around regiment's *Stab 200 zbV*, was a predominantly infantry unit that could either support the others or seize and secure any area they had captured. Both *Kampfgruppen* A and B began to move to Bir Chatria at 1200hrs on 21 November, while *Kampfgruppe* C followed one hour later (the rest of the division moved at 0300hrs on 22 November). In spite of this hurried arrangement, the night marching, poor road conditions and enemy activity, by 0730hrs on 22 November all three battlegroups had reached their targets without problems.

COMMUNICATIONS

In fast, mobile warfare, communications were essential for both command and control. In 1941–42 the German field communications systems and equipment were the most advanced in Europe, though in North Africa some shortcomings were experienced. The use of radio communications appropriate for mobile units moving in the desert was not without its problems. In some cases, as during Rommel's 'dash to the wire' in November 1941, the short range of radio equipment caused contact to be lost. Also, to make radios mobile appropriate communications vehicles were needed, which the DAK were always short of. Moreover, radio communications could be intercepted by enemy's signal intelligence, and often they could be deciphered as well. On the other hand, field telephones and wire communications were more functional and reliable, though lacking the flexibility of the radio communication. That was especially true in the Western Desert, where large spaces and the limited availability of a local wire communications net severely limited their use. For example, only from early 1942 did Panzer Group Africa's communications largely rely on wire communications. Just before the attack against the Gazala Line, Panzer Army Africa's communications net was largely based on wire, and it was also ready to be moved forward as soon as the advance began. In practice, the Panzer army's HQ served as a kind of giant switchboard connecting all the subordinate units and commands through its communications systems. In particular, those at the front line were connected using both the wire and the radio communications nets, since they would have clearly lost most of their wire links after the advance.

LEFT: Three combatants from the North African theatre demonstrate the varieties of combat dress, including some camouflage patterns that had crept in by 1942–43. They are (from left to right) an *Oberfeldwelbel* of the Panzer Regiment *Hermann Göring*, a *Leutnant* of the *Jäger* Regiment *Hermann Göring* and a *Jäger* of the *Fallschirmjäger* Brigade 'Ramcke'. (Ron Volstad © Osprey Publishing)

The radio communications net, though functional in most cases, had some serious shortcomings. For example, only the Panzer army and DAK's HQs, plus the 104th Artillery Commander unit, had a direct link with the Luftwaffe's liaison officer. Yet German troops in North Africa were well aware of how important a direct link with Luftwaffe units was, especially to contact the close-support Stuka aircraft and the aerial reconnaissance. A system of visual signals was used, though without great success. Only in March 1942 did Rommel order the creation of a number of *Flieger Funk Truppe* (airborne radio troops), land-to-air radio communications squads destined to serve with several divisional and regimental HQs. However, the lack of suitable vehicles, one of the DAK's greatest shortcomings, prevented their widespread use.

Wheeled communications vehicles were not much suited for frontline service, especially when moving off-road and under enemy artillery fire. In particular, the special-purpose radio vehicle Kfz 17 was especially prone to breaking springs. Half- and fully tracked vehicles were preferred, though as we have seen they were always in short supply, and in early 1942 the rifle companies were stripped of them to equip the divisional *Nachrichten Abteilungen* (Intelligence Battalion). Mostly equipped with the *Funkgerät 7*, a 20-watt radio with a range of 50km, the various SdKfz 250 and 251 variants worked along with the *Panzerbefehlswagen* III SdKfz 267 and 268 equipped with the *Funkgerät 8*, a 30-watt radio with a similar range.

Limited range was one serious shortcoming. The arrangement of the communication net was another one. Only divisional HQs could directly contact subordinate units, while neighbouring units, like those giving and receiving fire support, had to contact each other through higher HQs. Things actually worsened during the not-uncommon cases of friendly fire, when quick contact was badly needed. German troops had to revert to the obsolete system of pre-arranged smoke and flares signals to stop friendly artillery fire from pounding their own positions.

INTELLIGENCE

Aerial reconnaissance and signals intelligence (SIGINT) provided much of the intelligence material used by the Panzer Army Africa and the DAK. Aerial reconnaissance was the quickest and most immediate intelligence source. It was widely used since in the dust-raising environment it could easily spot practically any moving vehicle, especially columns and large concentrations, though it also had some serious failings. First, because of the lack of land-to-air radio links, it was often very hard to distinguish whether such concentrations were friendly or enemy forces. Second, the large and extensive use of camouflage rendered vehicles visible only when moving, and hence aerial reconnaissance was therefore limited only to active battlefields.

The only intelligence source capable of giving a deep, inside view of the enemy situation was therefore SIGINT, in which Germans forces in North Africa excelled. The first signals intelligence unit to arrive in North Africa was the *Horchzug* (radio monitoring platoon) attached to the 5th Light Division's 3rd Company, 39th Intelligence Battalion. In late April 1941 this was absorbed into Oberleutnant (then Hauptmann) Alfred Seebohm's 3rd Radio Monitoring Company, 56th Intelligence Battalion, itself a radio interception unit. One year later, in April 1942, this was eventually renamed 621st Radio Monitoring Company (Motorized), most of which was eventually captured at Tell el Eisa on 10 July.

British carelessness in radio communications – particularly their use of simple codes, easy to decipher – was of great help to German SIGINT. German SIGINT's first success came almost at once when, thanks to the information it supplied, Rommel was well aware there only were British rearguards at Mersa el Brega. After he had started his drive into Cyrenaica, his intelligence units also revealed that these rearguards were withdrawing.

In the months to follow, German SIGINT saw a series of ups and downs. Rommel's reaction to the British *Battleaxe* offensive in June 1941 was greatly helped by SIGINT, which informed him of the actual start date of the operation and also of British intentions during the battle. On the other hand, one of SIGINT's greatest failures was Operation *Crusader*, which came as a complete surprise. In the first half of 1942 many of Rommel's successes were due to both his SIGINT's activity and to the information provided by the 'good source' – the deciphered messages sent by the American military attaché in Egypt.

The long distances travelled by Germany Army vehicles in North Africa, such as these Panzers, caused significant issues with maintenance as well as logistics. Air filters were clogged easily by dust, and any moving parts were worn by sand, increasing the frequency of repairs and cleaning.

In North Africa, British reconnaissance tactics tended to rely on stealth to acquire information, while the Germans were always prepared to fight for it if necessary. All of their armoured cars were usually armed with a 2cm cannon (later upgraded) and this gave them a distinct advantage over those of the British. Here, an SdKfz 232 and an SdKfz 222 from 3rd Reconnaissance Battalion advance towards Benghazi. (Jim Laurier © Osprey Publishing)

The fact that this intelligence source eventually ran dry in July 1942, when most of Seebohm's Radio Monitoring Company was also destroyed, certainly suggests that a good deal of Rommel's failures at El Alamein were due to the lack of intelligence.

LESSONS LEARNED

In a similar way to its campaigns of 1941–42, the image of the DAK has both lights and shadows. Rommel's brilliant leadership and superior German tactics made early successes possible – principally the first drive into Cyrenaica and the defence of the Sollum–Halfaya line. On the other hand, lack of experience and incomplete wartime training, as well as inadequate weaponry and equipment, especially compared to those available to DAK's enemies, ultimately provided the backdrop to early defeats at Tobruk and during Operation *Crusader*. Experience gained was not, however, wasted and in 1942 many changes were introduced. Training was improved, taking advantage of experienced personnel and proven tactics. Unit organization was altered, making good many shortcomings; in 1941 German units greatly suffered from their unbalanced organization, which saw three different divisional assets none of which was actually suitable for the Western Desert. Changes introduced in September 1941, though useful, were only a provisional remedy, but those introduced in April 1942 brought many decisive innovations. DAK's divisions were now well balanced and, thanks to a larger weapons allotment and to the introduction of new and more powerful weapons, they turned into extremely powerful and successful units. Not that every shortcoming had been eliminated: a lack of motor vehicles, especially

SUPPLY ISSUES

Another critical cause of Germany's defeat in North Africa was supply problems. Bringing supplies across the Mediterranean was hard enough, with interdiction of shipping by Allied aircraft and naval vessels, but those supplies then had to be carried from harbours to the front and had to reach every division and unit. Only motorized columns could accomplish that, though they were extremely exposed to British air attacks, especially in the summer of 1942. Estimating daily divisional needs is quite hard, but an acceptable figure is no less than 300–400 tonnes (water excluded) for a Panzer division. The amount was mainly made up of ammunitions (about 100–200 tonnes) and petrol, oil and lubricants (POL, c.150 tonnes). The rest consisted of food, spare parts for vehicles and weapons, medical supplies and every other kind of supply needed by men and machines. Consumption of ammunition was extremely high when divisions were in combat, and stocks could be exhausted in a few days. For example, between 28 and 30 May 1942, the 21st Panzer Division consumed about 2,300 artillery rounds, 1,900 tank-gun rounds, 600 rounds for the 8.8cm guns and 340 more rounds for the 5cm anti-tank guns. During the ten days of the last Alamein battle, the division consumed about 10,000 tank-gun rounds and 12,000 artillery rounds, plus some

80,000 litres of water and 260,000 litres of fuel. Fuel was a major problem, especially because transport columns also burned it while moving from depots to the frontline. In 1941 the 5th Panzer Regiment needed as much as 4,400 litres of fuel for a single day of combat, about one-third of the fuel needed by all combat units (between 10,000 and 12,000 litres). Services and supply units included, the daily consumption of the entire division was about 33,000 litres. Water consumption too was extremely high, given the daily allowance of 3 litres per man in mid-1942 – vehicle-cooling water included. This figure had already been reduced from the daily allowance in 1941 of 5 litres per man.

Logistics therefore played a major role in the Western Desert. Their importance is clearly shown by 21st Panzer Division's experience during the last German offensive that eventually stopped at Alam Halfa. Problems had already been encountered while crossing the minefields, which were deeper than expected. Also, while trying to reach their objectives, units ran into a sandstorm that slowed down the pace of the advance and increased fuel consumption. Eventually, in the late afternoon of 30 August, the 21st Panzer Division halted its march and deployed for defence. Logistics had won the battle over the warriors.

suitable ones, could only be made good thanks to the large amount of captured enemy equipment. Also the new divisional organization, based on the principle of 'more weapons, less men', coupled with strengths perpetually below establishment, eventually imposed too severe a strain on the relatively few available men. The result was that when the Alamein Line was reached, the DAK had to face a simple reality: it had gone beyond its limits.

Nevertheless, the fact remains that the stunning victories of May–June 1942, obtained against a superior enemy, were the result of a decisive evolution that, in a few months, brought the DAK to remarkable levels of capability and efficiency. As a matter of fact, had the DAK seized Tobruk in 1941 we may very likely suppose that given its then lack of experience, its faulty organization and all other shortcomings, it might not have been able to continue with its offensive into Egypt, at least successfully. And that was not just a matter of weapons and equipment: some of DAK's most stunning successes were achieved when it faced a superior enemy and before modern and powerful weapons became available in quantity. Both drives into Cyrenaica were conducted with scarce resources: the defence against operations *Brevity* and *Battleaxe* was successful thanks to the ingenious use of the 8.8cm Flak, and the victories of May–June 1942 were obtained before large quantities of the newest, most powerful, tanks were available. It is once more a matter of light and shadow. In October 1942 the DAK was in comparison stronger and much more skilled than it had been in 1941, yet it was finally defeated because its own doctrines and tactics had to be surrendered in favour of those imposed by its enemy.

The failure of logistics was a principal cause of the eventual German defeat in North Africa. Supplies of fuel and ammunition became particularly troubled along stretched supply lines, and Allied advances from October 1942 captured hundreds of vehicles, as illustrated by this photograph of requisitioned German trucks.

Pioneers from 5th Light Division struggle to locate mines whilst under fire from nearby defence posts during the 1 May 1941 assault on the Tobruk perimeter. The careful camouflage of the Australians' defence posts made the task doubly difficult and with the armoured units having charged through the perimeter defences, the pioneers were left without adequate support. (Jim Laurier © Osprey Publishing)

A war of movement and penetration, the type of conflict preferred by the Germans, became a battle of attrition, which ate into German resources, manpower and logistical capabilities. At the very end, neither weapons nor experience could assure success on the battlefield, though they certainly influenced defeats.

What then were the real secrets of the DAK, those that made possible its many successes? Rommel was certainly one; no matter whether his strategic and tactical skills can be criticized or not, the fact remains that his personality, his brilliant leadership and his capability to face changing situations proved decisive in many cases. Also, one should not forget that his subordinates, as well as most of the DAK's senior and junior officers, possessed remarkable skills, and leadership capabilities. Undoubtedly, it was thanks to the combination of these two factors that the DAK became such a solid, strong and welded group and, in spite of its shortcomings, such a successful fighting force. Beyond any doubt, this is the true lesson that should be learnt from the history of the DAK. Ingenuity, skills, leadership, capability to face changing situations and to react appropriately were the qualities that made Rommel, his subordinate commanders and most of the DAK's men capable of dealing with a hostile environment and a superior enemy.

THE BALKANS

The war in North Africa was not the only theatre around the Mediterranean into which the German Army was drawn in 1941. On 28 October 1940, Mussolini invaded Greece from Albania, opening a new Balkan front. Yet damaging Greek counterattacks, the

German paratroopers and supply containers spill from a Ju 52 transport aircraft during the invasion of Crete. The *Fallschirmjäger* parachutes gave little control over direction and landing, and by consequence dozens of German troops were either drowned in the sea off the Cretan coast, or injured themselves when landing on the rocky landscape.

British occupation of Crete on 31 October (which threatened Romanian oil-fields vital to the German war-machine), the arrival of a 53,000-strong Allied 'W' Force in Greece on 7 March 1941 and a pro-Allied military coup in Yugoslavia on 27 March forced Hitler to activate Operation *Marita* – the invasion of the Balkans – to prevent Greece and Yugoslavia aiding the Allies.

For the invasion, German forces comprised the 2nd Army (Generaloberst Maximilian von Weichs), with four corps – LI, LII, XXXXVI Panzer, XXXXIX Mountain – and most of the 12th Army (Generalfeldmarschall Wilhelm List), with five corps – XVIII Mountain, XXXX Panzer with XI, XIV Panzer and XXXXI Motorised Corps in 1st Panzer Group (Generaloberst Von Kleist). These forces totalled 24 divisions: eight infantry, seven Panzer, four mountain, two motorized, one light infantry and two SS motorized, assisted by Italian and Hungarian units.

German troops of the 2nd Panzer Division advance warily into Greece. The division was formed in 1935, and went on to serve until in the end of war in theatres such as Poland, France, the Balkans, the Eastern Front, Normandy and the Ardennes.

The invasion commenced on 6 April, and showed a pattern of success that had eluded Italian forces. The 2nd Army reached Zagreb on 10 April, Belgrade on 12 April, Sarajevo on 16 April and Dubrovnik on 17 April. The 1st Panzer Group's XI and XIV Panzer Corps captured Belgrade on 12 April, meeting XXXXI Motorized Corps advancing from Romania. Yugoslav Macedonia was occupied by the XXXX Panzer Corps and elements of XVIII Corps, taking Strumica on 6 April, Skopje on 7 April and Monastir on 9 April before pivoting southwards towards Greece.

The 30 Yugoslav divisions were easily defeated by German tactical superiority. In the north some Slovene and Croatian units refused to fight, but Serbian divisions in the south

ABOVE: A Panzer *Feldwebel* (centre) is flanked by an infantry *Obergefreiter* (left) and a mountain regiment *Gefreiter*, all figures from the Balkans campaign in April and May 1941. The tankman wears regulation field uniform, consisting of the M1934 special tank crew uniform modified in 1936 with three lapel button-holes, with the Iron Cross 1st Class medal and 2nd Class ribbon and silver battle badge. (Stephen Andrew © Osprey Publishing)

The Balkans remained a long-term commitment for German occupation forces, on account of their vigorous guerrilla forces. Here we see *Sturmgeschütz* III (StuG III) Ausf. G assault guns on the streets of Salonika, Greece, in 1944. The StuG III served in both infantry support and tank-destroyer capacities.

counterattacked briefly into Italian-held Albania. On 17 April the Yugoslav High Command surrendered, but many troops joined Nationalist Chetnik and later communist partisan guerrilla forces.

Facing the Germans in Greece was the Greek Army, which comprised 21 divisions in 1st (Epirus) Army, 2nd (Eastern Macedonian) Army and the troops of 'W' Force. On 6 April, the German 12th Army's XXX Corps advanced into western Thrace against the Greek 2nd Army, taking Xanthi on 9 April. By 4 May they had occupied the Aegean islands. On 9 April, XVIII Mountain Corps stormed the Metaxa Line in Greek Macedonia and advanced through eastern Greece, reaching Larisa on 19 April. Meanwhile XXXX Panzer Corps pushed through western Greece, taking Kozani on 14 April and Ioannina on 20 April, forcing the outflanked Greek 1st Army to surrender on 23 April. The victorious Germans then set off in pursuit of 'W' Force, taking Lamia on 20 April, Thermopylae on 24 April and Athens on 27 April. On 30 April the Peloponnese were secured and 'W' Force had evacuated to Crete.

The epic German invasion of Crete – Operation *Merkur* (Mercury) – commenced on 20 May 1941, when the Luftwaffe's 7. *Flieger Division* (7th Parachute Division) parachuted onto Crete, and from 22 May 5th Mountain Division and 6th Mountain Division's 141st Mountain Regiment were flown in by glider. The 41,500 Allied defenders fought tenaciously, but on 1 June the Germans secured the island (see below), and effectively completed its takeover of the Balkans. Hitler's armies had notched up another great campaign victory, although furious partisan resistance, particularly in Yugoslavia, meant the Balkans remained an active combat zone until late in the war.

CRETE AND THE *FALLSCHIRMJÄGER*

The capture of Crete brought the world's attention to Germany's airborne forces, who had already made something of a name for themselves during the campaigns of 1940. The men of the 7th Parachute Division who spearheaded the assault on Crete in May 1941 were all volunteers. Tough, physically fit, well trained and with excellent officers at every level, they were highly disciplined and motivated and encouraged to use their initiative whenever possible. They rightly considered themselves an elite corps.

The call for volunteers to form the first *Fallschirmjäger* (paratroopers) battalion had gone out in 1936, with a paratrooper training school established at Stendal-Bostel airfield outside Berlin. By the outbreak of war, having consolidated control of the parachute, glider and air transport forces, the Luftwaffe had enough men to form the nucleus of an airborne division under the command of Generalmajor Kurt Student and based at Tempelhof airfield, near Berlin.

Hitler's new parachute forces distinguished themselves as an elite during the campaigns in Northern and Western Europe in 1940. In Denmark, the 1st *Fallschirmjäger* Regiment captured the two Aalborg airfields and Vordingborg bridge in Copenhagen, while in Norway paratroopers took the Fornebu airfield outside Oslo and the Sola airfield at Stavanger. For the campaign in the Netherlands, troops of the 1st and 2nd *Fallschirmjäger* Regiments took and held the Dordrecht and Moerdijk bridges on the approaches to Rotterdam and the airfields at Ockenburg, Valkenburg, Waalhaven and Ypenburg. Belgium provided their most daring success, however, when four sections of *Sturmabteilung Koch* (Assault Battalion 'Koch'), formed from the 1st *Fallschirmjäger* Regiment and named after its commander, Hauptman Walter Koch, stormed (using glider deployment) and captured the powerful fortress of Eben Emael and the bridges at Kanne, Veldwezelt and Vroenhoven.

Hitler was much inspired by his new airborne warriors. By 1941, it had grown into a full division, commanded by Generalleutnant Willhelm Süssmann, consisting of three parachute regiments and a semi-autonomous *Luftlande Sturmregiment* (Airborne Assault Regiment), supported by artillery, anti-tank, machine-gun and combat engineer battalions. The three parachute regiments had three parachute battalions apiece, while the air assault

regiment had three parachute battalions and a glider battalion. The strength of each parachute battalion averaged around 700 men and comprised three infantry companies, a headquarters company, a support company and a signals section. The entire battalion, along with all its heavy equipment – including radios, heavy weapons, ammunition, medical supplies and rations – was airdropped. The equipment was dropped in lightweight containers. Neither the paratroopers nor the containers could be controlled while they descended, as the majority of parachutes used were still the older RZ16 that lacked the lift webs or 'risers' of American and British designs.

Fallschirmjäger troops eagerly study maps of landing areas for the forthcoming invasion of Crete. Their transport is the Junkers Ju 52, a workhorse transport aircraft that also performed airborne landings, air supply drops and even bombing roles during the war.

For the Crete operation, Hitler would use the airborne troops of General Student's XI *Fliegerkorps* (XI Air Corps), which incorporated both para and airlanding troops, the latter deployed by gliders and Ju 52s. Operation *Merkur* (Mercury) began on 20 May with glider and parachute landings from a fleet of 500 transport aircraft. The British had failed to defend the island during a six-month occupation and most of the 35,000-strong garrison, commanded by the New Zealand World War I hero Lieutenant-General Bernard Freyberg VC, had just escaped from Greece with nothing but their own light weapons.

On 20 May, the skies above Crete were choked with the gently falling figures of German *Fallschirmjäger*. The first assault by 3,000 paratroopers failed to capture the main objective, the airfield at Maleme, but after the New Zealanders withdrew from one end during the night the Germans began to land reinforcements the next day, despite still being under intense artillery and mortar fire. For the first days of the operation, the possibility of disaster hung over the Germans. Whole units were wiped out before landing, or soon after before they could reach their weapons, and the Royal Navy stopped a supplementary seaborne landing on the second night. Nevertheless, the Germans were able to land a steady stream of reinforcements, and after a week of bitter fighting Freyberg ordered a retreat and evacuation.

5. *GEBIRGS* DIVISION

Instead of the 22nd Airborne Division (which was guarding the Ploesti oilfields in Romania), the paratroopers on Crete would be reinforced by the 5. *Gebirgs Division* (5th Mountain Division) under the command of Generalmajor Julius 'Papa' Ringel. The majority of troops in this division were volunteers and had combat experience, having come from a number of other divisions that had seen service in the Low Countries and Norway before the 5th had started forming in Salzburg in October 1940. The majority of the soldiers were recruited from Austria and the alpine region of southern Germany and were tough, intelligent men. The division was organized along similar lines to a conventional infantry division, although it had only two *Gebirgsjäger* (mountain rifle) regiments – the 85th and 100th – each with three battalions, and the 95th Mountain Artillery Regiment with two artillery battalions along with signals, reconnaissance, anti-tank and engineer battalions. With just under 14,000 men, the division was weaker in manpower than a standard infantry division. However, for the Crete campaign, it was reinforced with the 141st Mountain Rifle Regiment from the 6th Mountain Division. Each battalion had the usual three rifle companies, headquarters company and support elements. Neither Ringel nor his men expected their sudden transfer to Student's *Fliegerkorps* XI (XI Air Corps), as none of them had any experience in airborne warfare, but their contribution to the outcome of the battle cannot be underestimated.

The 2nd Battalion, 1st *Fallschirmjäger* Regiment, landing just west of Heraklion airfield, Crete, on the afternoon of 20 May 1941. Heraklion was to be the target for *Gruppe Ost*, consisting of Oberst Bruno Bräuer's 1st *Fallschirmjäger* Regiment, reinforced with a battalion from Oberst Alfred Sturm's 2nd *Fallschirmjäger* Regiment and strong supporting units. (Howard Gerrard © Osprey Publishing)

The airborne invasion of Crete was one of the most spectacular and audacious events of the war. The Luftwaffe men, once unshackled from their parachute harnesses, worked superbly as assault troops, utilizing air-dropped firepower to overcome what should have been a virtually unbreakable Allied defensive advantage. The paratroopers eventually won through, but it was an extremely costly for the Germans. Several hundred planes had been destroyed or damaged during the battle, and there were 7,000 casualties out of the 22,000 troops landed, more than the entire Balkan campaign. The Germans considered themselves lucky to have captured Crete, and Hitler was shocked by the

OVERLEAF: German mountain troops are given their orders after being airlanded on Crete in May 1941. A total of ten *Gebirgs* divisions were raised between 1938 and 1945, although two divisions were given the title of 9th *Gebirgs* Division, and the combat status of these divisions is uncertain.

General Kurt Student, commanding general of XI *Fliegerkorps*, consults a map with his staff during the invasion of Crete. Student was one of Hitler's most capable generals, although he could be ruthless towards local civilians if they resisted his forces.

losses. He concluded that the days of paratroops were over and scrapped plans for an airborne invasion of Malta, which would have proved more beneficial to German strategy. From this point on, Hitler's parachute units – which eventually expanded to several divisions strong – served principally as elite infantry regiments. They gave good service in North Africa, Italy and on the Eastern and Western Fronts, but as the war ground on their casualties increased and the quality of the replacements, as in all Wehrmacht formations, significantly declined.

RIGHT: A typical German paratrooper and his equipment, c.1940. 1) Helmet showing liner with straps; 2) Parachutist's jump badge; 3) Zeiss binoculars; 4) MP 40 submachine gun; 5) Leather MP 40 magazine pouches; 6) Leather map case with stitched-on pockets for pencils, ruler and compasses; 7) Water bottle and drinking cup; 8) Front and rear views of the external knee pads; 9) Luger holster; 10) First pattern side-lacing jump boots showing cleated sole. (Velimir Vuksic © Osprey Publishing)

APPEARANCE AND EQUIPMENT

Fallschirmjäger clothing and equipment were designed to be practical, comfortable and well suited to the battlefield of the 1940s. Unfortunately, the main distinguishing feature of a German paratrooper's apparel was his bright golden-yellow *Waffenfarbe* (arm of service colour) applied principally to collar patches and shoulder boards. Men of the *Hermann Göring* units wore white. Both colours were wildly impractical on a battleground – they gave a convenient target marker for enemy riflemen – and were frequently removed or carefully muddied other than when an official photographer was around. *Waffenfarbe* apart, most paratroopers wore largely standard Luftwaffe uniform and insignia.

Starting at the top, the men's *Fallschirmhelme* (jump helmets) were originally cut-down Wehrmacht helmets with the brims removed. This measure was taken partly to prevent the air flow of the initial descent from an aircraft lifting the helmet and half-strangling the men, and partly to eliminate the risk of the relatively sharp edges from severing a shroud line. The helmets were initially painted Luftwaffe blue-grey and featured the national tricolour and air force eagle on either side. Battle experience soon caused them to be repainted green or, in North Africa and Italy, dull yellow, and the insignia disappeared. In winter, they were simply whitewashed, since this would scrub

Wounded *Fallschirmjäger* and mountain troops are loaded aboard a Ju 52 for the flight out of Crete. Medical treatment for the German Army would be the responsibility of *Armee Sanitätsabteilung* (Army Medical Battalion), with each company of the battalion operating a field hospital just behind the front line. Soldiers who needed any type of surgery would be transported to a general hospital further behind the lines.

off easily in the spring. A variety of camouflage cloth helmet covers were issued as the war progressed. Men also made their own disruptive patterns using cut-down string vests or chicken wire, into which they inserted seasonal foliage. After 1941, with the virtual abolition of the paratroopers as genuine airborne soldiers, an increasing number of men in the later-numbered divisions simply wore ordinary army helmets.

Other *Fallschirmjäger* headgear was standard Luftwaffe issue – sidecap, field cap with brim and both styles of officers' peaked cap, in either blue-grey or tropical tan. For winter, especially in Russia, the men were issued with long woollen toques, tubular garments which fitted over their heads and necks rather like Balaclava helmets. A stylish peaked fur cap with ear flaps modelled on those issued to mountain troops also made an appearance, but it does not seem, from photographic evidence, to have been widely issued to the *Fallschirmtruppen*. One hat which did single out a *Fallschirmjäger* officer in the Afro-Mediterranean theatres was the so-called Meyer cap, a comfortable, lightweight, loose, air-vented design with a detachable neck flap to protect against sunstroke.

Linen underwear, woollen socks, PE kit, fatigue overalls and white (parade), blue-grey or tropical tan shirts were standard for all ranks and no different from those issued to other Luftwaffe personnel. One other individual item that became something of a *Fallschirmjäger* trademark in North Africa and later, was a brightly coloured neckerchief or silk scarf. Some regiments even adopted uniform colours: FJR 5's, for example, were dark blue with white polka dots.

Jackets and tunics were, again, standard Luftwaffe issue, either the stylish tapered-waist *Fliegerbluse* (Flying Service Blouse) or the four-pocket *Tuchrock* (Service Tunic); only the latter appears from photographs to have been issued in tropical tan material.

Jackets were belted at the waist and all ranks normally wore a holstered sidearm. Over the jacket, the paratroopers wore the *Fallschirmkittel* (jump smock), a practical garment made of heavy duck cotton or, later, herringbone weave, which was designed to prevent clothing or equipment getting snagged in the aircraft or entangled in the parachute shroud lines at the moment of opening. The first pattern smock was not, however, easy to put on or take off, because it had short integral legs. The paratrooper had to step into the legs, pull the garment up to his shoulders and then struggle into the sleeves before buttoning up the front. On landing, after freeing himself from the parachute harness, the paratrooper then had to pull the smock down to his waist in order to undo his equipment belt and buckle it back on outside the smock. To add insult to injury, he had to take the smock off again, or at least pull it down to his knees, in order to relieve himself. The first pattern smocks differed slightly from one another in the number of pockets they had, and were produced in either pale green or grey.

Most men involved in the 1940 campaigns wore the first pattern smock even though by this time the second had emerged. The later model was of a more practical design that

Soldiers of the 7th Airborne Division on Crete. Note the two types of submachine gun on display here: the soldier in the foreground on the left has a Swiss/Austrian Steyr-Solothurn MP 34, while the man behind him has the more modern MP 40.

omitted the legs of the first pattern smock, and which buttoned all down the front. On a jump, the lower half buttoned round the upper legs to recreate the earlier legs and prevent the smock billowing up as the soldier fell. The smock also had two large chest and thigh pockets and was manufactured in a green or tan/brown splinter camouflage pattern. A later variant of this garment, although not designated 'third pattern', was produced in more subtle brownish water camouflage after the Crete operation, and combat trousers were also introduced in this material.

Finally, after 1942, with the virtual abolition of the paratroop mission, an increasing number of *Fallschirmtruppen* (especially in the higher numbered divisions) were issued with the same single-breasted *Kampfjacke* (combat jacket), made of a rayon/cotton mix in splinter camouflage, as that issued to the Luftwaffe field divisions. Reports of a jump smock being produced in tropical tan are unsubstantiated, although some officers may have had these

RIGHT: The main part of the illustration (1) shows a *Fallschirmjäger*'s descent after jumping from a Ju 52. After hooking their static lines to the anchor cable in the aircraft, the men shuffled forward on command to brace themselves in the doorway. At the command 'Jump!', they launched themselves in a spread-eagled position to prevent tumbling and perhaps snagging the static line; this posture also reduced the shock when the parachute opened, at which point the men found themselves being dragged backwards until they were lying almost horizontally. After oscillating for a few seconds, the 'chute would steady and the men would begin dropping vertically (or nearly so, depending on the wind strength). Neither the RZ1 (2 and 3) nor RZ16 parachute had lift webs, or 'risers', as on British and American designs, but two ropes converging into one from behind the shoulder blades. This unwieldy arrangement made it impossible to control the descent, leaving the men helpless until they were on the ground, at which point they could find and access the contents of the supply containers (4), as shown. (Velimir Vuksic © Osprey Publishing)

tailored privately. Other smocks were, however, sewn from Italian camouflage material after the armistice in 1943. The only insignia worn on any smocks or combat jackets (except on parade, when decorations were permitted) were the Luftwaffe breast eagle and cloth rank patches on the sleeves. Other special clothing issued after the first disastrous winter in Russia included at least two patterns of quilted jacket and trousers in reversible white/mouse-grey colours. These garments were designed to give the *Fallschirmtruppen* more freedom of movement in extreme weather conditions than the standard double-breasted greatcoat, but they were never available in sufficient quantity. It should be noted that the greatcoat was never worn over the jump smock.

For most of the war, the *Fallschirmtruppen* wore combat trousers in a slightly darker grey-green material than their smocks. *Hosen*, as they were called, were relatively loose fitting for comfort and ease of movement, and fastened at the ankles with tapes. They had two side and two hip pockets plus a small fob pocket under the waistband, and could be held up with either braces (suspenders) or a belt, depending upon personal preference. Uniquely, on the outside of each knee there was a vent through which the paratrooper could withdraw the rectangular kapok filled canvas pads that were worn to protect the knees in the heavy frontal fall dictated by the absurd parachute design. The system,

Fallschirmjäger take a break from the fighting in a Cretan alleyway. Out of a total force of 22,000 men, the Germans lost 3,250 dead and 3,400 wounded. These figures are higher than the Allied totals, despite the German victory.

A dramatic image of the *Fallschirmjäger* in action on Crete, with one soldier providing covering fire around a corner with his MP 40 submachine gun, while the other members of the squad prepare to make an advance.

however, proved ineffective, so external pads were also later strapped on. Both sets of pads were quickly discarded after landing to give more freedom of movement.

A final distinction of the *Fallschirmjäger's* trousers was the small pocket fastened with plastic press studs on the right thigh, and which carried the so-called 'gravity knife'. Unlike an ordinary clasp knife, which requires two hands to open, the *Fallschirmjäger* knife had a weighted blade that slid free automatically as it was taken out of the pocket, and was locked in place by a simple thumb catch. It was specially designed to allow a paratrooper, who already had one hand fully occupied trying to gather in his billowing 'chute, to cut the shroud lines and quickly free himself. The knife could, of course, also be used in combat or for eating. In North Africa and elsewhere, the *Fallschirmtruppen* were issued with tropical trousers or shorts in a comfortable lightweight but hard-wearing cotton. The trousers were particularly baggy to increase air flow and prevent chafing, and had both two generous hip pockets and a map pocket on the left thigh.

A *Fallschirmjäger's* uniform was also distinguished by the *Handschuhe* (gauntlets) and *Fallschirmschnürschuhe* (jump boots). The soft black leather gloves, elasticated at wrist and cuff, were designed to keep his hands warm both inside the unheated cabin of the Ju 52/3m transport aircraft and during the drop itself. They were also sufficiently supple to be worn in combat. The boots, made of black leather with cleated rubber soles for grip, were originally laced at the side under the mistaken belief that this would offer extra ankle support. The second pattern had standard frontal lacing. Canvas ankle gaiters could be worn with either. However, on parade and as the war dragged on, in the field too, the Fallschirmtruppen wore the standard calf-length Wehrmacht jackboots.

FG 42

The FG 42 was one of the most remarkable weapons of the war and, although only about 7,000 were manufactured due to its complexity and cost, its gas-operated mechanism, and the open/closed bolt system which allowed for single-shot or automatic fire, has been copied in most post-war automatic rifles. The story of its genesis is a lengthy one, but in brief it was inspired by the usual rivalry between the *Heer*, which had introduced the world's first self-loading automatic rifle in the form of the Haenel/Schmeisser 7.92mm (kurz) MP 43/StG 44, and the Luftwaffe, which wanted one of its own for the *Fallschirmtruppen*. The result was a very light (4.5kg) weapon with a straight line barrel-to-butt layout, sloping pistol grip (later discarded because of cost in favour of a more conventional pistol grip), ergonomically designed plastic shoulder butt, integral bipod for use in the LMG role, muzzle-flash eliminator and even a special 'spike' bayonet rather like an ice pick. The weapon's only real drawback in use was the side-mounted 20-round box magazine, which unbalanced the weapon unless the bipod was used and tended to snag on relatively loose clothing such as the jump smock. Its main advantage in the field compared with the MP 43/StG 44 was that it used the same long 7.92mm cartridge as in the standard Gew/Kar 98 rifle and carbine, so reloading the magazine was never the problem it was in the early days of the army rifle.

Field equipment for the individual *Fallschirmjäger* was more or less the same as that issued to army and Luftwaffe field divisions, although in the early days the paratrooper was issued with a soft canvas carrying bag for his gasmask instead of the rigid cylindrical metal one, which could have caused injury during a drop. A special ammunition bandolier was also developed for the *Fallschirmtruppen*. Personal weapons were identical to everyone else's, with the exception of the specially designed *Fallschirmgewehr* 42 (FG 42) assault rifle.

In addition to the FG 42, the *Fallschirmtruppen* also had a higher allocation of other automatic weapons, including the MP 40 and MG 34/42, and pockets or waistbelts bulged with grenades. They also had a cut-down lightweight version of the army's standard 8.8cm mortar, the *kurzer Granatwerfer* 42 (Short Grenade Launcher 42).

Because of the limitations on what a paratrooper could carry on his person during a drop, the Germans developed a rigid lightweight container to protect weapons and

RIGHT: *Fallschirmjäger* sidearms and personal weapons. 1) 9mm Luger P'08, shown field-stripped into its component parts; 2) 9mm (kurz) Parabellum Walther PP; 3) 7.65mm Sauer *Selbsladepistole* (self-loading pistol) Modell 38H; 4) 9mm *Pistole Automatique Browning, modèle à Grande Puissance* 1935 (German designation Pistole P620[b]); 5) 9mm Parabellum Walther P 38; 6) *Stielgranate* M1924; 7) *Eiergranate* (egg grenade) M1939; 8) Bayonet Modell S84/98 and 8a canvas and mild steel belt frog; 9) Bayonet Modell S98/04 in leather and mild steel frog; 10) *Fallschirmjäger* gravity-operated knife. (Velimir Vuksic © Osprey Publishing)

A Ju 52 plunges to earth in flames after being hit by ground fire during the invasion of Crete. Hundreds of German troops were killed in the initial landings, many as they floated to earth virtually helpless through storms of small-arms fire.

ammunition on their descent. Rifles and bandoliers, submachine guns and ammunition pouches, machine guns, mortars and ammunition boxes were all stowed away in these devices. Other containers, clearly marked with red crosses, carried medical and surgical equipment.

Because the *Fallschirmtruppen* needed to get at their weapons very quickly once on the ground, the supply containers were normally thrown out of the aircraft before the first man jumped, giving him an aiming point. However, not all weapons went in the containers and, despite the risks, about one man in four dropped on Crete carried an MP 40 tucked under his parachute harness or strapped to his outer thigh. Similarly, during demonstration jumps for the 'brass' at Stendal, carbines were carried very unsafely in the hands. Nevertheless, despite the clumsiness of the German container system, the *Fallschirmtruppen* never imitated the British practice of stowing weapons and other equipment in a kitbag which could be dangled on a rope below each man, but given the impracticality of the RZ parachutes, this might have posed an unacceptable hazard.

As a result, the *Fallschirmjäger's* uniform and equipment was the typical mix of the practical and the awkward. Yet regardless of what they wore or carried, the German paratroopers were superbly trained, not only in their airborne roles but also in infantry assault tactics. In their later career as infantry, they were frequently used in a 'fire brigade' capacity, rushed between threatened sectors to bolster a defence or attack. As with many elements of the German Army, the *Fallschirmjäger* were much respected by their opponents.

The war in North Africa, although it ended in a German defeat, was one in which the German Army fought with distinction and nobility. The theatre itself was conducive to a 'clean' war (if such a thing exists), with few civilians to get in the way of the fighting and little of the ideological and racial baggage that hung over other theatres. The same could not be said of the Balkans – the internecine fighting in Yugoslavia, for example, would take more than a million lives by the end of the war. From June 1941, furthermore, the German Army would be locked in an epic struggle against Soviet Union, a war of unimaginable proportions that would reveal the very best and very worst of Hitler's fighting men.

SS paratroopers in Yugoslavia. They belong to the 500. *SS-Fallschirmjägerbataillon* (500th SS-Paratrooper Battalion), which was formed in 1943 and, on account of its dangerous mission profile, used 50 per cent personnel from disciplinary battalions.

OPERATION *BARBAROSSA* AND THE WAR IN THE EAST, 1941–43

O**N 23 AUGUST 1939, HITLER HAD CONCLUDED AN ALLIANCE OF CONVENIENCE** with the Soviet dictator Stalin to protect Germany's eastern borders during the 1939–40 western campaign. Nevertheless, the Soviet Union remained Germany's ideological arch-enemy, a territory for ever marked in Hitler's mind as holding the promise of true *Lebensraum* (living space) for the German people. On 18 December 1940, Hitler told his commanders that Operation *Barbarossa*, the attack on the Soviet Union, would commence on 15 May 1941, a date postponed to 22 June 1941 by the invasion of Yugoslavia and Greece.

Barbarossa would be the biggest conflict in military history, with some three million German troops and about 900,000 allies facing almost 4.7 million Soviet troops. Its outcome was to colour post-war European history for 50 years. For the Wehrmacht, however, the Eastern Front would be a war totally unlike anything experienced so far on the Western Front or in North Africa.

INVASION AND FIRST DEFEAT

For Operation *Barbarossa*, the German Army, supported by the Romanian, Finnish, Hungarian and Slovak armies, would attack the Soviet Union with three army groups spearheaded by Panzer and motorized divisions organized in four reinforced army corps, designated as Panzer groups. The plan was that these would trap and smash the bulk of the Soviet Red Army in Belorussia and occupy the three key cities of Leningrad (the cradle of Soviet communism), Moscow (the nerve centre of political power) and Kiev (capital of the agriculturally rich Ukraine and gateway to the Caucasian oilfields). The German Army would then advance to the Ural Mountains–River Volga line, some 2,100km from the German border, build a 3,000-mile defensive line against Soviet Siberia and Central Asia, and occupy European Russia. Soviet Karelia would be awarded to Finland and Romania would annex Bessarabia, northern Bukovina and 'Transnistria' (Moldova and Odessa). The remaining territory would be divided into four huge *Reichskommissariate* (Reich provinces): *Ostland* (Estonia, Latvia, Lithuania, Belarus and north-western Russia), *Moskau* (northern and central Russia), *Ukraine* (Ukraine and southern Russia) and *Kaukasus* (Transcaucasia, Armenia, Georgia and Azerbaijan). Local populations would be ruled by up to 100 million German, Dutch and Scandinavian settlers, who would ensure permanent Nazi domination of the Eurasian land mass.

Thus ran the theory, and its attempted realization was certainly not hampered by lack of resources. Operation *Barbarossa* was the greatest land campaign in history, dwarfing the scale of all previous operations since September 1939. The sheer scale of the German invasion, plus the very size of enemy territory and forces the Wehrmacht faced, would make it a very different theatre to Western Europe and North Africa. Before looking at the nature of the German forces on the Eastern Front, an overview of the Barbarossa campaign to mid 1943 is instructive for exploring the Wehrmacht's experience of warfare on the *Ostfront* (Eastern Front).

Despite the scale of the invasion forces, the Germans achieved almost complete surprise when they pushed across the Soviet border at 0415hrs on Sunday 22 June 1941. The German forces were arranged into three army groups. Army Group North (Generalfeldmarschall Von Leeb), with 16th and 18th Armies, totalled 20 divisions, plus the 4th Panzer Group (Generaloberst Hoepner) with three tank and three motorized infantry divisions. It was to drive through the Baltic States towards Leningrad. Army Group Centre (Generalfeldmarschall Fedor von Bock) confronted Soviet West Front in Belorussia, with Moscow as it ultimate goal. Von Bock had nine Panzer, six motorized and 35 infantry divisions under his command. He planned for his two Panzer groups (1 and 2) to advance 400km into Belarus and converge east of its capital, Minsk, to crush Russian forces between themselves and the infantry of 4th and 9th Armies. Army Group South (Generalfeldmarschall Von Rundstedt) had Panzer Group 1 and the 6th and 17th Armies in Poland, and three armies (German 11th, Romanian 3rd and 4th) in Romania. It was to drive through the Ukraine and take Kiev. The five Panzer, three motorized, and 26 infantry divisions in Poland invaded Ukraine south of the Pripet Marshes, while

The German Army was woefully unprepared for the Russian winter of 1941–42, the Wehrmacht leaders having expected a short campaign as in the West. These troopers have improvised winter camouflage from white smocks and sheets tied over the helmets; an official winter uniform did not appear until the following winter.

the seven German and 14 Romanian divisions in Romania waited in case the Ploesti oilfields needed their protection, and did not move until 29 June.

Barbarossa got off to a formidable start. By 8 August 347,000 prisoners had been taken, and 3,400 tanks and over 3,000 guns destroyed or captured. In the next two weeks another 78,000 prisoners were snared, and in two months Army Group Centre had covered two-thirds of the 1,200km from the frontier to Moscow.

The Germans now had to decide what to do next, particularly as Soviet resistance stiffened and German losses rose. With the additional stresses of distance, heat and dust, over half of Army Group Centre's tanks and trucks were out of action, while the infantry and the horses pulling their carts and guns were nearing exhaustion. The *Barbarossa*

The 7th Panzer and 29th Motorized Infantry Divisions link up, closing the Smolensk *Kessel* (cauldron), 16 July 1941. The 7th Panzer Division (which had been commanded by Erwin Rommel during the Western campaign of May–June 1940) led Hoth's 3rd Panzer Group during the first three weeks of *Barbarossa*. (Peter Dennis © Osprey Publishing)

This scene shows infantry and engineers of the 137th Infantry Division negotiating the defences near Voronino almost due south of Moscow, between Maloyaroslavets and Serphukov, on 17 November 1941. The infantry first fought their way across a steep-sided anti-tank ditch and then through the primitive earthen field works beyond, losing many men to mines and machine-gun fire. The Soviets quickly launched counterattacks, often supported by tanks. (Peter Dennis © Osprey Publishing)

directive had indicated that after routing the enemy forces in Belorussia the emphasis was to shift to destroying those in the Baltic, and taking Leningrad. Only after that would Moscow be considered. Hitler's adherence to this plan sat ill with Von Bock and Guderian (in charge of Panzer Group 2 in Army Group Centre), but he rejected their pleas to go immediately for Moscow.

Army Group South made tough headway in the Ukraine, but its fortunes improved after mid July, when Von Rundstedt directed two of Panzer Group 1's three corps south-eastward from Berdichev to Pervomaysk, to get behind three Soviet armies. The 17th and 11th Armies helped close this, the Uman 'pocket', on 2 August, and six days later 103,000 trapped Soviet troops surrendered. The rest of the Soviet South Front had no choice but hasty withdrawal across the Dnieper, leaving Odessa as an isolated fortress.

Arguments about going for Moscow continued, but Hitler succumbed to further diversions before the offensive resumed in earnest in the autumn. By this time, Leningrad's defence was crumbling, and by 8 September it was completely isolated, except for a perilous route across Lake Ladoga. By 14 September the Germans were on the Gulf of Finland, less than 7km from the city's outskirts, but an offensive on 17 September failed, and on 25 September Army Group North settled for one of the longest sieges in history.

MOSCOW

The assault on Moscow, Operation *Typhoon*, began on 30 September, and immediately smashed through the defenders: Western, Bryansk and Reserve Fronts. But the Panzer groups, now renamed Panzer armies, were seriously short of tanks. At the end of September, 2nd Panzer Army had only 50 per cent of war establishment and the 1st and 3rd about 75 per cent; only the 4th Panzer Army had its full complement. There was also a 30 per cent shortage of lorries, and manpower in 54 of Germany's 142 Eastern Front divisions was more than 3,000 (20 per cent) below establishment. Nevertheless, Army

RIGHT: A German motorcycle soldier demonstrates the serious business of protecting himself against the Russian winter of 1941–42. A gas mask has been adapted as a face protector against temperatures as low as -40°C, while his body is wrapped in sheepskin.

INFANTRY REGIMENT *GROSSDEUTSCHLAND* (GD)

This elite army formation began as a Berlin guard company with ceremonial duties; by the war's end it had grown into a complete mechanized corps. Its name, meaning 'Greater Germany', indicated that its soldiers were chosen from all over the country rather than from a specific *Wehrkreis* as with the rest of the army. In 1941 it was much stronger than its official designation suggested; *Grossdeutschland* had three infantry battalions, each with three line companies, a machine-gun company and a heavy company. A fourth battalion grouped a light infantry gun, an antitank, a heavy infantry gun and an assault gun company; reconnaissance, pioneer, signal and Flak companies made up the 5th Battalion; and the regiment also had an artillery battalion and a logistics column. The regiment fought in France in 1940 and with Army Group Centre during the first months of *Barbarossa*, but suffered massive losses outside Moscow in late 1941. The regiment was reformed and took divisional status in 1942, then became Panzergrenadier Division *Grossdeutschland* in 1943, eventually being equipped with Tiger tanks. In 1944 the division came to be part of the new Panzer Corps *Grossdeutschland*. In the thick of the fighting on the Eastern Front, by the time the war ended the division consisted of just a few thousand weary men.

Group Centre, reinforced by Panzer and motorized divisions from Army Groups North and South, and five infantry divisions from South, had 14 Panzer, eight motorized and 48 infantry divisions, about half of all Germany's Eastern Front force, outnumbering the defenders in tanks and aircraft by almost three to one, and in guns by two to one.

Guderian attacked on 30 September, broke through Bryansk Front's southern flank, and advanced more than 210km in two days, to Orel. Bryansk Front's three armies were encircled by 6 October, and on the 8th were ordered to break out eastward. Some did, but more than 50,000 were captured. Western and Reserve Fronts fared even worse. The 3rd and 4th Panzer and 4th and 9th Armies attacked on 2 October, and here too broke through at once. On 7 October they met west of Vyazma, encircling 45 Soviet divisions, and by 19 October had claimed 673,000 prisoners. Post-Soviet research confirms a lower but still immense figure: 514,338 to the end of November, 41 per cent of the two fronts' strength. On 18 October, XL Panzer Corps took Mozhaisk, only 100km from Moscow.

Two factors, however, now intervened to slow the Germans. The first was the weather. Snowfalls began on 6 October, and from the 9th sleet and heavy rain was almost continuous. Vehicles and carts bogged down, and the infantry, often up to their knees in mud, frequently outran their ammunition and rations. The weather was no better on the Russian side, but the slowing favoured the defenders, particularly by immobilizing the Panzers. The German advance could speed up again only after the mud froze. Secondly, the Soviets strengthened their defences around the capital in preparation for the German assault.

Soldiers of the *Grossdeutschland* Division operate a PaK 40 anti-tank gun on the Soviet steppes. The PaK 40 could deliver effective armour-piercing fire over a 2,000m range, although its high-explosive range was more than 7,000m.

As the ground hardened in mid November, the Germans recovered mobility, but met new problems. Few had winter clothing or white camouflage suits, and there were 133,000 cases of frostbite. Supplies of fuel, anti-freeze and winter lubricants for aircraft and vehicles were inadequate. Frozen grease had to be scraped off every shell before it could be loaded, and maintenance of aircraft, tanks and trucks in the open air was a

The final defence along the Don River by *Leibstandarte SS Adolf Hitler*, Rostov, 25 November 1941. The Soviet infantry attacked in three waves. Successive lines stumbled over piles of dead from earlier attacks, each getting closer to the defenders on the bluff above the river who fought desperately to keep control of the River Don bridge. Finally the fourth wave broke through the 2nd and then 1st Companies of SS men. The assault guns of the German infantry immediately counterattacked. They captured 400, mostly wounded, while more than 300 Red Army soldiers lay dead on the battlefield. Total cost to the *Leibstandarte* Division was two dead and seven wounded. But two days later Marshal Timoshenko attacked along the entire southern front line and the 1st Panzer Army reeled back to the River Mius position. Their retreat represented the *Ostheer*'s first operational defeat of World War II. (Howard Gerrard © Osprey Publishing)

A Waffen-SS sniper of the Totenkopf Division scans for targets. The Totenkopf soldiers were known to be fanatical fighters wherever they were deployed, although like all *Waffen-SS* formations their effectiveness degraded under the effects of continual heavy losses.

nightmare. Stalin and Marshal Zhukov had ordered 'scorched earth' – as much destruction of buildings as possible – before retreats. The German troops, therefore, often went both frozen and unfed.

At the end of November, the German offensive petered out, then faced a new experience – a major Soviet counterattack in the sector. In 34 days of heavy fighting, the Germans were pushed back a minimum of 100km, in some places up to 240km. Moscow was not Hitler's only problem. Army Group South was equally beset by weather, and was halted on 11 October 1941, as much by mud as by the seven armies of South and South-west Fronts. As with Army Group Centre, the southern German forces were also then compelled to make limited withdrawals in the face of Soviet offensives.

The battle of Moscow was the Wehrmacht's first major land defeat of the war, and marked the beginning of the failure of *Blitzkrieg* as a strategy. The Red Army had suffered enormous losses, but was still very much in business, and of 1941's three 'symbolic' objectives, Leningrad, Moscow and Kiev, only Kiev had fallen. Germany's losses had been much smaller, but so was Germany's capacity to replace them. In the coming months, Soviet machinery evacuated to the Urals and Siberia would help the recently established industries there to begin replacing the equipment losses. From December, American entry into the war would provide the Soviet Union with a major supplier of the necessities of war. Note also that by December 1941, the Wehrmacht had suffered more than 730,000 casualties, nearly a quarter of the manpower of *Barbarossa*.

STALINGRAD

In early 1942, the Soviets continued with offensives, particularly in the south, and by 20 April, when the spring thaw imposed a standstill, the Germans were well back from Moscow. (In balance, the Germans had by now developed formidable talents in the defence.) Hitler's plan for 1942, therefore, focused exclusively on the south. Almost all Soviet oil at that time came from three oilfields in the Caucasus, and reached the heartland by tankers up the Volga and railways along its banks. The Don, the European Soviet Union's second biggest river, sweeps through a right angle just south of Voronezh to run south-east for about 400km, before turning south-west to flow into the Sea of Azov. On this second 'Big Bend' it is only 72km from the Volga. The plan was for Army Group South to advance east along the Don, then cross to the Volga north of the major industrial city of Stalingrad, thus cutting the Soviet oil supply route. The second phase would be an advance into the Caucasus to capture the oilfields. This plan did not require Stalingrad to be taken, but Hitler ideally wanted it because of its symbolic name.

German troops at Stalingrad clearly showing signs of exhaustion in their faces and in their uniforms. The Soviets deliberately chose to fight the Germans in Stalingrad with close-quarter tactics, 'hugging' the enemy units close at all times to deny the Wehrmacht the effective use of supporting fire.

For the main offensive, Von Bock had four German and four satellite armies. The northern pincer, along the Don, had 4th Panzer and 6th Armies. The southern had 1st Panzer (Kleist) and 17th Armies, and the 11th Army was to become available after capturing Sebastopol. Satellite armies – 2nd Hungarian, 8th Italian and 3rd Romanian – were to guard the German flank along the Don. Von Bock had 89 divisions, including nine Panzer, most at or near full strength. On 9 July, just after the offensive actually began, Army Group South was divided into Army Group A, which was mainly to strike down into the Causasus and occupy Soviet oilfields, and Army Group B, which would strike along the Donets Corridor and reach the Volga.

The offensive, Operation *Blau* (Blue), began on 28 June, and although progress was solid a pedestrian German pursuit produced few encirclements, and far fewer prisoners than expected. Hitler, however, ignored evidence that South-west and South Fronts were withdrawing across the Don. On 13 July he ordered 4th Panzer Army transferred to Army Group A, to cross the Don at Konstantinovka and move down its east bank to Rostov, to encircle Soviet forces he believed still west of the river. Heavy summer rains and fuel shortages hampered movement, but South Front had already crossed. In mid July Halder confided to his diary that Hitler's underestimation of the enemy had become so grotesque as to make planning impossible.

As history now knows, the German offensive of 1942 culminated in the apocalypic struggle for Stalingrad, which Hitler had suddenly designated a major objective on 17 July. The German 6th and parts of the 4th Army were trapped in fighting the type of battle that was least suited to its skills – close-quarters, small-unit urban fighting that stripped away the advantages of armour and mechanization. Although the Germans captured much of the city, it could not complete the process. More significantly, on 12 November the Soviets launched a bold and unexpected counterattack, driving westwards in a pincer movement from north and south of the city and capitalizing on the weaknesses of Germany's satellite armies, which were providing flank protection. On 23 November, the pincers met just south of Kalach, encircling German 6th and part of 4th Panzer and 4th Romanian Armies, totaling 20 German and two Romanian divisions.

A propaganda photograph from Operation *Barbarossa* shows a German Army officer demonstrating offensive spirit. Indicating his bravery, around his neck he wears the Iron Cross 1st Class, of which about 300,000 were granted to Wehrmacht personnel during World War II.

An assault on the Red October steel plant, Stalingrad, on 23 October 1942. The plant was one of the most contested sites of the battle. In this environment, hand-to-hand fighting and close-quarter assaults were the order of the day, and hand grenades and submachine guns were the weapons of choice. (Peter Dennis © Osprey Publishing)

On 22 November Hitler ordered 6th Army's commander, Generaloberst Paulus, to move his headquarters into Stalingrad and prepare to defend it. Paulus complied, but that day notified Army Group B's commander, Generalfeldmarschall Von Weichs, that he had very little ammunition and fuel, and only six days' rations. If supplied by air, he would try to hold out, but unless he could fill the gap left by the Romanians, he wanted permission to break out south-westwards. Von Weichs considered an immediate breakout imperative, and so did Paulus' five corps commanders. On 23 November, Paulus, with Von Weichs' support, radioed Hitler, seeking permission to abandon Stalingrad. Hitler refused, bolstered by Göring's assertion on 24 November that the Luftwaffe could supply Stalingrad by air, a boast subsequently proved totally unrealistic. A rescue mission by

Manstein failed to materialize, and by 2 February 1943, all German forces in the city had surrendered. Nor was Stalingrad the only German setback. On 13 January, the Red Army troops of the Voronezh Front had smashed the Hungarian 2nd Army.

Axis losses in the Stalingrad campaign, including the fighting along the Don, included the whole of the 6th Army, part of 4th Panzer, most of Romanian 2nd and 4th, and the Hungarian 2nd and Italian 8th Armies. In Stalingrad itself, 91,000 surrendered, but weakened by starvation, cold and typhus most of them died in captivity – fewer than 6,000 survived to go home. In the city, 147,200 German troops died. The Germans flew out about 84,000, mostly wounded, but many died in shot-down aircraft. The Germans' net loss (dead, captured, missing or invalided, minus replacements) was 226,000, and the replacements were generally inferior to those lost. The surviving remnants of the Romanian, Hungarian and Italian armies were withdrawn, an additional net loss of at least 200,000. It was not only the German forces that were paying heavily for fighting a war on the Eastern Front.

Barbarossa had now conclusively failed. As in the 1939–40 Western Europe campaign, but to a far greater degree, there was a tension between two strategies – Guderian's 'armoured concept', whereby armoured troops had to advance rapidly to capture the enemy power centres, and the classic 'decisive manoeuvre' strategy of Army High Command, which needed time to destroy pockets of trapped enemy forces. In the event, neither of the strategies achieved their objectives. The rapidly advancing tanks wasted precious days waiting for supporting infantry to catch up, allowing Red Army units to reform and consolidate their defences. 'Decisive manoeuvre' inflicted heavy losses during 1941 – Soviet sources suggest 3.1 million killed and taken prisoner, German sources 7.5 million – but Moscow, the Soviet capital, was not captured, and the bulk of the Red Army was able to retreat, re-group and counterattack. Hitler's caution prevented the Panzer forces advancing as fast as they wanted, and he stubbornly forbade local tactical withdrawals that might have avoided disasters such as Stalingrad.

Yet nothing in the Western campaigns had prepared the Wehrmacht for the defiance, tenacity and resourcefulness of the Red Army. Stalingrad marked a reversal of German fortunes and the turning-point in World War II. Henceforth, it would be the Wehrmacht that was outnumbered, outequipped and outmanoeuvred, and the Allies who would take, and retain, the strategic initiative until the German surrender on 8 May 1945.

THE DEVELOPMENT OF ARMY UNITS

The German Army in Operation *Barbarossa* was organized largely as for the Western and Balkan campaigns, with three (from 1942, five) army groups deployed. Each army group, initially averaging one million troops commanded by a *Generalfeldmarschall*, controlled Army Group HQ troops and three to four armies. An infantry army, about 200,000 strong under a *Generaloberst*, comprised Army HQ troops and two to five infantry corps and sometimes a reinforced armoured corps (a Panzer group, by January 1942 upgraded to Panzer army) with Panzer and motorized (in June–July 1942 also designated Panzer) corps. The independent 20th Mountain Army operated on the Arctic front under OKW control.

Infantry, motorized, mountain and Panzer corps comprised about 60,000 men under a *General der Infanterie* (or equivalent), with corps HQ troops and two to five divisions. In September 1942, the 61st and 62nd Reserve Corps were formed to control reserve divisions in *Ostland* and Ukraine respectively. The infantry division retained its 1939 organization, with three 3,049-man infantry regiments and five divisional support units – an artillery regiment and reconnaissance, anti-tank, engineer and signals battalions. It had fewer divisional services, however – about four horse-drawn and motorized transport (soon replaced by Russian *panje* cart) columns, medical company, field hospital, veterinary company, military police troop and field post office. From January 1942, many infantry divisions were reduced to two infantry regiments, theoretically offsetting this reduction with increased firepower, and as we have seen on 15 October 1942 all infantry regiments were redesignated 'elite' grenadier regiments to boost morale.

Sicherungs Divisionen (security divisions) were formed from an infantry regiment, territorial rifle battalions and various divisional support units to garrison the occupied

GERMAN WAR ESTABLISHMENT CHARTS: THE *KRIEGSSTÄRKE NACHWEISUNGEN*

Organization, strength, weapons and equipment allowances are normally dictated by war establishment charts or tables of organization and equipment (TO&E). In general these are laid down starting with the main combat unit, namely the division, to every subunit. However, the German Army issued its own war establishment charts, or *Kriegsstärke Nachweisung* (KStN), based at the lowest level (companies and platoons). This sometimes led to two divisions of the same kind having different organizations and strengths, in spite of the fact they were fighting alongside one another. Such an elaborate system actually enabled the Germans to reorganize their units according to both their needs and to available manpower, weapons and equipment, right down to the lowest level. Occasionally, single units within the divisions were reorganized, or others maintained their current organization when other units underwent reorganization. Regularly updated, the KStN were put into effect during rest periods or when the unit was pulled out from the front to rest and refit – often months after they had been issued.

22 June 1941. On the very first day of the *Barbarossa* campaign, a group of mechanized infantry disembark from their SdKfz to throw stick grenades at a point of resistance.

territories. They were joined after September 1942 by units of the home-based Replacement Army; 16,000-strong reserve divisions with two to three reserve infantry regiments and divisional support units had the role of training recruits and undertook garrison duties. *Feldausbildungs Divisionen* (training divisions), with two to four regiments comprising 16,000 recruits, underwent advanced combat training and awaited allocation to frontline units.

The 14,319-man M1940 Motorized Division had two motorized regiments (on 15 October 1942 redesignated Motorized Grenadier) and motorized divisional support units (including a motorcycle reconnaissance battalion) and services. The army's most prestigious unit, the *Grossdeutschland* Motorized Regiment, actually an independent reinforced regiment with four motorized battalions, support and artillery battalions and services, fought in Belarus and central Russia. On 12 March 1942 it became a motorized division and then deployed to southern and central Russia.

The 13,000-man light infantry division, first formed in December 1940 as an elite non-motorized 'pursuit' unit, had two infantry regiments, and from 28 June 1942 was redesignated a *Jäger* (hunter) division. The 14,131-man mountain division had two mountain regiments with mountain-equipped divisional support units and services.

THE *SCHÜTZEN*/PANZERGRENADIER REGIMENT

The basic organization of the 1941 *Schützen* (rifle) brigade included two rifle regiments and the motorcycle battalion, later to became the divisional recce unit. The new rifle regiment, according to establishments of 1 February 1941, was much stronger than its 1940 counterpart, as was the brigade as a whole. Each regiment included an HQ company with an intelligence, a despatch rider and a pioneer platoon, plus two rifle battalions each with three rifle companies, a machine-gun company and a heavy weapons company (with an engineer and an anti-tank platoon with three guns). The total strength of the regiment was 2,571, and its weapons allowance included 119 light and 28 HMGs, 18 light and 12 heavy mortars, six anti-tank guns, eight light and two heavy infantry guns.

Experiences in the field and losses suffered during winter 1941/42 led to another reorganization: a three-gun PaK platoon replaced the pioneer platoon in the regimental HQ company, while machine-gun companies were phased out, and revisions of 1 November 1941 brought a completely different weapons allowance. Total strength of the rifle/Panzergrenadier Regiment decreased to 2,223 with an overall weapons allowance of 141 light and 24 heavy machine guns, 12 heavy mortars, nine anti-tank guns, eight light and four heavy infantry guns, 24 anti-tank rifles and 12 anti-aircraft guns. From late 1942, when all the brigade HQs were either disbanded or detached, the Panzer divisions were left with two Panzergrenadier regiments only.

A *Waffen-SS* gun crew, clad in leaf-pattern camouflage uniforms, opens fire with a 2cm Flak 30 anti-aircraft gun on a wheeled mount. As with many German anti-aircraft weapons, the Flak 30 made a serviceable ground-fire weapon, with an effective range of about 2,000m.

A flamethrower team attack a Soviet position in the winter of 1941/42. The operator is using the *Flammenwerfer* 38, which had a burn time of about ten seconds and a range of up to 25m. An improved version, the *Flammenwerfer* 41, began to be issued during the first year of the German campaign in the East.

From August 1940 to January 1941 the number of Panzer divisions was expanded to 20 at the cost of weakening existing divisions. The M1940 Panzer Division now had 1 x 2-battalion armoured regiments (instead of two); nine divisional support units, namely two motorized rifle regiments (on 5 July 1942, redesignated mechanized Panzergrenadier regiment), one artillery (later Panzer artillery) regiment, motorcycle reconnaissance (including an armoured-car company) and motorized reconnaissance battalions (ordered to merge in 1941), motorized anti-tank, armoured engineer, armoured signals and later anti-aircraft battalions; and motorized divisional services.

IDEOLOGICAL VOLUNTEERS

Apart from its Romanian, Hungarian, Finnish, Slovak and Italian allies, the German Army deployed huge numbers of non-German volunteers in German uniform on the Eastern Front, fighting to earn a favoured place in a post-war settlement after an expected German victory.

On 20 July 1941, Francisco Franco, the ruler of Spain (a neutral country) allowed the 250th Infantry Division – the 'Blue Division' – to be formed from 18,693 Spanish Army and fascist Falange political militia volunteers, in gratitude for German assistance in the

Spanish Civil War. It fought on the Leningrad and Volkhov fronts until 20 October 1943, when Franco, responding to Allied pressure, had it repatriated. From the Balkans, the 369th Reinforced Croatian Infantry Regiment was created from 3,000 Croatian and Bosnian volunteers in July 1941, and after a lengthy training period in Germany joined the 100th Light Infantry Division in Ukraine – it fought and surrendered at Stalingrad in January 1943. The 3,000-strong 638th Reinforced French Infantry Regiment (a grenadier regiment from 15 October 1942) was formed on 27 October 1941, and fought with the 4th Panzer Army attacking Moscow. Thereafter it was relegated to the grim work of anti-partisan operations in occupied Poland and Belarus, and was transferred to the *Waffen-SS* on 1 September 1944. The Walloon Legion was organized as the 373rd Walloon Infantry Battalion on 8 August 1941 from 860 French-speaking Belgian members of Leon Degrelle's fascist Rex Party. It served in South Russia with the 100th Light Infantry Division and in the Caucasus with 97th Rifle Division before transferring to the *Waffen-SS* on 1 June 1943. During this period Danish, Dutch, Finnish, Flemish and Norwegian volunteers also served on the Eastern Front with the *Waffen-SS*, which became something of a repository for foreign formations (see below).

Despite the racial objectives of Hitler's war in the East, German divisions fighting in the Soviet Union were surprised and delighted to accept a continuous stream of civilians and surrendered Soviet troops offering their services. Soon these men were unofficially employed as manual labour in all units and, in emergencies, as combat reinforcements. In September 1941, Hitler officially sanctioned recruitment of Soviet citizens as *Hilfswillige* (auxiliaries, usually abbreviated to *Hiwis*) unsuccessfully insisting that they remain unarmed. *Hiwis* were still joining German divisions up to May 1945, and in 1943 their numbers were estimated at 250,000: German divisions were permitted to recruit them at up to 15 per cent of divisional strength.

On 29 August 1941, the Germans organized the first volunteers into armed units – ten Estonian, Russian and Ingermanland security battalions and the *Freijagerregiment* (Anti-Partisan Regiment) in Army Group North, and five *Kampfbataillone* (combat battalions) in Army Group Centre. Attached to German divisions on anti-partisan duties or as frontline reinforcements, these troops consistently proved their commitment and combat value. Hence on 6 October 1941, mass recruitment of Soviet nationals as *Ostruppen* (Eastern Troops) was permitted. The first Cossack unit in the German Army was the Red Army's 436th Infantry Regiment, which defected on 22 August 1941, and from October 1941 11 Cossack cavalry squadrons were raised for anti-partisan duties with security divisions, or mounted reconnaissance for Panzer divisions, usually with one squadron per division: in late 1942 these expanded to 11 battalions. In 1942 three mounted regiments, three infantry regiments and six infantry battalions were recruited with Cossack field officers.

Latvian volunteer soldiers with the *Waffen-SS* break for cover during fighting in Russia. Eastern Europeans, particularly those from the Baltic States, came to form a high percentage of the *Waffen-SS* combat strength by 1943, although their fighting performance was mixed.

From 15 November 1941, seven security companies were raised from inaccurately labelled 'Turkic' Caucasian and Soviet middle-eastern nationalities, and in 1942 they expanded into six *Ostlegionen* (Eastern legions) in occupied Poland: Armenian, Azerbaijan, Georgian, North Caucasian (Ossetians, Ingushes, Chechens, etc.), Turkestan (Kazakhs, Kirkhiz, Tajiks, Turkmens, Uzbeks, etc.) and Volga-Tartar (Kazan Tartars, Bashkirs, Chuvashes, Udmurts, etc.) Up to the fall of Stalingrad, the legions recruited civilian volunteers into five ordnance, construction and transport battalions and 200 supply and transport companies. Ex-Red Army troops joined 34 infantry battalions numbered in the 783–844 series, and 28 field battalions carrying the divisional number, but only 28 battalions saw action on the Eastern Front, mostly in the Caucasus.

RIGHT: Infantrymen in 1941 were similarly equipped to those in 1939, but there was a tendency to carry less in the field. The man on the left (a) is dressed in the standard infantry uniform, and carries the Kar 98k 7.92mm rifle (1). The man on the right (b) wears the shelter quarter issued to every man. It could be used in a number of ways, one of which was as a rain cape, as it is seen here. The cape was more effective than any other issued to armies of the time, in that it had more than 60 buttons and 30 button holes, letting the individual choose how he wanted to wear it. It could act as a single weather shield if propped with sticks or vegetation, and could also combine with three others to make a very effective four-man tent. Also shown: 2) A clip of five rounds of 7.92mm ammunition for the rifle; 3) A complete set of belt kit; 4) The standard army belt buckle; 5) A set of three leather ammunition pouches, each capable of holding 15 rounds in clips; 6) The standard German water bottle; 7) and 8) The issue German Army gas mask and container; (9) front and back of a tin of issue concentrated chocolate; (10) The knife, fork, spoon and tin opener which were standard issue to troops. (Elizabeth Sharp © Osprey Publishing)

From 1 October 1942, Estonian, Russian, Belarussian and Ukrainian units were designated as 'Eastern Battalions', mostly with Army Group Centre. Each *Ostbataillon*, about 950 strong, was allocated a German commander and a cadre of 36 German officers, NCOs and men. In January 1943, the 48 Eastern Battalions (except those numbered 658–660) and all Russian, Belorussian and Ukrainian *Hiwis* were nominally united as the *Russkaya Osvoboditel'naya Armiya* (ROA; Russian Liberation Army).

INFANTRY

Despite the theoretically dominant position often occupied by armoured divisions during World War II, it was the infantry branch that bore the brunt of the Nazi–Soviet War. The *Ostheer* (Eastern Army) suffered 300,000 killed during *Barbarossa* – the equivalent of one regiment per day – and the majority of them were infantrymen.

The German infantry regiment on the Eastern Front in 1941 was little changed from that which went into Poland in 1939. Divisions consisted (with the exception of Wave 15 divisions and later) of three infantry regiments, each of three battalions. The regimental organization was a mirror, on a small scale, of the divisional organization, in that every regiment had an infantry (and field engineer) component, an artillery component and anti-tank elements, together with all the services needed to supply the troops with ammunition, food, water and the myriad other items needed to keep the regiment effective in the field. Regimental headquarters included the commanding officer and his staff officers, plus a supply train (including the regimental medical officer, the vet, the armourer, the blacksmith and the field kitchen) that was partly motorized. Under the command of this HQ were the field engineer platoon, the intelligence platoon (including signals platoon) and the band (acting as stretcher bearers in battle).

The three battalions of infantry were themselves divided into three rifle companies, a machine-gun company, infantry engineer platoon, supply troops and a pack train. The regiment also had the following under its command: an infantry gun company, an anti-tank company (from March 1940 known as *Panzerjäger*) and a light infantry supply column.

HORSES AND RATIONS

Although contemporary audiences like to picture the German infantry as a mechanized force, in actual fact all regimental vehicles were horse-drawn with the exception of the machine-gun company in each infantry battalion. All rear services (butchery, bakery, postal services, ammunition trains etc.) were dependent upon horse-drawn wagons. Thus the German Army that marched into Russia (as opposed to the armoured and mechanized units that drove) could proceed at approximately the same pace as a Roman

legion nearly 2,000 years earlier. This fact alone was to contribute to problems on the Eastern Front that were never effectively resolved.

Each infantryman in the German Army was familiar with the platoon horse; this beast went everywhere with the platoon, pulling the platoon cart into which packs were loaded together with any extra items that soldiers could manage to fit on. Often the carts in the West had carried the booty of the conqueror, for example: French wines, Dutch cheeses, Belgian chocolates. In the East, however, the wagons carried the bare essentials, for there was little loot to be had, and warm clothing soon became more important than any fine wine. The German Army went into Russia with more than 700,000 horses, yet only a few thousand tanks.

In every company eight horse-drawn wagons were needed for movement, plus a further company wagon at regimental level to carry extra (heavy) company equipment. These eight wagons were used as follows: three one-horse wagons to carry the machine guns and mortars for the three heavy platoons of the company; two four-horse wagons: one for ammunition, one for the field kitchen (later reduced to a two-horse wagon); and two two-horse wagons for back packs; and one two-horse wagon for rations.

Horses were integral to German logistics on the Eastern Front (750,000 were used at the beginning of *Barbarossa*), but the beasts themselves, unused to the Soviet winters and the terrible labour, died in their hundreds of thousands – about 1.5 million by the end of the war in 1945.

This arrangement meant that a number of men (21 in all, including NCOs in charge) spent the majority of their time looking after horses and driving wagons. The wagons themselves were of good design, but the concept, in a so-called mobile army, was archaic. The other problems that arose for the German Army in Russia were the vulnerability of the horses to the intense cold, and the need for constant supplies of fodder for the animals when the army itself was desperate for ammunition, clothing and other supplies. Furthermore, the horses were very easily injured.

Training for horse handlers was less intense than that for cavalrymen, but involved acquiring a basic ability to ride, the care of the horse in the field, and dietary training to ensure that the animals were fed and cared for and so were able to pull their loads.

In the matter of rations, the German Army, like all others, had ration scales laid down for both men and horses. However, once the Russian campaign had started, ration supplies were often erratic, and the men in the field had to scavenge for themselves. Quite often the horses became food, especially during the siege of the encircled 6th Army at Stalingrad.

The following is an intelligence report on ration scales. It applied whenever possible, but was never more than a guide when means were in short supply:

a. Human rations scales

The daily ration quantity [*Portionsatz*] is the amount of food consumed by one man for one day. It consists of three meals, the noon meal amounting to one-half of the total, the evening meal to one-third, and the next morning's breakfast to one-sixth. The OKW has laid down an overall plan specifying the maximum amount of any ration item that may be served. The amount depends upon two factors: the duty class of the man receiving the ration, and the component class of the particular item being served.

There are four main types of rations served to troops. Ration I [*Verpflegungssatz* I] is for troops committed to combat, for those that are recuperating from combat, and for troops stationed in Norway north of 66° North. Ration II is for occupation and line of communication troops. Ration III is for garrison troops within Germany. Ration IV goes to office workers and nurses within Germany. Hospital cases may fall within any of these classes depending on the seriousness of the cases.

The most important items of the component classes are as follows:

(a) bread;

(b) meats, soy bean flour, cheese, fish, and eggs;

(c) vegetables;

(d) puddings and milk;

(e) salt, mustard, vinegar, and other seasonings;

(f) spices such as pepper, cinnamon, and cloves;

The horse and the *Landser* (soldier) were almost inseparable throughout World War II. Here infantry and their platoon cart march side by side on the long road east. The cart is the two-horse Hf. 1/7 with pneumatic tyres. The horses are Pomeranian draft horses, well known for their strength, although even this type of horse found the wagon too heavy when fully loaded, and many times the hitch had to be augmented by manpower or by additional horses or oxen. (Elizabeth Sharp © Osprey Publishing)

(g) butter, lard, marmalades, fats, and bread spreads;

(h) coffee and tea;

(i) sugar;

(j) spirits and wines;

(k) tobacco.

Substitute issues may be made within a component class but not among different component classes. Thus the daily maximum allowance of vegetables for a soldier is 60 grams of dried vegetables, or 1,200 grams of kidney beans, or 400 grams of salted vegetables, or equivalent quantities of any of about 30 other substitutes. It is not possible to predict which items will be served on any given day. The following chart, however, sets forth a likely breakdown of these maximum ration allowances.

OVERLEAF: A horse-drawn field kitchen trundles along in the wake of the German advance. Such a kitchen typically had a 200-litre pot for cooking stews plus a 90-litre kettle for making coffee. This contraption was affectionately known amongst the troops as the *Gulaschkanone* (goulash cannon).

b. Special types of human rations

(1) March ration [*Alarmverpflegung*]. The march ration is a cold food ration issued for not more than three or four consecutive days to units in transit either by carrier or on foot. It consists of approximately 700 grams of bread, 200 grams of cold meat or cheese, 60 grams of bread spreads, 9 grams of coffee (or 4 grams of tea), 10 grams of sugar, and 6 cigarettes. Thus it has a total weight of about 987 grams.

(2) Iron ration [*Eiserne Portion*]. An iron ration consists of 250 grams of biscuits, 200 grams of cold meat, 150 grams of preserved vegetables, 25 grams of coffee and 25 grams of

The main meal of the day for the German soldier was at midday. This was prepared, often on the march, by the company cooks who travelled with the *Gulaschkanone* (goulash cannon) or, as it was officially known, the *Feldkuche* (seen in the background). The field kitchen was horse drawn and served hot stews. Bread was supplied by regimental bakeries, which were centralized. (Elizabeth Sharp © Osprey Publishing)

salt. Total weight is 650 grams without packing and 825 grams with packing. An iron half-ration is composed of 250 grams of biscuits and 200 grams of preserved meat: thus its total weight is 450 grams without packing and 535 grams with packing.

(3) Combat Package [*Grosskampfpäcken*] and Close Combat Package [*Nahkampfpäcken*]. The Germans have begun to use these types of ration for troops engaged in combat. They include chocolate bars, fruit bars, sweets, cigarettes and possibly biscuits.

c. Animal rations

An animal ration is the amount of food consumed by one horse, draft ox, dog, or carrier pigeon for one day. The quantity of an animal ration allowance [*Rationssatz*] depends on the type of animal, the area in which it is serving, and the content of the ration it is being fed. Horses, for instance, are divided into four groups: draft horses of the heaviest breed, draft horses of heavy breed, saddle horses and light draft horses, and small horses. On the Eastern Front, draft horses of the heaviest breed receive a maximum ration allowance of 5,650 grams of oats, 5,300 grams of hay, and 5,750 grams of straw (including 1,500 grams of bedding straw). The allotments to other horse groups are proportionately less. On fronts other than the Eastern Front the allotments for all horses are generally smaller. In addition, substitutes such as preserved forage, barley, corn, etc., may change the ration weight. If the horse is being fed an iron ration, it is given a single item such as oats or hay or straw.

d. Rations in the field

Local stores obtained by purchase or confiscation play a greater part in the supply of rations in the field than is the case for any other class of supply. It is part of the German planning principle to live off the land as much as possible and to obtain only the remaining requirements from stocks procured through channels. The Germans fully appreciate the difficulty of employing such methods during periods of combat and do not count upon local stores during operative periods. Usually a normal reserve of about 10 days' rations for each man of an army is maintained within the army. The rations consist of full and iron rations, although the latter may be eaten only upon the receipt of special orders.

Rations carried in an army for each man

	Full rations	Iron rations
With the man	–	1 (half)
On a combat vehicle	–	1
In the field kitchen	1	1
In the unit ration train	2	–
In the division train	1	–
In the army dumps and train a total of about 3		

A German catering crew prepare food on the cook's wagon of a supply train heading through Russia. German supply trains were often most vulnerable in rear areas, where they became prime targets for Soviet partisans.

Ordinarily there are two full and two iron horse rations carried either on the horse or in unit supply columns. Other rations are carried by the army and the division.

For staff planning purposes, the weights of rations are computed by the Germans as follows:

Type of rations	Weights (grams)	Weight (pounds)
Human rations:		
Standard ration with packing	1,500	3.3
Iron ration with packing	825	1.82
Iron half-ration with packing	535	1.18
Horse rations		
Standard ration	10,000	22
Iron oat ration	5,000	11
Iron hay ration	5,000	11
Iron straw ration	2,500	5.5

This report was published at the latter end of the war, but the information was current throughout World War II. Actual amounts supplied on the Eastern Front in 1941–43 varied from full rations at the beginning of the campaign to nearly nothing later on, particularly during the last days of the battle of Stalingrad. The troops in Stalingrad, for example, were eventually starving and freezing to death. By December they had eaten most of their 7,000 horses, and their daily ration was down to just 200g of horsemeat, 70g of bread and 14g of margarine or fat.

MOVEMENT

Troops of the infantry thought that the campaigns in the West had been arduous, and that they had seen all they needed to see of the long roads to the front. In the Soviet Union, however, the roads were seemingly endless. The infantry's complaints were exaggerated by the fact that the armoured and mobile units sped ahead from the start of the operation, and the infantry following behind were almost constantly engaged in marching to catch up with them.

Sleep, when it came, was often no more than a short break. One soldier complained: 'Sleep was a precious and often elusive commodity. Personal equipment was pulled on and all straps and accoutrements secured. Unnecessary clothing would be placed in packs and handed across to be ferried by the light infantry supply column. Some companies marched as many as 50km in one day.' One veteran calculated a single step covered 60cm – men took shorter or longer paces, but this was the average – so 50km meant an estimated 84,000 paces.

The infantry were constantly being rushed, trying to catch up at 5km/h units that could travel at five times that speed or more. Meals and rest periods were consequently short. The marching soldiers were also exposed to whatever the environment threw at them, from choking, tiring dust during the summer months to blizzard conditions in the winter. The sheer physical toil of the trudge to the Eeast was exacerbated by the damage to men's feet, while daunting Soviet Russian and Ukrainian landscapes sapped morale. Further weather complications came with the autumn and spring mud – the *rasputitsa*. The mud prevented movement: no man, horse or vehicle (even tanks) could cope with the 2ft depth of mud that was produced by the first vehicles over any stretch of track. The Germans installed corduroy roads – log roads – but these soon sank into the quagmire, and constant efforts had to be made to re-lay more and more logs.

Then came the winter, bringing temperatures lower than those experienced by even mountain troops. With temperatures of -30°C and beyond, and inadequate uniforms (see below), German troops suffered appallingly from environmental injuries. There were an estimated 100,000 cases of frostbite in the German Army between November 1941 and January 1942, with 1,500 amputations. Gun and vehicle lubricants froze solid, immobilizing weapons and vehicles alike; often fires had to be started beneath engines to thaw them out. German troops spent more of their time just surviving the cold, hence drawing away any offensive energy they still possessed.

ABOVE: Figures from Army Group Centre, 1941, including a Panzer officer (right) and two artillerymen from the 51st *Nebelwerfer* Regiment. The soldier on the far left is handling a 28cm high-explosive rocket shell. (Stephen Andrew © Osprey Publishing)

UNIFORMS

To add to its misery, the German Army in 1941 stood in the snow and ice in the remnants of the same uniforms they had worn when they started the move to the East in July. From the invasion of the Rhineland on 7 March 1936 to the attack on the Soviet Union on 22 June 1941, German units maintained a high degree of uniformity of appearance, and this continued up to the surrender of the Stalingrad pocket on 2 February 1943. Thereafter the OKH began to introduce new bravery awards, encouraging elite units with non-standard

Paratroopers in a bunker in Russia, 1942. Bunkers were dug 3–4m into the earth, sometimes deeper. The walls were shored up by rough-hewn pine or birch logs and they were roofed with felled tree trunks, above which the excavated earth was tamped back. A properly constructed bunker like the one shown could withstand direct hits by 105mm shells. (Velimir Vuksic © Osprey Publishing)

uniforms and insignia, and increasingly tolerate unofficial and security-compromising units in ordinary divisions, in order to boost morale and self-confidence severely dented by the Stalingrad defeat.

The conditions experienced by infantry on the Eastern Front led to some changes in field uniforms. The M1935 field tunic and trousers proved uncomfortably hot for the stifling temperatures encountered from June to August 1941, and so in summer 1941 many troops adopted the M1940 reed-green drill fatigue uniform as a summer field uniform. This consisted of the off-white cotton herringbone twill tunic, with five buttons and two patch hip pockets, and trousers introduced on 1 April 1933, and from 12 February 1940 manufactured in reed-green. Officers and NCOs added shoulder-strap insignia and all ranks wore the breast-eagle. Its popularity led to the production of the M1942 reed-green drill tunic with the same cut as the M193 field tunic, introduced in early 1942 but not common until summer 1943.

The only issue clothing available for the first Soviet winter, from November 1941 to March 1942, consisted of nine uniform items. These were the *feldgrau* tube-shaped woollen balaclava; extra-thick woollen underwear; the M1936 round-neck or V-neck grey-white woollen sweater, introduced 15 March 1936 and replaced by the M1942 high turtle-neck sweater; *feldgrau* woollen mittens; the *feldgrau* sentry's water repellent, ankle-length, six-button double-breasted guard coat with reinforced leather shoulders, and felt overshoes; the vehicle crew's M1934 or M1940 *feldgrau* water-repellent surcoat, cut as for the M1935 greatcoat but ankle-length and wide enough to be worn over field equipment; three-fingered fur-lined mittens in *feldgrau* surcoat cloth; and the driver's and motocyclist's greenish-brown calico fingerless overgloves.

LEFT: An exhausted-looking German soldier takes a bite to eat. He is clad in a splinter-pattern camouflage jacket and the net on his helmet allows him to fit improvised field camouflage, a good idea in the presence of talented Soviet snipers.

THE MG 42

Introduced in 1942 as a more cost-efficient replacement for the MG 34, the 7.92mm MG 42 machine gun quickly proved itself to be one of the best infantry weapons of World War II. It was a short-recoil, air-cooled weapon with an extremely high rate of fire of up to 1200rpm, which produced devastating area effects against exposed enemy infantry. A barrel change could be performed in just a few seconds through a quick-change system, and the gun could fire from a variety of mounts (e.g. bipod, tripod, vehicle mount) to change its role from assault weapon through to anti-aircraft gun or medium machine gun (MMG). On the Eastern Front, it proved far more resistant to the effects of dirt and dust than the MG 34. Such was the quality of the MG 42 that it was essentially put into post-war production for the *Bundeswehr* (the German armed forces), recalibred to suit the 7.62x51mm NATO round and labelled the MG 3.

German infantrymen, one armed with an MP38/40 submachine gun, interrogate a Soviet civilian. Although the Wehrmacht did not gain the same horrendous reputation for war crimes as the *Waffen-SS*, German Army soldiers could also handle civilians brutally, particularly in the requisitioning of houses.

The clothing, while sufficient for Central Europe, proved totally inadequate for the Eastern Front. Many troops improvised with German and Soviet civilian fur coats and captured Red Army fur caps and padded field uniforms, but on 19 April 1942 new white and *feldgrau* fully reversible padded winter clothing had been approved and was issued in three weights – light, medium and heavy. The thigh-length six-buttoned hooded winter tunic had two hip pockets, the only permitted insignia being coloured sleeve field signs. There were also reversible high trousers and mittens, but the reversible hood and face-mask and white-webbing snow boots proved unpopular and were often discarded.

Other issue winter clothing consisted of ankle-length sheepskin overcoats without insignia; various styles of white, brown or black sheepskin, rabbit and articificial fur caps with service cap insignia; plain brown quilted jacket and trousers worn over the field uniform and under the greatcoat; and leather-reinforced felt calf-boots. Of course, what

LEFT: Winter clothing in Stalingrad, ranging from the official to the improvised. One big problem, noted by the Finns early on in the war, was that the Germans had studs going into the soles of their boots. In sub-zero conditions, these studs had no grip and worse, they conducted the cold straight into the wearer's feet. The man on the left has wrapped sacking round his boots in the vain hope that this will keep him warmer. (Elizabeth Sharp © Osprey Publishing)

was produced and what men actually received could vary considerably, particularly with such long supply lines stretching across the Soviet Union. Yet it is undoubted that the humble German soldier went into the winter of 1943/44 far better prepared than he had the previous winter.

PANZER DIVISIONS ON THE EASTERN FRONT

Shortly after the conclusion of the 1940 campaign in the West, Panzer commanders at every level were requested to submit detailed reports about their own experiences in the field. These were used to improve the 1938 technical manual, which was reissued on 3 December 1940 under the title *Directives for Command and Employment of a Panzer Division*. It was reprinted in 1942 without further changes, and its guidelines remained unaltered until the end of the war. It stated that the main task of the Panzer division was to seek decision on the battlefield. A Panzer division was required to attack every kind of enemy position and to exploit the success using either in-depth penetration behind enemy lines or attacking an enemy's rear positions, and pursuing any enemy remnants. Attack was the only combat method suited to the Panzer divisions; even in defence they were to counterattack enemy breakthroughs. Only when facing fixed or fortified defence lines were the Panzer divisions to give way to the infantry, not only to avoid severe losses but also to avoid eschewing the decisive advantage of their speed and manoeuvrability.

There were several ways in which the Panzers and infantry could co-operate, though initially the preferred one was for mechanized infantry to closely follow up the Panzer attack. Heavy fire and fast movement were the keys to a successful attack. First, suitable terrain had to be chosen (wooded and built-up areas were quite unsuitable); second, while the artillery kept pace with the Panzer and infantry advance, attacking units were to reach their firing positions quickly. Third, as soon as a breakthrough had been made, the enemy forces had to be encircled and attacked in their rear.

It did not take long before the war on the Eastern Front exposed the shortcomings of German doctrine. The lack of an adequate road network and accurate maps, the erroneous estimates for fuel consumption (60,000 litres of fuel daily for a 200-tank Panzer regiment soon turned into 120,000 and 180,000 litres daily) and the wear and tear on the vehicles greatly influenced the Panzer divisions' capabilities, along with the inability of the infantry to keep pace with the armoured advance. Until 27 June 1941, Panzer Groups 2 and 3 advanced 320km with a daily rate of 64km, but this shrank to 20km a day in early July. Likewise, the 8th Panzer Division's daily rate of advance was 75km until 26 June, but this dropped to 32km in the first half of July. Autumn brought the first bad weather, and the resulting quagmire, which restricted the Panzer divisions

to movement on the main roads, and made manoeuvre and encirclement practically impossible. Winter combined with improvements to the Soviet defences, with their anti-tank guns deployed forward, further reduced the mobility of the Panzer divisions. Eventually, the severe losses suffered during the first Soviet counteroffensive and the subsequent reorganization of the Panzer divisions crushed any German hopes of victory.

In 1942 the Panzer divisions were still an effective fighting force, despite having only part of their established strength. Along with improvements made to the Red Army, this eventually tipped the balance in favour of firepower rather than movement and, in order to spare tanks, German attacks were led more often by the infantry with artillery support. The Panzer was no longer the decisive weapon and was now used rather for support and exploitation, while infantry and artillery were deemed the best weapons for breaking through. The structure of the battlegroup changed accordingly, as more Panzer units were broken down to company level. Although the Panzer divisions were still capable of manoeuvring and striking in depth, even if to a reduced extent, the rest of the German Army was no longer able to support them in these roles. Eventually, this reshaped the entire notion of armoured warfare, as the doomed Operation *Zitadelle* (Citadel) – the battle of Kursk – would eventually show (see Chapter 5).

A Soviet soldier inspects a destroyed Tiger tank. Note the burst barrel, indicating that the tank crew had been forced to abandon the vehicle, possibly on account of mechanical failure, and had destroyed the vehicle's combat capability as they left.

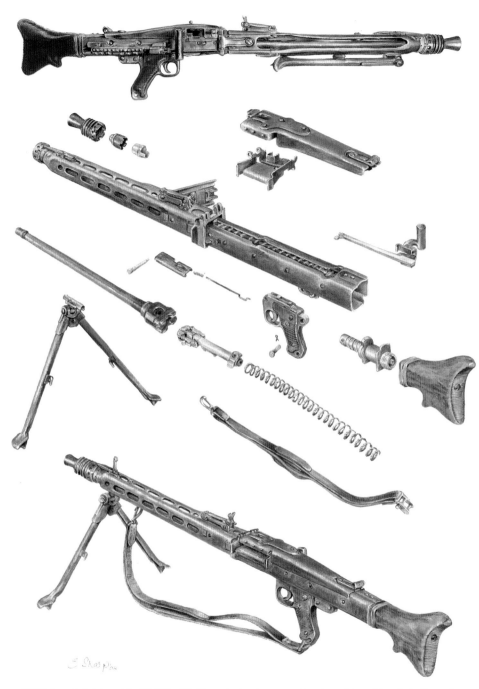

ABOVE: An exploded view of the MG 42. The MG 42 was designed to operate in quite awful conditions: it fired in mud, water, snow, heat and dust. As long as the machine gunner handling it knew how to maintain his weapon, about the only time it refused to fire was when the metalwork of the action was frozen. The ingenuity of the Germans then solved even that problem, with the aid of sunflower oil, which lubricated the working parts at sub-zero temperatures. (Elizabeth Sharp © Osprey Publishing)

REORGANIZING THE PANZER DIVISIONS

Even before the end of the campaign in the West, the OKH started to plan a reorganization of armoured and motorized divisions. The first figure of 24 Panzer and 12 motorized infantry divisions drafted at the end of May 1940 was reduced by mid June to 20 Panzer and ten motorized infantry divisions, though in April 1941 a new plan for the post-*Barbarossa* army envisaged the creation by the following autumn of another four to six new Panzer divisions, four of which were actually formed during the year. Although no overall establishment was laid down, the reorganization of the ten old Panzer divisions and the creation of ten new ones followed the guidelines dictated by the experiences made during the campaign in the West, in addition to an attempt to obtain uniformity. As a result, every Panzer division now had one two-battalion Panzer regiment, one rifle brigade with two regiments, each with two battalions, plus a motorcycle battalion and a three-battalion artillery regiment which, in the old Panzer divisions, simply led to the permanent attachment of the artillery battalion already available before May 1940. As before, every division also included a reconnaissance unit, anti-tank, engineer and communications units, plus a field replacement battalion and divisional supply and service units.

Complete uniformity was not attained, however, and heavy losses suffered during the winter of 1941/42 and the subsequent reorganization of those Panzer divisions scheduled to take part in the new summer offensive brought new changes, mainly affecting the number of Panzer battalions in the Panzer regiment. Also the *Panzer Aufklärungs Abteilung* (Panzer reconnaissance battalion) was disbanded and merged with the motorcycle battalion, now turned into the divisional recce unit, and a *Heeres-Flak Abteilung* (army anti-aircraft battalion) was attached as a fourth battalion to the artillery regiment. In late 1942 practically every *Schützen* – or Panzergrenadier, as they had been renamed – brigade HQ was disbanded or detached.

Following the crisis of Stalingrad and the appointment of Guderian as *Generalinspekteur der Panzertruppen* (Inspector General of Armoured Troops) in January 1943, a new reorganization took place. The motorcycle battalion was renamed Panzer reconnaissance battalion and, most importantly, Panzer regiments reverted to the standard two-battalion organization. However, since one Panzer battalion from every regiment was to be re-equipped with Panther tanks, most Panzer regiments were left with a single battalion for many months to come.

Lacking overall establishments, and given that several war establishment charts were lost, it is extremely difficult to assess the Panzer divisions' overall strength. By June 1941 it stood at about 13,300 for the standard two-Panzer battalion division, though it eventually rose to 15,600 including the third Panzer battalion, the army anti-aircraft battalion and the full-strength Field Replacement battalion. Armoured fighting vehicles (AFVs) apart, overall weaponry, including artillery resources, increased dramatically between 1941 and 1943.

OVERLEAF: German troops advance behind an StuG III through the devastated landscape of Stalingrad in 1942. The destruction of Stalingrad was so complete that during the severe winter of 1942/43 the soldiers within the city had difficulty in finding any combustible materials to make camp fires.

ABOVE: Army Group South soldiers, June–November 1941. They are (from left to right) a *Hilfswilliger* from the 13th Panzer Division, a *Leutnant* with the 230th Infantry Regiment and an *Oberschütze* from the 203rd Infantry Regiment. (Stephen Andrew © Osprey Publishing)

ABOVE: The Eastern Front, December 1941–March 1942. The figures here show the challenges of the first Russian winter. The *Feldwebel* in the centre wears the inadequate standard winter uniform, while the infantryman to his left has improvised camouflage and the man to his right is wearing straw overboots on his feet for extra protection. (Stephen Andrew © Osprey Publishing)

In 1941, the Panzer pioneer battalion was one of the Panzer divisions' strongest support elements with its 900 men and 200 vehicles. Its first two light pioneer companies, mounted on the 2-tonne *Pionier Kampfwagen* III lorries, each had three light pioneer platoons armed with nine LMGs (18 in 1942) plus combat engineer equipment. In January 1941, the third Panzer pioneer company was reorganized as a fully armoured company with a fourth light platoon providing support; the first two platoons each had five PzKpfw I Ausf. B (plus one in the company troop) modified to carry a detachable *Ladungsleger* (explosive load), while the third platoon had six SdKfz 251 equipped with the *Wurfrahmen* 40 rocket launcher, a device capable of firing 280mm high-explosive and 320mm incendiary rockets. Bridging equipment was provided by specialist columns, which could build bridges some 100m long for use by tanks.

In winter 1941/42, all the PzKpfw Is were lost and, lacking suitable replacements, the first two Panzer pioneer platoons shrank to a single light pioneer platoon, thus leaving the third as the only armoured platoon, now equipped with six SdKfz 251/5 and one SdKfz 250/3. A major reorganization took place in March/April 1943; both the light and Panzer pioneer companies had a *Granatenwerfer* and a HMG troop attached and were now armed with 18 light and two heavy machine guns, six flamethrowers, two heavy mortars and three anti-tank rifles; the Panzer pioneer companies were also equipped with two SdKfz 250/3, 23 SdKfz 251/7 and two SdKfz 251/2. In July 1943, all but six divisions had one Panzer pioneer company, and 7th Panzer Division had two.

FIGHTING CAPABILITIES

Three factors in particular affected the armoured component of the *Panzerwaffe* during the first stage of war on the Eastern Front; first, attrition; second, inadequate tank production and replacement; and third, the technical superiority of the Soviet tanks. Attrition took its toll as early as the first months of war, though apparently tank losses were not due only to enemy action but rather, to a greater or lesser extent, to mechanical breakdown. By 9 July 1941, the 6th Panzer Regiment, 3rd Panzer Division, had permanently lost 13 of its 58 PzKpfw II, 24 of its 110 PzKpfw III and eight of its 32 PzKpfw IV; two PzKpfw II and seven PzKpfw III were in repair, and the division still had some 144 tanks fully operational. By the end of the month, the same regiment had another four PzKpfw III write-offs and had about 50 tanks under repair, which along with tanks handed over to other units, brought its total strength to 35 PzKpfw II, 35 PzKpfw III and 16 PzKpfw IV. Other formations fared worse. On 21 July 1941, the 25th Panzer Regiment, 7th Panzer Division reported it had lost all of its 53 PzKpfw II, 112 of its 167 PzKpfw 38(t), 15 of its 30 PzKpfw IV and eight of its 15 PzBefh vehicles, although many of those were undergoing repair. Clearly the Panzer divisions were still able to fight on, in spite of the constant attrition, due to their efficient field maintenance system that enabled prompt recovery in most instances. However, in the long run this did not prevent a constant reduction in their combat effectiveness. A full recovery required either a long period of rest or adequate replacements. The Panzer divisions received neither.

In mid July 1941, Hitler released only 70 PzKpfw III and 15 PzKpfw IV, plus the available Czech tanks, to the Eastern Front as replacements, in spite of reports that showed how tank losses were as high as 50 per cent of the actual strength (though this figure probably included tanks in repair). The decision was made to preserve tank production for the new Panzer divisions being raised. Thus, in spite of the gloominess of the situation, by September 1941 137 replacement tanks had made their way to the Eastern Front; a statistic from 5 September reported that out of a total tank strength of 3,397 only 1,586 Panzers, about 47 per cent, were still fully operational. Total losses amounted to 702 write-offs and about another 542 tanks in repair along with 557 tanks whose fate was uncertain, though estimates reported that as much as 30 per cent of total strength had been permanently lost while about 23 per cent was undergoing repair. On average, the Panzer divisions had just 34 per cent of their established tank strength.

A long rest or adequate replacements would have spared the Panzer divisions from the predations of attrition, yet the only improvement was the arrival on the Eastern Front in September of the last two uncommitted Panzer divisions, which added some 380 tanks. The already depleted tank strength would shrink even further during the attack on Moscow, until the Soviet offensive of December 1941 eventually brought about final disaster. By mid December, the 2nd Panzer Army had only 40 tanks left out of the 248 that were available

PzKpfw III tanks advance in the Ukraine, with infantry in support. The soldier at the front is carrying a Teller anti-tank mine, which contained 5.5kg of TNT or Amatol high-explosive and was capable of wrecking any enemy vehicle, including main battle tanks.

in mid October; and Panzer Group 3 had only 34 left out of the 259 previously available. By January 1942 only 1,138 replacement tanks had reached the Eastern Front, or 35 per cent of the total loss suffered of 3,252 tanks in the same period, itself a figure too close for comfort to the 3,377 tanks deployed in June 1941.

A reorganization of spring 1942 introduced the two-tier concept that saw some divisions being brought up to strength to take part in the new offensive, while other divisions were left untouched, if not further depleted by detachments. As a result, only a few Panzer divisions recovered some kind of full effectiveness, while most were only partially operational and some others were unable to take part in offensive operations. Tank production was partly to blame for this state of affairs. Since the victory in France

PzKpfw III advancing at speed across the Russian steppe, summer 1941. The markings on the fender of this tank show that it belongs to the 14th Panzer Division. The basic colour of German tanks at this period in the war was the so-called 'Panzer grey'. This was not a particularly effective camouflage, but as shown here, the tank soon became covered with a thick coating of dust, which muted its dark colour. (Velimir Vuksic © Osprey Publishing)

in June 1940, tank production had been steadily increasing, though it never reached peak levels, and the outputs for 1941 were only marginally higher than in 1940.

The *Panzerwaffe* also suffered from issues with its tanks. The PzKpfw III was now the main German battle tank, yet it was no longer a tank capable of dealing with enemy armour on equal terms. When the Germans first met the Soviet KV and T-34 tanks in June 1941 they were stunned. Although they had already experienced fighting against enemy tanks with heavy armour; given its speed, mobility, invulnerability and powerful gun, it was the T-34 that most impressed the Germans. It did not take long before the German tankers began referring to the T-34 as a 'war-winning weapon', which it could have been had it not suffered from the same shortcomings that affected the French tanks

Soldiers of the 269th Infantry Division used captured anti-tank guns to destroy Soviet T-34 tanks in July 1941. In the early days of the campaign, common German anti-tank weapons failed miserably against the new Soviet armour. It was not unusual for Soviet tanks to receive many dozens and even hundreds of hits with no appreciable effect. (Peter Dennis © Osprey Publishing)

in 1940 (namely a lack of radio equipment, available only in command tanks, and a two-man turret that interfered with the tank commander's main role) and, above all, if their crews had not suffered from a lack of training and experience. Additionally, in the early stages of *Barbarossa* the T-34s were used in small groups, pairs or at most five tanks, which the Germans could deal with. Bigger problems arose in autumn 1941 when the Soviets began using their tanks en masse, which presented yet more defensive problems.

The German tanks in 1941 were easy prey to the T-34s, which could only be disabled if the Panzer placed a hit close to the rear sprocket wheel at a very close range, between 100m and 200m. The T-34s could easily hit (both on the sides and front) and destroy the German tanks at 1,000m or more. Since even the 5cm PaK 38 was all but useless against the T-34s and the KVs, the only readily available solution was a stopgap one: to use captured Soviet 76.2mm anti-tank guns, preferably mounted on the chassis of otherwise obsolete tanks. The first self-propelled *Panzerjäger* were produced from April 1942, either on the PzKpfw II chassis (Marder II, from June 1942, also armed with a 7.5cm PaK 40 gun) or on that of the PzKpfw 38 (t) – (Marder III, from November 1942, also armed with a 75mm PaK 40 gun). In 1942, 184 Marder II with the 7.62cm gun and 327 Marder II with the 7.5cm gun (figures for 1943 are respectively eight and 204) were built, plus 344 Marder III with the 7.62cm gun and another 110 with the 7.5cm gun (in 1943, 19 and 799 examples were produced). Production of the already obsolete 3.7cm PaK 35/36 was finally halted in 1941 (though 32 more were produced in 1942), while production of the 5cm PaK 38 rose from 388 in 1940 to 2,072 in 1941 and eventually to 4,480 in 1942 (in 1943 only 2,626 examples were produced). The 7.5cm PaK 97/38, a captured French gun, was introduced into service in large quantities to fight against the Soviet T-34 and KV tanks (2,854 in 1942), but it was only with the new 7.5cm PaK 40 that the Germans acquired a suitable anti-tank weapon (2,114 produced in 1942 and 8,740 in 1943). From 1942, the Panzer divisions' *Panzerjäger* battalions were made up of a mixture of towed and self-propelled anti-tank guns, ranging from the 3.7cm PaK 35/36 to the newest 7.5cm PaK 40, and only ten divisions had a self-propelled anti-tank gun company. Yet anti-tank guns were a defensive weapon and, to maintain some offensive capabilities, improvements were badly needed for the tanks.

With the long-barrelled 5cm and 7.5cm guns mounted on the PzKpfw III and IV in 1942, it was possible to restore some kind of offensive power to the Panzers. Although the former was only effective against the T-34 at very short range if firing frontally (100m), it was otherwise effective at about 500m when firing against the sides, the same range at which the long-barrelled PzKpfw IV could effectively engage the T-34 frontally. Also, long-barrelled PzKpfw IV were able to engage the side of a T-34 at about 1,000m. Matching these performances with the improved armour on the German tanks, which reduced to 500m the distance at which a T-34 could effectively engage them frontally,

it is clear that some kind of offensive power had been restored. However, the peak had been reached and, until the Panther tank became available to the Panzer divisions (which happened in September 1943), their main battle tanks could improve their armour but not their guns. In fact, the new models of PzKpfw III and IV introduced in 1943 maintained their guns unaltered but, thanks to increased armour, now reduced to about 100m the effective range at which the T-34 could challenge them frontally. This was not done without cost, since the reduced speed, mobility and manoeuvrability of the German tanks also affected the capabilities of the Panzer units.

The production picture regarding tanks is mixed for the first two years of the war. Production in the first half of 1942 saw only 256 PzKpfw II, 1,339 PzKpfw III (of which 1,042 were armed with the 5cm L/60 gun), 195 PzKpfw 38 (t) (production ceased in June), 362 PzKpfw IV (of which 237 were armed with the 7.5cm L/43 gun) and 14 PzBefh built. By 1 June 1942, the German tank inventory included 979 PzKpfw II (deemed non-battleworthy but still in high demand for their role in reconnaissance), 454 PzKpfw 38 (t) (again non-battleworthy, though hard to replace), 2,306 PzKpfw III, 681 PzKpfw IV and 264 PzBefh. As opposed to the figures of the year before, these

The view from the other side. Soviet troops, well clad in winter clothing, watch as a PzKpfw IV explodes under the impact of an anti-tank round. Many German infantry often adopted captured Soviet small arms, which proved to be more durable in the local climate.

reveal how overall tank strength increased (5,385 versus 5,262 in 1941), though the German Army still largely depended on obsolete tanks since the battleworthy ones only numbered 3,251 against the 4,198 of June 1941.

By 1 July 1942, total tank strength on the Eastern Front was 2,535, which is one-quarter fewer than it had been the previous June. Between late June and mid July, overall tank strength in the Panzer divisions included 297 PzKpfw II, 614 short-barrelled PzKpfw III, 380 long-barrelled PzKpfw III, 296 PzKpfw 38 (t), 205 short-barrelled PzKpfw IV, 89 long-barrelled PzKpfw IV and 52 PzBefh. With about 2,000 tanks, the Panzer divisions were still the main spearhead of the German Army in the East.

A Panzer crew cautiously guide their PzKpfw III vehicle across a pontoon bridge. The soldiers are wearing the classic all-black armoured vehicle crew uniform issued from 1935. The berets were padded to serve as protective helmets inside the tank.

LEFT: Army Group North soldiers in 1942. The figure on the far left is actually a field vet seconded to the 81st Infantry Division's veterinary company. He is accompanied by a pioneer (centre), armed with a Teller mine, and a *Jäger* wrapped in a camouflage pattern *Zeltbahn* shelter quarter. (Stephen Andrew © Osprey Publishing)

Production of the PzKpfw II ceased in July 1942 with the last 20 examples built, and given the lack of any suitable replacement, this was a tank that the Panzer divisions would miss in the months to come. However, tank production was now steered to meet the demands of the battlefield. In the second half of 1942, 1,266 PzKpfw III were produced, now armed only with the 50mm L/60 gun (production ceased in December) or with the 7.5cm L/24 equipping the PzKpfw IV (449 produced in 1942). Production of the PzKpfw IV now stood at 632, all armed with the L/43 gun (36 PzBefh were also produced).

Tank strength on the Eastern Front on 18 November 1942 shows how the situation had changed since *Barbarossa*; in total there were 164 PzKpfw II (135 with the Panzer divisions), 107 PzKpfw 38 (t) (all with the Panzer divisions), 264 short-barrelled 5cm gun PzKpfw III (261 with the Panzer divisions), 381 long-barrelled 5cm gun PzKpfw III (287 with the Panzer divisions), 93 PzKpfw III with the 7.5cm gun (65 with the Panzer divisions), 99 short-barrelled 7.5cm PzKpfw IV (91 with the Panzer divisions), 183 long-barrelled 7.5cm gun PzKpfw IV (128 with the Panzer divisions) and 50 PzBefh (43 with the Panzer divisions). The sharp difference between production and actual strength was explained partly by losses, which in 1942 included some 287 PzKpfw II, 1,501 PzKpfw III (against 2,605 produced), 196 PzKpfw 38 (t), 502 PzKpfw IV (against 994 produced) and 99 PzBefh. The increased number of Panzer divisions and the demands from the other fronts added further strain to the *Panzerwaffe*.

The PzKpfw VI Tiger tank was also making its presence felt on the battlefield. The Tiger actually began its development journey prior to the war, when the OKW began to think about a heavier, more powerful replacement for its PzKpfw III and IV. A long development process began involving Krupp, Porsche and Henschel, the latter's design winning through to become the basis of the PzKpfw VI Tiger Ausf. E, which went into production in August 1942.

The Tiger was a battlefield monster. It weighed an astonishing 55 tonnes with armour reaching a maximum depth of 110mm. The Tiger's gun was an adaptation of the 8.8cm Flak, and it could destroy virtually any armoured opponent on the battlefield. Hitler was eager to get the Tigers into battle, hence they were thrown into the cauldron of the Eastern Front in the high summer of 1942, and thereafter served in North Africa, Italy and Northern Europe.

The Tiger's experience in combat sent mixed messages. When everything was working well, the Tiger was a terrifying beast to fight, its accurate, powerful gun dispatching Allied tanks in disproportionate numbers. In one incident in 1943, during the battle of Kursk, a single *Waffen-SS* Tiger engaged about 50 T-34s, destroying 22 and compelling the rest to retreat. A feat that would be replicated when, following the Normandy landings, one Tiger tank destroyed 25 Allied vehicles before it was finally overcome, holding up an

LEFT: On the Eastern Front in 1941, Generaloberst Heinz Guderian (left) has a lighter moment with Generaloberst Hermann Hoth, commander of the 4th Panzer Army. Hoth, like many generals, had a stormy relationship with Hitler, and was dismissed after the battle of Kursk in 1943, although he was reinstated to a command position just before the end of the war.

entire divisional advance in the process. Matters later became even worse for the Allies with the later introduction of the Tiger II, which had an even more powerful 8.8cm gun and much thicker, sloped armor.

Yet ultimately, the Tigers fell short of expectations. Their sheer size meant they had no battlefield agility, and were limited in their abilities to cross soft terrain and keep up with more mobile formations. Mechanical breakdown was a serious issue, the tank's weight resulting in overstressed engines, brakes and transmissions. On the Eastern Front, mud and snow would be trapped in the overlapping wheels and freeze overnight in winter, rendering the vehicles immobile by the morning. The tanks also had a voracious appetite for fuel, overstretching logistics. So on balance, the Tiger was arguably more of a drain on German resources than was warranted. Nevertheless, in open combat most Allied tanks were at a serious disadvantage if they faced a Tiger.

Tigers, being special vehicles, were generally assigned purely to special heavy tank battalions, which were packaged out to reinforce other units during a campaign. Tiger battalions were given an elite status, and hence only a few divisions ever received them, including Panzergrenadier Division *Grossdeutschland* and *Panzer Lehr* Division.

It is worth noting that, in spite of their problems, the Germans still held the upper hand against Red Army armour. On 1 January 1942, the Soviets had 7,700 tanks and self-propelled guns, 2,200 of which were with the field forces; another 24,500 were produced during the year. Yet the Germans destroyed some 15,100 of them by the end of the year, nearly 47 per cent of the entire availability – although it is hard to say how many can be credited to the Panzer divisions (and also which weapon actually destroyed them).

By July 1943 most of the Panzer divisions had only a single Panzer battalion left and were still equipped with a mixture of old and new tank models. Most importantly, looking at the actual tank strength on the Eastern Front on 1 July, one can see not only that with 3,524 tanks and assault guns this was the highest figure since the beginning of *Barbarossa*, which shows how the Germans had been able to recover even from the Stalingrad disaster, but also a closer look at the total number of tanks in the Panzer divisions (1,451) reveals how by then they were no longer the main and only instrument of warfare available to the German Army. Rather, they had now become just one of the many instruments of warfare that included, amongst others, the combined-arms Panzergrenadier division, both army and *Waffen-SS*, plus the independent tanks and assault gun units (the three *Waffen-SS* Panzergrenadier divisions had a total tank strength of 494; 90 Tiger tanks were in two independent heavy Panzer battalions and 305 assault guns were in the independent *Sturmgeschütz Abteilungen* – assault gun battalions). Along with such fragmentation, there is another factor to take into account. As the breakdown of the Panzer divisions' tank strength reveals, in spite of the still heavily mixed composition, the trend was now unmistakable. In fact, those 1,451 tanks included

90 PzKpfw II, 611 PzKpfw III (all types), 12 PzKpfw 38(t), 665 PzKpfw IV (short- and long-barrelled) and 73 PzBefh. There could no longer be any doubt; the age of the light, fast-moving tanks was coming to an end, and the age of the heavily armoured and strongly armed tanks had begun.

PANZER TACTICS

Although the basic tactical principles of German armoured warfare did not change much during the first two years of war on the Eastern Front, the way these were put into practice by the Panzer divisions varied to a greater extent owing to several factors. First, terrain and climate began to influence operations and tactics as early as autumn 1941. The same happened on account of the Panzer divisions' shrinking fighting power, a consequence of the increasing losses and the lack of replacements. Tied as they were to the (few) major paved roads, the Panzer divisions were no longer able to drive deeply into enemy territory as they had done the previous summer. Additionally, tracked elements such as the Panzer regiment and the armoured infantry battalions not only took the lead, but, given their unique movement capabilities, soon turned into the only available units able to spearhead

A German supply train, filled with anti-tank guns, staff cars and trucks, begins its roll east. German trains, manufactured with more sensitive engineering than Soviet models, broke down in their thousands during the Russian winter of 1941/42, rendering up to 80 per cent of them inoperable.

the attack. Attrition caused both by the enemy and the weather, unmatched by adequate reinforcements, eventually took its toll until Red Army counteroffensives of winter 1941/42 brought the first real change to the Panzer divisions' tactics. Not only were the Panzer divisions forced to fight on the defensive for the first time, but they also primarily had to do it with their non-armoured units, since most of the armoured ones had practically ceased to exist as such.

German defensive tactics, based on the 'hold fast' principle (in which units facing an enemy attack had to maintain their positions regardless of what happened on their flanks and rear) coupled with the need to counterattack enemy breakthroughs immediately, proved particularly suitable for the Panzer divisions, though heavy losses further reduced their combat efficiency. This efficiency was never fully recovered, even after reorganizations. There was a consequent significant reduction to the Panzer divisions' speed and manoeuvre capabilities. Balance in the two elements of the attack – fire and movement – significantly shifted in favour of fire. The main consequence was the inability to drive deeply into enemy territory, at least at a tactical level, plus the development of tighter command and control at every level. The Panzer divisions, which were still superior to their opponents in the field, remained the spearhead of the German Army, but they were no longer able to assure breakthrough and the ensuing encirclement of enemy forces. The summer of 1943, particularly the failure at Kursk, marked the turning point of the evolution of German armoured tactics, which from that point turned the Panzer divisions into 'fire-fighters'.

Speed, manoeuvre and flexibility were the key factors that enabled the Panzer divisions to win their battles during the rapid advances of the early war. The implementation of these on the battlefield was made possible by the German command system, which had in *Auftragstaktik* (mission tactics) and the 'lead forward' concepts two highly efficient tools. In practice, a Panzer division on the battlefield was divided into a series of different battlegroups, each one behaving independently, focusing exclusively on its own task and ignoring all else. Every battlegroup commander was to take care of his own assigned route and target, determining how best to attain it and, by keeping in close contact with his subordinate units, how to deal with any unexpected situations. Unless directly threatened, he was not to concern himself with his flanks and rear and, above all, he was not to concern himself with what other battlegroups were doing. This was a task reserved for the division commander.

Supported by his HQ, the division commander was the only one intended to have a complete picture of the situation on the entire divisional front. He could give direct orders to the battlegroup commanders to help them deal with the situation they were actually facing on the basis of his knowledge of the bigger picture. Yet in a general way the division commander would only intervene if a position held by his subordinate units was endangered or if a situation could be exploited by switching units from other battlegroups, which could not be attained by moving an entire battlegroup from elsewhere. Speed, manoeuvrability and flexibility would be assured with the higher commanders dealing with the overall conditions on the battlefield. The system worked practically at every level, from the battalion upwards, yet it was at the divisional level that control required the greatest care and attention, since any failure at this level could affect the division as a whole.

These HQ command detachments moved closely with the combat elements, following up the spearhead march and battlegroups, establishing a command post in a suitable position and maintaining contact with the single commanders and the divisional rear and supply units. When needed, the commander himself would lead forward, joining the groups, talking to their commanders and assessing the situation at first hand, putting him in position to make the right decision at the right moment. Seeing their commanders on the battlefield in the heat of battle also served as a boost to the morale of the soldiers, especially when facing overwhelming odds.

Yet the command system soon turned into a critical issue for the Panzer divisions. Heavily relying on skilled and capable unit commanders at almost every level, not to mention the skilled and well-trained men supporting them (in the field of communications, as one example alone), the Panzer divisions would feel the shortages of such men following the heavy losses suffered in the winters of 1941/42 and 1942/43, a situation further aggravated by the rapid growth in the number of the Panzer divisions. As the war went on, it became more difficult to keep up with the standards of the *Blitzkrieg* years, and the Panzer divisions' command system would eventually turn towards the direct control of subordinate units by higher commanders.

PANZER HQ

In 1942 the HQ of a Panzer division was neither large nor cumbersome. In total it was only 61 strong, including 17 officers, 11 officials, 17 NCOs and 16 other ranks. The actual command echelon, directly entrusted with the task of leading the division on the battlefield, was even smaller and included, other than the division commander and his orderly, only three officers, two NCOs and one other ranks in the operations department and four officers, one NCO and three other ranks in the intelligence department. They would form the advanced command detachment – *Führungs Staffel* – which had the task of leading forward the combat elements of the Panzer division while the logistics detachment (*Quartiermeister*) followed up with the divisional rear and supply units.

ABOVE: Soldiers of Army Group Centre receive their orders from an armoured signals battalion NCO. The man in the centre has the M1941 flamethrower, while his infantry companion shows a typical load-carrying arrangement. (Stephen Andrew © Osprey Publishing)

WAFFEN-SS

By the launch of Operation *Barbarossa*, the German Army was not the only major land combat force on the battlefield. In fact, since the opening shots of World War II, it had been accompanied by another, more ideologically focused force – the *Waffen-SS*. The *Waffen-SS* (meaning 'armed SS') had emerged by the outbreak of September 1939 from the umbrella *Schutzstaffeln* (SS or 'protection squad') NSDAP security organization. This formation traced its origins to the early 1920s, when a small bodyguard unit for Adolf Hitler was formed alongside the Nazi Party's mass uniformed paramilitary force, the *Sturmabteilung* (SA; Storm Detachment). In 1929, the whole SS numbered less than 300 men; by 1933 this figure had increased to some 30,000. Under the national command of Heinrich Himmler the SS, with three battalions of armed gendarmerie, provided the key personnel for the internal coup against the SA leadership carried out on 30 June 1934.

An 8.8cm Flak in action on the Eastern Front. Such guns claimed thousands of T-34 tanks and other Soviet armoured vehicles; this particular gun indicates its armour kills via white rings on the barrel, while anti-aircraft kills are shown by the aircraft symbol. The soldier is using a 1m base stereoscopic range-finder.

Thereafter the growth in the size and influence of the SS in most areas of German public life was massive, complicated and virtually unchallenged. Nevertheless, at the outbreak of war in 1939 the armed units of what were then termed the *SS-Verfügungstruppe* (SS-VT; Dispositional Troop) were still few and militarily insignificant. They were regarded by the armed forces with some suspicion, as a political gendarmerie with no true role to play on the battlefield. Early combat experience in the West, and particularly in the first year of the Russian campaign, changed that perception, leading to a number of different cycles of expansion of what was now the *Waffen-SS*. By late 1943 this battle-proven organization was fielding several complete armoured and mechanized divisions.

SS formations became the trusted spearhead of Germany's armies on the Eastern Front, and served on every other major front except North Africa. Between early 1943 and spring 1945 the ostensible order of battle of the *Waffen-SS* grew from eight to no less than 38 divisions 'on paper' – though many of the higher numbered (mostly foreign) formations fell far below the standards set by the early divisions. A number of corps-level formations, and even one or two nominal 'SS armies' containing both SS and Army units, would see action in 1943–45.

The *Waffen-SS* stood apart from the army in many ways. As a whole it earned a dual reputation: for remarkable aggression and stamina in combat, and for murderous atrocities against civilians and prisoners. Although its divisions came under the tactical command of the OKW in the field, the *Waffen-SS* had its own unique internal command structure, at the pinnacle of which sat the *Reichsführer-SS*, Heinrich Himmler. Operational command of the entire SS came under the auspices of the *SS-Führungshauptamt* (SS Leadership Main Office), a new main office created in the summer of 1940 around the time that the *Waffen-SS* itself emerged from its forerunner, the SS-VT.

The rank structure and rank titles of the *Waffen-SS* were directly adapted from those of the administrative *Allgemeine-SS* (General SS), although the *Allgemeine-SS* method of displaying rank banding by single straps on the right shoulder only was eventually replaced by matched pairs of straps in the army fashion. The old *Allgemeine-SS* style of left-hand collar patches showing specific rank was retained, with only minor changes, until May 1945.

As well as the adoption of army-style shoulder straps, a further move to emphasize the 'military' nature of the *Waffen-SS* was marked when the original SS ranks equivalent to army generals were given a suffix indicating the equivalent general's rank of the *Waffen-SS*. Thus, the original rank of SS-Brigadeführer became in the *Waffen-SS* the *SS-Brigadeführer und Generalmajor der Waffen-SS*.

Generally speaking, in the army and *Waffen-SS* similar positions were held by soldiers with equivalent ranks. Thus a *Hauptmann* (captain) commanding a company-sized unit in the army would have as his equivalent in a *Waffen-SS* unit an officer with the rank of

LEFT: An infantryman and despatch rider of the *Das Reich* Division, a *Waffen-SS* formation. The *Waffen-SS* had begun experimenting with camouflage combat uniforms as early as 1938, and here we see one of the early camouflage smocks. They were originally designed to be worn over belt equipment, but many soldiers put the belt over the top, as seen here.

ABOVE: Four soldiers of the SS *Totenkopf* Divison, 1940–43. They are: 1) *SS-Oberscharführer*, *Feldgendarmerie*, 1940; 2) *SS-Sturmbannführer* of infantry, late 1941; 3) *SS-Sturmmann* of infantry, 1942; 4) *SS-Rottenführer*, 6th SS-Panzergrenadier Regiment, late 1943 (Stephen Andrew © Osprey Publishing)

SS-Hauptsturmführer. Similarly, an *Oberst* (colonel) in the army, commanding a regiment, would have as his equivalent an *SS-Standartenführer*. The original SS ranks indicated precisely the size of the unit that the soldier would command, suffixed by the term *Führer* or leader: thus *Scharführer, Sturmführer, Sturmbannführer, Standartenführer, Gruppenführer*, etc.

It should also be noted that within the later-raised 'non-Nordic' volunteer formations, the rank prefix 'SS-' was replaced by '*Waffen-*'. Thus a French SS volunteer with the equivalent rank to captain should technically have been referred to not as an *SS-Hauptsturmführer* but as a *Waffen-Hauptsturmführer*. In the case of the various foreign volunteer national legions, the prefix '*Legions-*' was used, thus *Legions-Hauptsturmführer*. Most of this nonsensical and unnecessary complication was due to Himmler's bizarre racial beliefs and the insistence that those SS volunteers who were not considered racially 'Aryan' should not be permitted to use the 'SS' prefix. It was also primarily for this reason that many foreign volunteer units were forced to adopt special unit collar patches in place of the SS runes. German cadre staff in these units were entitled to wear the runes on the left breast pocket to indicate their status as true members of the SS.

What, then, motivated a man to join the *Waffen-SS* rather than going into the regular army? Most often the answer was simple ambition and the desire to belong to an elite. After the reintroduction of conscription in 1935, the army's standards were somewhat

PzKpfw IV Ausf. E tanks of a *Waffen-SS* unit roll over the Russian steppes. The landscape and dimensions of the Russian and Ukrainian hinterlands deprived German armour of the ability to concentrate itself effectively, as it had done in the Western European campaigns.

lowered. An ambitious man who also realised his own limitations would, quite naturally, prefer to be a big fish in a small pond rather than a small fish in a large one. Army leaders also realized this, and exercised tight controls over the number of men eligible for national service whom they would permit to join the SS. Seeing what was happening, Hitler put the entire SS on to the police rather than the army budget. This gave the army more money to play with and helped reduce their animosity towards the growth of the SS, an animosity based on the fact that the army was traditionally the sole arms bearer for the state and undiminished by the fact that the pre-war *Waffen-SS* was a relatively tiny organization.

There were two other significant differences between volunteers for the *Waffen-SS* and for the army. Although the SS physical requirements were higher, their educational ones were lower. Nearly half of all *Waffen-SS* recruits had received only minimal schooling, and officer candidates especially were accepted with far lower academic qualifications than their counterparts in the army. This, of course, made them more amenable both to the tight discipline and to ideological indoctrination.

The other difference is that the majority of volunteers for the *Waffen-SS* came from rural areas, whereas the bulk of the army's ranks were composed of city dwellers. This process of natural selection vindicated itself later in a way which seems rather surprising, until you remember that fifty-odd years ago rural living conditions were far more primitive and, literally, closer to the earth than they are today. Thus it soon became apparent, particularly on the Eastern Front, that the majority of men in the *Waffen-SS* divisions were more comfortable living in the field, and more adept at field- and woodcraft, than their urban comrades. Since one of the basic requirements of a soldier is to survive in order to be able to fight, this was a not insignificant asset. Recruits for the *Waffen-SS* – at least in the early days, before wartime demands forced a relaxation of standards – had to satisfy stringent physical and moral conditions. 'Sepp' Dietrich, the commander of the *Leibstandarte SS Adolf Hitler* – Hitler's SS bodyguard – wanted mature men rather than insecure teenagers, so only recruited from those aged between 23 and 35, at least 1.8m tall, and in peak physical condition. No man was accepted if he had a criminal record, and he had to be able to prove pure 'Aryan' ancestry with no 'taint' of Jewish blood.

Until the need to replace casualties forced him to relax his own standards, Dietrich would not even accept a man into the *Leibstandarte* if he had a single tooth filled. He was determined that the regiment would be the toughest, fittest and most highly disciplined unit in the *Führer's* service, and right to the very end it attracted the cream of volunteers for the *Waffen-SS*.

However, despite the tough physical, racial and moral entry requirements, there was no shortage of volunteers. But in the early days, what the *Waffen-SS* badly lacked was experienced officers, and this was to be a contributory factor to their high casualty rate during the 1940 campaigns.

LEFT: *Waffen-SS* troops in Russia in 1941, seen as the winter begins to close in. By November 1941 the *Waffen-SS* had taken some 30,000 casualties, and by the mid point of the following year many of the divisions were in need of rest and refit, having been used intensively in the 'fire brigade' role at crisis points on the Eastern Front.

TRAINING AND FIGHTING CAPABILITIES

Initial *Waffen-SS* training was carried out in depots outside each regiment's home town. To begin with there was no consistency in training, so in 1936 Himmler created a *Waffen-SS* Inspectorate headed by a highly experienced former army officer, Paul Hausser. Brand new officer training schools were built at Bad Tolz and Braunschweig with light and airy barracks and classrooms.

Hausser was helped in initiating the training programme by two men in particular: Felix Steiner and Cassius Freiherr von Montigny. Steiner had been a member of a *Strosstruppe,* or assault troop, during World War I, and wanted to instil the *Waffen-SS* with a similar style and élan. These assault troops had consisted of small bodies of volunteers armed to the teeth not only with the first SMGs but also with improvised weapons such as clusters of grenades wrapped around a single stick, shields like a medieval knight and entrenching tools with their edges sharpened like razors. They were true light infantry, just as the *Waffen-SS* grenadiers were to become, going into action in daring trench raids unencumbered by the usual weight of kit, just carrying weapons, ammunition and water bottles. This, Steiner decided, would be the style of the SS; let the army provide the cannon fodder was no doubt his thinking.

Montigny, a World War I U-boat skipper, had similarly strong ideas on discipline. Between them, he and Steiner were determined to create a force of men who would be tough, ruthless and self-disciplined, and to a large degree they succeeded. What they also created was a force of men who were almost recklessly brave and totally callous where human life was concerned, factors which were to have repercussions on the battlefield, in the form of a number of appalling atrocities.

Training in the *Waffen-SS* was consistently tough. Once the men were familiar with their weapons they would begin learning infantry assault techniques, charging at sandbags with fixed bayonets. The instructors put great emphasis on aggression, constantly stressing fierceness in the attack both as a means of winning battles quickly and of minimizing casualties. To this end the men were taught the techniques of unarmed combat by qualified martial arts instructors and, later, when they were sufficiently skilled to be able to practise against each other without causing injury, they would fight mock battles using rifle and bayonet, or just the bayonet on its own. To further encourage aggression, boxing featured as a major part of the curriculum, helping the men to get over the instinctive fear of being hurt and teaching them to get their own blow in first.

LEFT: Personnel from the SS-Volunteer Mountain Division *Prinz Eugen*, seen in typical *Waffen-SS* dress for the second half of the war. They all wear mountain boots, and the soldier on the left has the M1940 reversible SS camouflage smock in its distinctive 'plane tree' pattern, the spring/summer side outwards, and a matching first type helmet cover. (Stephen Andrew © Osprey Publishing)

In fact, sport played a major part in the *Waffen-SS* training programme, much more so than in the army. All forms of field and track sports were encouraged, not just for relaxation as in the army but as part of the training itself, as a means of enhancing physical fitness and reflexes. And, of course, there were endless route marches and cross-country runs, both with and without full kit, to develop stamina and endurance.

In terms of ideological training, there were formal lectures at least three times a week covering the policies of the NSDAP and intense indoctrination in SS philosophy, particularly the theories of racial superiority that supposedly destined them to rule over the *Untermenschen* – the so-called 'sub-human' Jews, Slavs, gypsies and communists. Shortly after the invasion, when loses began to bite, the SS hierarchy began changing its mind on some racial ideas. Latvians, Lithuanians and Estonians, it was decided, were not 'Slav' but essentially 'Germanic'. So, it turned out, were Ukrainians, Azerbaijanis and anyone else who hated Moscow, almost regardless of their origins, because casualties created such a huge manpower demand.

Into this melting pot would also flow Indians and Palestinians, as well as men from every European country (Britain not excepted with a handful of volunteers), who all swore variants of the basic *Waffen-SS* oath and adherence to its motto, *Meine Ehre heist Treue*, which can be translated either as 'my loyalty is my honour', or 'honour is my loyalty'. Thus, its initial idealism diffused, the *Waffen-SS* actually became a polyglot organization whose members fell far short of the standards demanded by Hausser, Dietrich, Steiner and the remainder of the 'old guard'.

Panzers of the *Das Reich* Division move through the mud of the Soviet spring in 1943. A Tiger tank is visible on the far left; at this time the Tiger was still attempting to resolve its mechanical issues, but it had already proved itself a formidable killer of Soviet tanks.

Once the *Waffen-SS* recruit had survived this basic training and ideological and 'spiritual' indoctrination, he could – like a trainee soldier anywhere – learn more complex skills. In particular, and more so than in any contemporary armed force before the emergence of the British Commandos and the American Rangers, for example, Steiner and his team of instructors intended that the SS grenadier would be able to handle himself and his weapons competently under any conceivable battlefield situation, by day or night, regardless of terrain or weather. Individual training still continued, but increasingly gave way to unit training, first at the squad level of eight men and gradually broadening out into exercises at company, battalion and regimental level. Finally, full-scale exercises would be held involving the whole of a division.

The only way in which this training differed from the army's was, as we have seen, in the emphasis on aggression and overwhelming firepower. The *Waffen-SS* had plenty of the former but, initially at least, were hampered in acquiring the latter. They were in a situation rather like the army's *Panzerwaffe* – knowing what they wanted, but unable to get enough in sufficient time. This situation changed as the war progressed and Hitler came to place increasing reliance on his *Waffen-SS* divisions to 'get the job done', giving them priority in the issue of new equipment; although in the early years of the war this was not the case.

The capabilities of the SS are illustrated by what would become the 1st SS-Panzer Division *Leibstandarte SS Adolf Hitler*, referred to previously in smaller incarnations. It had its origins back in 1933, reaching regimental size by July 1939. It proved itself in action in both Western Europe in 1940 and Greece in 1941, but it was with the invasion of the Soviet Union in June 1941 that the *Leibstandarte* was to be put to its greatest test. Now a brigade just under 11,000 strong, it formed part of Army Group South. After advancing through Cherson it captured Taganrog, and in November, Rostov, where it took over 10,000 prisoners. Here, SS-Hauptsturmführer Heinrich Springer earned the Knight's Cross of the Iron Cross for his daring seizure of the vital bridge over the River Don. As the end of the year drew near, however, the impetus of the advance faltered and Soviet resistance grew. Counterattacks put the *Leibstandarte* in danger, but Hitler refused to countenance a general withdrawal. Nevertheless, the SS was forced back out of Rostov, and into a number of grim winter defensive engagements in the area of the Donetz Basin as the Soviets counterattacked in considerable strength.

The *Leibstandarte* had greatly enhanced its reputation as a first-class combat unit, drawing praise from army generals who had formerly regarded the *Waffen-SS* with some disdain. The commander of III Panzer Corps is recorded as saying of the *Leibstandarte*, 'This truly is an elite unit.' This reputation was not achieved without cost, however: more than 5,200 of the brigade's soldiers had become casualties.

In June 1942 the *Leibstandarte* was pulled from its defensive positions along the River Mius and moved to France, where it was greatly reinforced and re-formed as a mechanized

A German sniper takes aim in the ruins of Stalingrad, the rubble-strewn battleground ideally suited to sniper warfare. Sniper rifles such as the 7.92mm *Scharfschützen Gewehr* 98 were capable, with the right scope and in talented hands, of hitting a human target at ranges in excess of 600m.

or Panzergrenadier division. The new division spent some months forming up and training before moving to occupation duties in the southern (Vichy) part of France – occupied by Germany in retaliation for the surrender of the French Army in North Africa to the Anglo–American landings in November. During this period the *Leibstandarte* was given its own detachment of the new PzKpfw VI Tiger heavy tanks. In early 1943 the *Leibstandarte* was rushed back to the Eastern Front as Stalingrad fell and the whole military situation deteriorated. Thereafter it would be rushed around battlefronts and theatres, giving impressive performance but being ground down in the 'fire-fighting' role.

APPEARANCE

In general terms, and certainly during the early part of the war, the *Waffen-SS* grenadier wore much the same clothing and carried the same personal equipment as his counterpart in the army, with minor variations in style and the SS divisional insignia. The *Waffen-SS*, however, were among the first German units to use what has become known as 'disruptive pattern' clothing, designed to help the men blend in with their background surroundings and make them less visible to their enemies. The idea of camouflage itself is, of course, hardly new, but in the modern sense only dates from the turn of the century when the

ABOVE: SS armoured personnel, 1942–43. Note that the *Waffen-SS* produced its own camouflaged version of the Panzer uniform (bottom left), cut in lightweight drill material and printed with the so-called 'pea pattern' camouflage colours; unlike the combat smocks it was not reversible. The other men here wear the regulation SS Panzer jacket.
[Stephen Andrew © Osprey Publishing]

British Army belatedly decided that red tunics made the men marvellous targets and adopted khaki, a practice which, with variations in shade, was rapidly copied by most other armies. Khaki, or the German *feldgrau* equivalent, are practical, neutral shades, but the *Waffen-SS* decided this was not going far enough. What was needed was a form of garment to allow the men to blend in not just with different types of countryside, but with seasonal changes in the coloration of grass and foliage.

From the very outbreak of war in September 1939 most *Waffen-SS* combat troops wore a loose, thigh-length pullover smock over their service tunic. Made of a rayon/cotton mixure, it was generously cut for ease of movement, and could be pulled tight at the waist with a drawstring, offering a degree of extra protection against the wind. The collarless head opening also had a drawstring, as did the cuffs, emphasizing the baggy appearance (which was quite deliberate) and a further form of camouflage in itself. Early pattern smocks had two chest vents to allow the wearer to reach the pockets in his tunic underneath, but it was soon found that this was impossible when webbing was worn, as it had to be, over the smock, so they were discontinued. Loops were also frequently sewn to the shoulders, upper arms and helmet cover to allow foliage to be attached as extra camouflage.

The smocks were reversible, and printed in a variety of patterns to match the changing seasons: light and dark green for spring, two shades of green and a purplish brown for summer, and three shades of russet and brown for autumn. Quantity fabric printing of such complexity had never been tried before, and special dyes and techniques had to be invented. Early smocks were screen printed, but because this took time, especially since the smocks also had to be waterproofed, later versions were machine printed. The patterns were carefully designed to break up the wearer's outline, with small hard-edged splodges of colour outlined in contrasting colours, so that a man standing still in a wood or hedgerow became virtually invisible. There were four basic patterns used as the war progressed, which for convenience are generally referred to as 'plane tree', 'palm tree',

RIGHT: *Waffen-SS* grenadiers sprint from a trench during action in Russia in 1941, obviously in the warmer summer months. These soldiers wear a mix of Wehrmacht and *Waffen-SS* uniform items; from 1941 the *Waffen-SS* began to issue its own field blouse, as well as wearing *Heer* versions.

FROZEN POSITIONS

The 1942 German *Taschenbuch für den Winterkrieg* (Pocket Book for Winter Warfare) acknowledged that a totally different system of cover had to be used on ground frozen hard. Here logs could be cut and bound together in low walls to form a three-sided enclosure, pierced by one or more weapons slots. Drifting snow provided some additional protection but, more importantly, served to make the position difficult to see. White cloths or a *Zeltbahn* covered with snow completed the illusion. Similar effects could be created with sandbags sunk into holes dug down through the snow and placed directly on the frozen ground.

ABOVE: SS winter uniforms of 1943–45. The figure at the top wears the SS reversible camouflage/white winter uniform, with the white side outermost, and special winter felt boots. The winter cap lined with rabbit fur was widely worn in both the Army and *Waffen-SS*. (Stephen Andrew © Osprey Publishing)

'oakleaf' and 'pea', although none gave significantly greater camouflage protection than the others, so the reasons for the changes seem to have been merely experimental.

In 1942 work began in designing a new uniform for the *Waffen-SS* grenadier. The result was the M43 drill camouflage uniform. This consisted of a single-breasted jacket and trousers in a rayon mixture, camouflage printed on one side only, the coloration being predominantly dull yellow with green and brown splodges. The M44 suit that followed the M43 was made of coarse herringbone twill, which was not as warm. The waterproof qualities of the M44 were also inferior to the M43. The introduction of the M44 field uniform marked the final stage in the simplification and deterioration of the dress of Germany's armed forces.

By 1944, shortages of materials and the need to make economies forced the German Army and the *Waffen-SS* to adopt a different type of tunic and trousers. The M44 field blouse was shortwaisted, closely resembling the British Army's battledress blouse. It was made from *Zeltbahn* material for cheapness, and was distinctly shoddy in appearance and less warm than earlier tunics. The accompanying trousers were also waist length and tighter fitting, being held up with a belt instead of braces.

CHANGES IN FORTUNES

The *Waffen-SS*, for all the horrors they visited upon innocents and POWs, added to the excellence of the German armed forces during Operation *Barbarossa*. Yet in conclusion, it is important to ask the overall question why did the German Army, victorious in Western Europe, fail to defeat the Soviet Union in both operations *Barbarossa* and *Blau*, a failure that would lead to the catastrophe at Stalingrad? It has been argued that this failure to defeat the Soviet Union was due to the German approach to warfare and their fighting methods. During World War II, the Wehrmacht's understanding of strategy still encompassed the 19th-century concept of *Vernichtungsschlacht*, which loosely translated means a strategic military victory in a single campaign. Having the ability to destroy an enemy army through tactical and operational excellence would quickly bring about victory at the strategic level and thus attain the political objectives of the war. During the inter-war period, as noted in the Introduction and Chapter 1, the German Army learnt a number of lessons from its experiences in the previous war, but they refused to believe that the Schlieffen Plan, itself a powerful example of the *Vernichtungsschlacht*, had failed because of tactical flaws in its execution, but rather that the British and French armies had failed to adopt a particular tactical approach.

The success of the German *Blitzkrieg* between September 1939 and June 1941 seemed to justify the continued use of the *Vernichtungsschlacht*. In the campaign for the Low Countries and France, both sides were evenly matched in terms of personnel, tanks and aircraft, but in six weeks, the Wehrmacht achieved what the Imperial German Army could not in four years. It appeared that to defeat the Soviet Union, the same principles could be applied again.

In many circles, the development and employment of what we call *Blitzkrieg* constituted a revolutionary advance in the techniques of war, but for the Germans, who rarely used the term itself, it was merely a new word used to describe already established fighting methods, albeit with new weapons. The German tactical approach to battle was again heavily influenced by the 19th-century concept of *Kesselschlacht* (roughly translated as a 'cauldron battle of annihilation'), which was the practical approach to achieving a *Vernichtungsschlacht* on the field of battle. In effect, it involved encircling the enemy army and destroying it. In the early years of the war, the Wehrmacht used the *Kesselschlacht* concept with signal success, although in fact there was nothing that was particularly sophisticated about it. It therefore followed that the number of encirclement operations would depend on the size and skill of the opponent.

The Wehrmacht concentrated on achieving tactical excellence through a combination of creativity, initiative, boldness and adaptability, in conjunction with a thorough understanding of the value of mechanization, airpower, artillery, communications and manoeuvre in order to encircle and destroy the enemy. However, the scale of the pockets that were created in the *Kesselschlachten* during the campaign in the East caused problems in that the Germans had essentially two armies – a mechanized force, which formed the minority, and an infantry force that formed the majority. The Panzer groups would need to undertake huge encircling movements in order to trap the Soviet armies and prevent them from escaping into

German supply trucks brave the icy roads on the Eastern Front. The lack of 'winterized' vehicles in the first year of fighting on the Eastern Front meant that trucks often had to be kept idling even when not moving, to avoid them freezing solid, a measure that ate into fuel supplies.

the interior, but would have to wait until they had been reduced by the infantry with the support of the Luftwaffe before moving on, which would eventually hinder forward momentum as the Panzer groups quickly outran the infantry. A slower advance would allow the proper elimination of the pockets but might invite an attritional struggle that would favour the Soviet Union. The widespread mechanization of the Wehrmacht was impossible at that point and so the Germans gambled on achieving a complete victory before the problem became too serious. If it worked, a campaign in 1942 (which would have to face the same problem) would be irrelevant. That the gamble came so close to success was thanks to Stalin, who did not allow the Red Army to trade space for time after *Barbarossa* had begun and so gave the Germans exactly what they had been hoping for.

A machine-gun team man an MG 34 in a trench in the Ukrainian city of Kharkov. The benighted city violently swapped hands several times during the war on the Eastern Front, destroying about 70 per cent of its buildings in the process and costing the Germans thousands of lives.

The Germans also failed to achieve victory because of the Soviet Union's vast manpower and industrial resources, as well as its ability to force the Germans into fighting an attritional battle over a particular objective, first at Moscow and then at Stalingrad. Furthermore, the invasion of the Soviet Union and operations on the Eastern Front involved problems that the Germans had not really confronted in the early campaigns.

These revolved around geography, distance, time and scale, and their effects were increasingly felt during the campaigns of 1941 and 1942. Geographically, the Pripet Marshes dominated the western part of the Soviet Union so that operations in the south were isolated until the army had advanced into the Ukraine. The size of the Soviet Union and the distances involved affected German operations and logistics. The Panzer force had suffered wear and tear during the battle for France but, as it was only some 320km from the Ardennes to the Atlantic coast, supporting the campaign was relatively easy. The distance from Warsaw to Moscow, however, is around 1,600km; from Leningrad to Rostov around 1,930km; and from Berlin to Stalingrad around 3,220km. Therefore supplies of food, ammunition and spare parts, fresh equipment and replacement personnel had to move much greater distances than before. The Russian climate limited mobile operations between the months of May and November, so the time of year also became important. All this, and the scale of operations that the Wehrmacht had to undertake, was greater than anything previously attempted in a country where the lack of a modern infrastructure hindered the logistic support of rapid mobile operations even under the most favourable of conditions.

The Eastern Front also saw the Wehrmacht became a more defensively oriented force, a point that is worth some elaboration. In December 1941, the Germans adopted a new defensive concept to deal with the desperate situation on the Eastern Front. The initial plan for the winter of 1941/42 was to drive the Red Army towards the Ural Mountains, seize the main population and industrial centres, and withdraw two-thirds of the German forces, leaving the rest to establish a line of strong points to defend the Third Reich's new frontier. The strong point defence was an economy-of-force effort to employ the smallest possible number of troops to cover the widest possible front. On 16 December Hitler issued his 'no retreat' order, putting a halt to local withdrawals then under way as units sought more easily defendable terrain in which to sit out the winter. The official term for a strong point was *Stützpunkt*, but Hitler preferred *Igelstellung* (hedgehog position): *Stützpunkt* generally remained in use in official publications though.

The 'no retreat' order denied commanders a proven, effective countermeasure to massed Soviet attacks. Regardless of the order, it was still carried out in some instances. When a Soviet attack was imminent the forward troops were pulled back prior to the artillery barrages striking the strong points. Depending on the terrain, a withdrawal of 800–2,000m back to second-line positions was all that was required. The barrages fell on empty positions and obstacles, as Russian infantrymen rushed forward supported by tanks. The Germans would then open fire with artillery, mortars and machine guns from long range and wait for the assault's momentum to slow, formations to become disorganized and disorientated, and then to either withdraw or stumble piecemeal into the prepared defences. The forward positions could usually be reoccupied following German counterattacks.

Army Group Centre had successfully employed this elastic defence in August and September, but by December German units were so severely under strength that such a defence could not be established other than as a thin screen. Sufficient troops were simply not available to man the multiple-zone, in-depth defence over such broad fronts, and the necessary mobile reserves did not exist. Panzer divisions fielded only a dozen tanks and the remaining crews were serving as infantrymen. Rear service units were stripped to provide infantry replacements. Infantry battalions were at less than company strength, and companies had 25–70 men. The infantry strength of entire corps was less than 2,000 troops with a 250-man battalion deemed well manned. Many units possessed only a quarter of their heavy weapons. Rather than the doctrinal 6–10km sectors, the hollow divisions were assigned 30–60km fronts against the unexpected Soviet counteroffensive. All three regiments had to be placed in the main battle line, often with all nine battalions as well, allowing no regimental reserves other than the battalions' reserve companies, which were also manning deeper strong points. The Germans called it 'putting everything in the shop window'. Scattered squads and platoons would be held in reserve by battalions and companies to conduct immediate, local counterattacks. An under-strength reconnaissance

A group of PzKpfw III and IV tanks act as transport for German Panzergrenadiers in the Ukraine in 1943. The nearest tank has *Schürzen* (armour skirts) mounted on the sides. These features, designed to enhance armour protection, became standard on most German tanks from the spring of 1943.

Troopers of the SS *Totenkopf* Division ford a stream on the Eastern Front in their Krupp Kfz 81 light truck. With its all-round independent suspension, the Kfz 81 gave decent cross-country performance, and was typically used as an artillery tractor for light field, anti-tank and anti-aircraft guns, as seen here.

battalion served as the division's only mobile reserve, although if possible divisions retained one infantry battalion in reserve. To make matters worse, the strained German logistics system was on the verge of collapse.

Under-strength companies might organize into two platoons with three 6–10-man squads, each with a machine gun and positioned in a cluster of 3–5 two-man firing positions. Additional machine guns were often provided from service units as a substitute for riflemen. Remaining 5cm mortars were concentrated 50m to the rear under company control. Anti-armour guns were held in the rear to deal with tank breakthroughs. In some instances anti-armour guns were placed in strong points, making few available to block breakthroughs in the rear.

Strong points were established around villages to control roads and provide shelter from the brutal weather until fighting positions and bunkers could be built. Other strong points were built on the little available high ground. Weapons were positioned to engage the enemy at maximum range, provide mutual support to adjacent strong points, and cover the gaps between strong points.

The little remaining artillery was positioned further forward than normal, increasing the danger of it being overrun, to cover the different strong points. Many divisions fielded only one under-strength artillery battalion, rather than four, causing the few batteries to be widely dispersed to cover all the strong points. This prevented artillery fire from being concentrated en masse on main attacks, as not all batteries could range the wide division front. Mortars were distributed among strong points rather than being concentrated behind the forward units, meaning they were unable to range all the strong points. They could usually cover adjacent strong points though. Light air-defence units positioned their 2cm Flak guns in strong points, which proved ideal for breaking up mass infantry attacks.

The strong point defence remained into mid 1943/1944 in some areas. After that the Germans were in steady retreat. Defences consisted of hastily established lines in scattered sectors without continuous front lines, little depth, and few if any reserves. As relentless Allied assaults hammered at the Germans on all fronts, time and resources rarely allowed anything close to a doctrinal defence to be established. Pioneer units often built defensive positions and obstacles to await withdrawing infantry. Defences were built on rivers to provide major obstacles; villages and towns were turned into strong points and cities into *Festung* (fortress, essentially a propaganda title). Some of these, though, were well defended with multiple rings of strong points protected by anti-armour ditches and minefields. In-depth defences were prepared on the roads leading into the fortress city. Switch positions were constructed between the fortified lines to protect against breakthroughs.

The Wehrmacht gained as great a reputation in the defence as for offensive actions, as the Allies would discover to their cost in 1944 and 1945. Yet for the Wehrmacht, the Eastern Front would truly prove to be its nemesis, one that no amount of defensive skill could control.

ITALY AND THE WESTERN FRONT, 1943–44

THE YEARS 1943–44 SAW THE WAR TIP IRREVOCABLY AGAINST THE GERMANS. By the end of 1943, the German Army was in a progressive retreat on the Eastern Front, unable to stop the Soviet juggernaut from building momentum. Adding to the burden was the fact that in the West new fronts were opened, first in Sicily and Italy then, most crucially, in Normandy in June 1944. From this point on, Hitler was locked in an unwinnable two-front war, which stretched his army to breaking point and beyond.

THE COLLAPSE OF ITALY

The battle for the 'soft underbelly' of Europe – as Winston Churchill memorably and inaccurately referred to the Italian campaign – began on 10 July 1943. British and US forces landed in south-eastern Sicily, defended by the Italian 6th Army and the German XIV Panzer Corps with three divisions in northern Sicily. German forces led a determined but ultimately futile Axis defence of the island, and on 17 August retreated largely intact to Calabria in southern Italy.

The approaching loss of Sicily shocked the Italian government, which on 25 July arrested Mussolini and appointed Marshal Pietro Badoglio as prime minister. Hitler, correctly suspecting a coming Italian surrender and the prospect of Allied forces rushing to the southern Austrian border, formed the highly mobile 10th Army around the divisions in Calabria on 15 August 1943. This army, reporting to Luftwaffe Southern Command in Rome, had ten divisions in 56 corps in Calabria, and three divisions – later under XIV Panzer Corps – in reserve in central Italy.

In September, the Allies widened the war to Italy itself. On 3 September 1943, they landed in Calabria and on 9 September at Taranto in Apulia, as the 10th Army conducted a fighting retreat northwards. Italy's surrender was announced on the 8th, prompting Hitler to send Rommel's Army Group B to occupy northern Italy. Meanwhile Allied forces landed at Salerno on 9 September, but the 10th Army attacked the bridgehead energetically until 18 September. Resuming its skillful retreat, the 10th Army evacuated Potenza on 20 September, Foggia on 27 September and Naples on 1 October, halting on 8 October on the Capua–Termoli 'Viktor Line'.

On 26 November 1943, Army Group C was formed under Generalfeldmarschall Albert Kesselring, with 18 divisions deployed under the 10th Army in central Italy and the 14th Army, formed 18 November 1943, in the north. The 10th Army defended the narrow Italian front with great skill and resourcefulness, exacting a high price for ground lost, before halting on 27 December 1943 on the 'Gustav' or 'Hitler Line' on the Sangro and Garigliano rivers through the Monte Cassino strong point.

The Allies threw themselves bloodily against the Gustav Line on 18 January 1944, and on 22 January landed at Anzio and Nettuno. Undeterred, the 10th Army held the line until 13 May 1944, and the 14th Army confined the Anzio beachhead until 23 May. Yet the German movement was inexorably northwards. Evacuating Rome on 4 June and retreating rather fast northwards, the Wehrmacht gave up Florence on 4 August and halted on the 'Gothic Line' on 19 August. Meanwhile, on 17 March 1944 the *Armeeabteilung von Zangen* (Von Zangen Reinforced Corps) was formed in northern Italy, expanding on 31 July 1944 to form the Liguria Army with two Italian and six German divisions.

In late August 1944, the Allies finally broke through the Gothic Line, taking Rimini on 21 September, but further advances were slow against determined opposition by Army Group C, which had halted south of Bologna on 29 December 1944. By this point, Allied victory in Italy seemed assured, but the German Army was making them pay a terrible price.

German troops disembark from a transport ship in Sicily in 1943, many still wearing the desert uniforms from their service in North Africa. Note the soldier in the centre – his *kleiner Spaten* (entrenching tool) is hung in the regulation manner from the left hip.

German paratroopers take cover behind their vehicle during street fighting in Rome in September 1943. Although by this time the *Fallschirmjäger* were almost exclusively employed as ground troops, they generally retained their Luftwaffe uniforms, including the cut-down paratrooper helmet.

D-DAY AND THE BATTLE FOR THE WEST

Italy would consume the lives of thousands of German troops, but by the end of 1944 the Wehrmacht had an even greater concern in the West. With Hitler expecting an Allied invasion of France; France, Belgium and the Netherlands had been garrisoned in June 1944 by Western High Command, controlling Army Group B covering northern France, Belgium and the Netherlands, and Reinforced Army Group G in southern France. Army Group B, commanded by Rommel, had two armies and the Netherlands garrison. The 7th Army had 12 divisions in Brittany and western Normandy, and the 319th Infantry Division on the Channel Islands. Further east, the 15th Army garrisoned eastern Normandy, the Pas-de-Calais region and Belgium with 18 divisions, while the Netherlands were defended by four divisions. Panzer Group West, on 5 August 1944 redesignated 5th Panzer Army, constituted Von Rundstedt's strategic reserve near Paris, with nine divisions. Together the German force was respectable, but it would soon be tested to destruction.

D-Day began just after midnight on Tuesday 6 June 1944, as the Allied 21st Army Group, with eight divisions (three airborne and five infantry), three armoured brigades and total air superiority, landed in western Normandy, which was defended by three static infantry divisions (352nd, 709th, 716th) of LXXXIV Corps, German 7th Army. Hitler's poor strategic instincts left his forces unprepared and his caution prevented a quick reaction or mobile deployment; thus only the 21st Panzer Division counterattacked decisively, near Caen. With daytime movement virtually excluded by Allied airpower, the deployment by late June of seven first-line mobile divisions from Panzer Group West and Army Group G was too late to destroy the Allied bridgehead. By early July this had been reinforced to total 28 American, British and Canadian divisions (three airborne, 19 infantry, six armoured) and five armoured brigades. The struggle was becoming unequal.

On 17 July, Rommel was seriously wounded by a strafing RAF fighter, Field Marshal Günther von Klugethen then served as Army Group B commander until his arrest following the failed 20 July 1944 assassination attempt, and replacement by Model, on 17 August. The Allied bridgehead expanded slowly against determined German counterattacks, but the eventual British capture of Caen on 10 July meant that the landings were now secure. On 25 July the Allies broke out of the bridgehead, and by 7 August German 7th Army had lost Brittany. The 1st Army was briefly assigned to Army Group B but was unable to stem the Allied advance, and on 20 August the 7th Army and 5th Panzer Army, which had extricated themselves only at huge cost from encirclement in the Falaise Pocket during the westward retreat, crossed the Seine. Paris was abandoned on the 23rd.

On 25 August 1944, the Allies attacked across the Seine. Western Command and Army Group B retreated rapidly eastwards under heavy Allied air attack, evacuating northern France by 6 September – but denying valuable Channel ports to the Allies

VON RUNDSTEDT'S WEAKNESSES

The commander-in-chief in the West (OB West) from March 1942 was Generalfeldmarschall Gerd von Rundstedt. The revered victor of the 1940 Battle of France was described by one of his Panzer commanders as 'an elderly man & a soldier of thorough training with adequate experience in practical warfare, but without an understanding of a three-dimensional war involving the combined operations of the *Heer*, *Kriegsmarine* and *Luftwaffe*. He was a gentleman and had the personal confidence and respect of his subordinate commanders and his troops. His authority was limited and quite handicapped. His chief of staff [General Günther Blumentritt] was not a suitable complement, either as to capability or character.' A post-war US Army study concluded that the lack of unified command in France following the Allied landings was a more serious weakness than shortages of troops and equipment.

The Allies advance towards the Gustav Line – the primary Axis defensive line in Italy – through the south.

A 3 September 1943: Landings by British Eighth Army
B 9 September 1943: Landings by British V Corps
C 9 September 1943: Landings by US Fifth Army
D 22 January 1944: Landings by US VI Corps

with isolated 'fortress' garrisons, some of which held out until May 1945. British progress through Belgium was even faster, with Brussels captured on 3 September, the city – but not the sea approaches – of Antwerp on 4 September and Luxembourg on 10 September. On 15 September, most of Army Group B, with minimal surviving armour and no reserves, had formed a defensive line just inside Belgium (still denying the Allies use of Antwerp's port facilities), and along the 1939 Siegfried Line (*Westwall*) fortifications on the Belgian–German border.

On 15 September, the weary and over-extended Allies, surprised at the speed of the German collapse and short of fuel, halted, allowing the Germans valuable time to reinforce their line with dwindling reserves of *Volkssturm* home guards, border guards and *Volksgrenadier* units of mixed value (see Chapter 5). On 4 September 1944, the 1st Luftwaffe Airborne Army with seven divisions had reinforced Army Group B in the Netherlands, just in time to help repulse – with the important assistance of II SS-Panzer Corps – the British airborne landings at Arnhem between 17 and 26 September. Yet by 21 October the Allies had occupied the southern Netherlands, and Aachen, the first major town in west Germany, had fallen. On 11 November 1944, Army Group H was formed under Luftwaffe Generaloberst Kurt Student to defend the remainder of the Netherlands with the 1st Airborne Army and 15th Army.

Then came a surprise for the Allies (explored in more depth in the next chapter). On 16 December 1944, the Wehrmacht attacked through the Belgian Ardennes with 24 under-strength divisions from Army Group B and Western Command's 6th SS-Panzer Army, and depleted Luftwaffe air support. It would prove to the the last offensive gasp of the German Army.

THE GERMAN ARMY IN 1944

A closer look at the German defenders of France in June 1944 serves to illustrate some wider problems faced by Hitler's forces. By the time of the Normandy landings in the summer of 1944, the Wehrmacht had been bled white by three years of brutal conflict in Russia. The enormous personnel demands of the Eastern Front led to the cannibalization of units in France. Hitler 'wanted to be stronger than mere facts', and so the Wehrmacht order of battle became increasingly fanciful, with impressive paper strength but increasingly emaciated forces.

In response to Von Rundstedt's strong criticism of the state of the forces in France in October 1943, Hitler issued *Führer* Directive 51 to reinvigorate the Wehrmacht in the West. From 2 October 1943 the M1939 infantry division was reorganized as a 12,772-strong M1944 Division, with 11,317 German personnel and 1,455 *Hilfswillige* auxiliaries from the Soviet Union, representing a 28 per cent reduction in manpower but

OVERLEAF: A *Fallschirmjäger* machine-gunner occupies a lonely outpost in Normandy, 1944. He is armed with the MG 42; here he has the top cover open and is laying the belt of 7.92mm rounds into the feed mechanism. The MG 42 fired so quickly that Allied soldiers nicknamed it 'Hitler's buzzsaw'.

a slight increase in firepower. The M1944 division had three M1944 infantry regiments, each 1,987 strong, with an anti-tank company, an infantry gun company and two infantry battalions. The six divisional support units were an artillery regiment (2,013 men), a bicycle reconaissance battalion with four fusilier companies (708 men), a field replacement battalion, an anti-tank battalion (484 men), an engineer battalion (620 men) and a signals battalion (379 men). The 2,380-strong divisional services consisted of horsedrawn and motorized transport columns, a medical company, field hospital, veterinary company, military police troop and field post office.

From 30 May 1944 existing independent reinforced infantry regiments were redesignated grenadier brigades, on 13 July 1944 expanded into grenadier divisions; and on 9 October renamed *Volksgrenadierdivisions* (People's Grenadier Divisions), joining other such units first ordered on 26 August 1944. The 10,072 strong People's Grenadier Division was created in the aftermath of the 20 July Bomb Plot, theoretically to provide politically reliable infantry under Himmler's direct command. Usually organized from combat-weary units, it was a M1944 division with a fusilier company instead of a battalion, but with 18 per cent less manpower and 16 per cent less firepower; fighting quality varied from good to wholly inadequate.

Under the reorganization, Von Rundstedt's command increased from 46 to 58 divisions, partly from the transfer of burned-out divisions from the Eastern Front to France for rebuilding, and partly from newly formed divisions. The units on the Cotentin peninsula, therefore, were second-rate formations. In 1942, Von Rundstedt had also initiated the formation of static divisions. These were under-strength compared to normal infantry divisions, lacked the usual reconnaissance battalion and had only three battalions of artillery. In addition, their personnel were mostly from older age groups.

Through much of the autumn of 1943, the better troops were siphoned off to satisfy the insatiable requirements for more replacements on the Eastern Front. In their place came a steady stream of *Ost* battalions manned by 'volunteers' from Red Army prisoners. Oberst Friedrich von der Heydte of the 6th *Fallschirmjäger* Regiment recalled that 'The troops for a defence against an Allied landing were not comparable to those committed in Russia. Their morale was low; the majority of the enlisted men and non-commissioned officers lacked combat experience; and the officers were in the main those who, because of lack of qualification or on account of wounds or illness were no longer fit for service on the Eastern Front.' The weapons were 'from all over the world and seem to have been accumulated from all periods of the 20th century.' For example, during the fighting along

RIGHT: Three soldiers based in northern France, 1944: (from left to right) Grenadier, 914th Grenadier Regiment, Omaha Beach, Normandy, 6 June 1944; *Gefreiter*, 901st Panzergrenadier Training Regiment, Barenton, August 1944; *Oberwachtmeister*, armoured rocket-launcher battery, Normandy, June 1944. (Stephen Andrew © Osprey Publishing)

Gerd von Rundstedt, the Commander-in-Chief West, consults with his officers in southern France. Von Rundstedt held the leadership of German forces in the West from 1942, and he was relieved of this post in July 1944, having failed to stop or contain the Allied landings.

a 2km stretch of the Carentan front, Von der Heydte's unit was equipped with four calibres of mortars from 78mm to 82mm, of German, French, Italian and Soviet design. General Erich Marcks summed up his assessment during the Cherbourg manoeuvres in 1944: 'Emplacements without guns, ammunition depots without ammunition, minefields without mines, and a large number of men in uniform with hardly a soldier among them.'

The occupation divisions were bedevilled by the petty mindset of an army assigned to years of peaceful occupation duty. General Karl-Wihelm von Schlieben, commander of the 709th Static Division, recalled:

For someone who had served only in the east, the flood of orders, directives, and regulations which continually showered the troops was a novelty for me. This paper flood impressed me more than the tide along the Atlantic coast. Higher headquarters concerned themselves with trivial affairs of subordinate commanders. For example, it became a problem whether a machine-gun was to be placed 20 meters more to the right or the left... A senior commander wanted to have an old ramshackle hut demolished to create a better field of fire so a written application had to be filed with the appropriate area HQ, accompanied by a sketch.

Bureaucratic inertia began to lift from February–March 1944 after Rommel's arrival, when he assumed control of the defences along the French coast. Rommel was insistent that beach defences be strengthened in anticipation of the Allied landings. There were not enough workers from the paramilitary *Organization Todt* (see below) to carry out this work, since they were involved in the construction of a series of massive concrete bases for the secret V-1 and V-2 missiles. Instead, the construction work was carried out by the infantry in these sectors, at the expense of their combat training.

The 709th Infantry Division defending Utah Beach was typical of the maladies creeping into German forces in the sector. The division had been formed in May 1941 as an occupation division and in November 1942 it was converted into a static division. One of its battalions was sent to Russia in October 1943, and in June 1944 three of its 11 infantry battalions were manned by former Red Army POWs. Two of these were attached *Ost* battalions formed from various Red Army prisoners while another was recruited from Georgian prisoners. The division was further weakened by the incorporation of a high percentage of 'Germanic' troops, mostly Poles from border areas incorporated into Germany after 1939. The divisional commander later noted that their reliability in combat was doubtful, and he did not expect that the eastern battalions would 'fight hard in cases of emergency'.

German troops in the division were over age, with an average of 36 years. In spite of the mediocre quality of the troops, the division was relatively large for a static division, with 12,320 men, and it had 11 infantry battalions instead of the nine found in the new pattern 1944 infantry divisions. Of these troops, 333 were Georgian volunteers and 1,784 were former Red Army POWs. The divisional artillery had three battalions: one with mixed French/Czech equipment, the second with French guns and the third with Soviet guns. For anti-tank defence, it had 12 towed 7.5cm anti-tank guns and nine self-propelled 7.5cm tank destroyers. Tank support was provided by the 101st Panzer Battalion, a training unit weakly equipped with ten *Panzerjäger* 35R, an improvised combination of Czech 4.7cm anti-tank guns on obsolete French Renault R-35 chassis.

The division was originally spread along the entire Cotentin coastline, a distance of some 240km. With the arrival of the 243rd Infantry Division in May, its frontage was reduced. It still stretched from Utah Beach all the way to the northern coast around Cherbourg, a distance of about 100km. As a result, its defences were simply a thin crust along the shore with very little depth. Rommel hoped to compensate for the paucity of men with concrete defences, but the construction along the Cotentin coast received less priority than in other sectors.

The other two main formations in the area were the 243rd Infantry Division and the 91st Airborne Division. The 243rd Infantry Division was formed in July 1943 as a static division and reorganized in January 1944. Two of its infantry battalions were converted from static units to bicycle infantry, though in the process the division lost an infantry battalion. The division was originally in reserve, but in late May was shifted to defend the western coast, taking over from the over-extended 709th Infantry Division. On D-Day it included about 11,530 troops, somewhat under strength. Its artillery was mostly captured Soviet types, but it had a self-propelled tank-destroyer battalion with 14 75mm Marder III and ten StuG III assault guns. The division was reinforced by the 206th Panzer Battalion, equipped with a hodgepodge of old French tanks including 20 Hotchkiss H-39, ten Somua S-35, two Renault R-35 and six Char B1 bis. This was deployed on the Cap de la Hague on the north-western tip of the Cotentin peninsula.

The 91st Airborne Division was formed in January 1944 to take part in Operation *Tanne* (Pine Tree), an aborted airborne action in Scandanavia planned for March 1944. When this mission fell through, the partially formed division was transferred to Normandy, arriving in May 1944 to reinforce the two static divisions. At the time of the invasion, it was under strength, with only two infantry regiments and a single fusilier battalion, and numbered about 7,500 men. However, the 6th *Fallschirmjäger* Regiment from the 2nd Fallschirmjäger Division was attached to the division during the Normandy fighting.

A German anti-tank gun fires during the battle for Normandy. Wehrmacht anti-tank teams utilized the convoluted terrain of the region much to their advantage, launching close-range ambushes against enemy armour on the narrow French lanes.

GERMAN BATTALION ATTACKS

German Army battalion attacks were frequently made on a narrow frontage of 400–1,000m, with a specific 'point of main effort' or *Schwerpunkt* as chief objective. Assaults could be *Frontaler Angriff* (frontal), or preferably *Flankenangriff* (flank attacks). Enveloping attacks with the front pinned were dubbed *Umfassener Angriff* – this German term contains the ideas of 'putting one's arm around' or encirclement. A *Flügelangriff* or 'wing attack' was also recognized; in this, though unable to attack the opposition flank at right angles, the German infantry would drive obliquely into the enemy wing. Flanks were obvious points to attack, and even where none existed at the start they could be created by manoeuvre, or by picking out a weak point from an otherwise continuous enemy line. Attacks could be made directly from the line of march, 'shaking out' into aggressive formations from the columns of advance. Although battalion commanders were encouraged to set up their command post in sight of the action, and company commanders were to 'arrange for constant close reconnaissance', time was vital; preparations were expected to take no more than 40 minutes from striking an obstruction to the assault. The common model was a threefold development: *Heranarbeiten*, or working forward until within range for the 'break in'; *Einbruch*, or breaking into the enemy position; *Kampf in der Tiefenzone*, or 'fighting in the deep zone', within the enemy position.

Colonel Von der Heydte considered that the combat efficiency of the division was poor, especially compared to his elite Luftwaffe troops. The division artillery was based around the 10.5cm *Gebirgs-haubitze* 40 mountain howitzer, which did not share the same type of ammunition as the normal 10.5cm divisional gun. Once the division had expended its one basic load of ammunition, its guns were useless. During the course of the fighting, its artillery regiment was re-armed with a mixture of captured artillery types including Czech and Soviet types. The 100th Panzer Battalion, headquartered at Château de Francquetot, provided armoured support. It had a motley collection of captured French tanks including 17 Renault R-35, eight Hotchkiss H-39, one Somua S-35, one Char B1 bis and one PzKpfw III.

There were a number of smaller formations in the area as well. Assault Battalion AOK 7 was an assault infantry battalion attached to the 7th Army headquarters. On D-Day, it was redeployed from Cherbourg to the 701st Infantry Division during its actions near the Vire River.

Even if the German units on the Cotentin peninsula were not the best in the Wehrmacht, they were still a credible fighting force. Training and tactics were based on hard-won battle experience, and there were Eastern Front veterans in many of the divisions. During the fighting, the American General Raymond Barton visited one of his battalions that had been stalled by the German defences and assured the officers that the German troops facing them were second-rate. A young lieutenant replied: 'General, I think you'd better put the Germans on the distribution list. They don't seem to realize that!'

SS paratroopers prepare to fire a GrW 34 8cm medium mortar. Mortars were ideal weapons for the fighting in the Normandy *bocage*, being able to deliver indirect fire from behind cover. The GrW 34 could hit targets at ranges up to 2,400m.

Besides the infantry formations, there were a significant number of coastal gun batteries located around the Cotentin peninsula. The army controlled two *Heeres-küsten-artillerie-abteilungen* (coastal artillery regiments), HKAA 1262 on the west coast of the peninsula and HKAA 1261 on the east coast. Some of these took part in the later land actions, most notably the Azeville and Crisbecq battery of HKAA 1261 near St Marcouf.

GERMAN FORCES AT OMAHA BEACH

As a counterpoint to the German forces on Utah Beach, the formations around Omaha Beach, another US landing area, are worth consideration. The US troops spilling out onto Omaha Beach on 6 June 1944 took the highest Allied casualties of that fateful day (3,000 dead and wounded) illustrating that even in mid 1944, after the depredations of the last three years, the Wehrmacht was still to be respected.

The 716th Infantry Division had garrisoned Omaha Beach, called the Grandcamps sector by the Germans, since June 1942. This static division was spread from Carentan to the Orne estuary and, therefore, defending all of the Normandy beaches except Utah in the west. The 726th Grenadier Regiment was responsible for covering the Omaha Beach area in 1942–43. The fourth battalion was the 439th *Ost* Battalion made up of former Red Army troops. The division was significantly under strength, with only about 7,000 troops compared to a nominal strength of over 12,000. On the other hand, most of its forces were deployed in bunkers or field fortifications with a large number of supplementary weapons, including 197 machine-gun pits, 12 anti-tank rifles, 75 medium mortars and 249 flamethrowers.

On 15 March 1944, the 352nd Infantry Division was ordered to take over the Bayeux sector of the Normandy beaches as part of Rommel's effort to strengthen the defences in this sector. This division had been formed in December 1943 near St Lô from the remnants of the battered 321st Infantry Division, which had been sent back from Russia to rebuild. Most of its personnel were recent conscripts from the classes of 1925/26, meaning young men 18–19 years old. Yet unlike the old 716th Infantry Division, the 352nd Infantry Division was at full strength. It consisted of three infantry regiments, each with two rifle battalions with their companies numbered 1 through 4 and 5 through 8 respectively. The 13th Company was a cannon company for direct-fire support equipped with two 15cm and six 7.5m infantry howitzers. The 14th company in each regiment was an anti-tank unit with *Panzerschreck* anti-tank rocket launchers. The 1944 divisional structure substituted a fusilier regiment for the old reconnaissance battalion, with one company on bicycles and one company motorized. The division's artillery regiment had four battalions, three with 12 105mm howitzers each and the fourth with 12 150mm guns. The division's anti-tank battalion had a company with 14 *Panzerjäger* 38(t) Ausf. M Marder III tank destroyers, another with ten StuG III assault guns and a third with improvised 3.7cm guns on Opel trucks.

Divisional training was hamstrung by the lack of fuel and ammunition as well as by the need to divert the troops to work on field fortifications to reinforce the Atlantic Wall. There was little opportunity for training above company level. This unit was reasonably well trained by Germany's 1944 standards, though not by US Army standards. The 1944 German infantry division had less manpower than its US counterpart but more firepower, especially in automatic weapons.

The reconfiguration of the defences along the Bayeux coast in late March 1944 more than tripled the divisions strength. The Omaha Beach area that had been held by two battalions from the 726th Grenadier Regiment was now reinforced by two regiments of the 352nd Infantry Division along the coastline and a reinforced regiment as corps reserve within a few hours' march of the coast. The two battalions of the 726th in the

Omaha Beach sector were subordinated to the headquarters of the 352nd Infantry Division and retained their mission of manning the coastal emplacements and trenches along the beach. The 914th Grenadier Regiment was responsible for the Isigny/Pointe-du-Hoc sector west of Omaha Beach, while 916th Grenadier Regiment was responsible for the Omaha Beach sector as well as the eastern section of Gold Beach. The third regiment, 915th Grenadier Regiment, and the division's 352nd Fusilier Battalion, were formed into Battlegroup Meyer and stationed behind the coast near St Lô to serve as the corps reserve.

The reinforced 352nd Infantry Division was responsible for defending 53km of coastline, far beyond what was considered prudent in German tactical doctrine. This led to a number of arguments between Rommel and the divisional commander, Generalleutnant Dietrich Kraiss. Rommel wanted all of the infantry companies deployed along the main line of resistance so they could fire on landing Allied troops. Kraiss wanted to adopt a more conventional defence with a relatively thin screen along the beach and most of the companies held in reserve behind the bluffs from where they could counterattack any penetrations. In the end a compromise was reached. In the Omaha Beach sector, one of its infantry battalions moved up to the coastline and deployed two of its companies in the forward defences alongside the 726th, with the other companies in the villages a few miles from the beach. The other battalion formed a reserve for the regimental sector along with the division's self-propelled anti-tank battalion.

Allied intelligence believed the entire 352nd Infantry Division was in corps reserve around St Lô when in fact only one of its three infantry regiments was in reserve on 6 June 1944. To explain its appearance in the fighting on Omaha Beach on D-Day, the myth developed that the division had been deployed near the beach to conduct training a few days before D-Day. This was not the case and the division had been in place near Omaha Beach for more than two months before D-Day.

As well as the small-arms of the infantry, Omaha Beach was covered by 1st Battalion, 352nd Artillery Regiment, headquartered at Etreham with three batteries of 10.5cm howitzers. This battalion had forward observation posts located in bunkers along the coast, significantly enhancing their lethality when employed against targets on Omaha Beach. The 2nd Battalion, 352nd Artillery Regiment, headquartered to the east at St Clement, also had Omaha Beach in range. The artillery battalions were provided with only one unit of fire, meaning 225 rounds per 10.5cm howitzer and 150 rounds for each 15cm gun. No resupply was available for a few days. The final element of the artillery in this sector was added on 9 May 1944 when a battery of heavy artillery rockets (*Nebelwerfer*) of *Werfer-Regiment* 84 (84th Rocket Regiment) was positioned in this sector. Behind the 352nd Infantry Division was the *Flak-Sturm Regiment* 1 (1st Anti-Aircraft Regiment) of the Luftwaffe 11th Flak Division, adding 36 8.8cm guns to the defence of this sector.

On the Pointe-du-Hoc promontory between Omaha and Utah Beaches was the 2nd Battery of the 1260th HKAA, equipped with six French 15.5cm guns and five LMGs. By June 1944, four of six casemates for the guns had been completed, but heavy Allied bombing raids had reduced the ground around the batteries to a lunar landscape of craters. After the 25 April 1944 bombing, the battery had withdrawn its guns from the casemates to an orchard south of the point. In their place the crews had fabricated dummy guns from timbers that fooled Allied intelligence into thinking the guns were still present.

Generalfeldmarschal Erwin Rommel inspects the Atlantic Wall defences prior to the Allied invasion of Europe in June 1944. Rommel's strategic priority was to prevent at all costs the Allies' securing a beachhead, but he had to compromise that goal by incorporating the views of commanders such as Von Rundstedt.

DEFENSIVE WARFARE

The intense casualties taken by the US forces on Omaha Beach was the result of a combination of factors – ideal fields of fire for defenders with automatic weapons; Allied problems getting adequate armour ashore; the enfilading fire of German artillery pieces. Yet it was also the product of improved German defensive constructions, which became increasingly important to the Wehrmacht as the war for them focused more on the defensive.

While we will go on to look at field defences in depth below, Omaha Beach gives a useful illustration of how the German Army constructed permanent defences when they had time to do so. The defences along Omaha Beach expanded continually after the autumn of 1943 when Rommel was put in charge of reinvigorating the Atlantic Wall.

Although Hitler and most senior German commanders expected the main invasion to take place on the Pas de Calais, Rommel believed that a case could be made for landings on the Normandy coast, or in Brittany around Montagne d'Aree. As a result, he ordered the construction of defences along the most likely areas of coastline.

Rommel believed that the sea itself was the best defensive barrier and the terrain around Omaha Beach presented ample defensive opportunities. The initial defensive work began at the water's edge with the construction of obstructions against landing craft. The outer barrier, about 100m above the low-tide mark and 250m from the sea wall, consisted of a string of steel obstructions, called *Cointet* gates by the Germans. These were designed to block landing craft from approaching the beach. The next line of barriers, about 25m closer to shore, were wooden stakes that were planted in the sand facing seaward and buttressed like an enormous tripod. These stakes were usually surmounted by a Tellermine 42 anti-tank mine and were designed to blow holes in the bottom of landing craft. In some sectors these were followed by *Hemmkurven*, called ramp obstacles by the Allies, which were curved steel structures designed to obstruct the landing craft. Finally there was a row of 'hedgehogs' of various types. The most common was the *Tschechenigel*, called 'Rommel's Asparagus' by the Allies, which was an anti-craft/anti-tank obstruction made from steel beams. The obstructions on the tidal flats were primarily intended to stop the approach of landing craft to the sea wall during high tide. These were submerged and invisible at high tide, preventing landing craft crews from steering easily through any gaps. There were a total of 3,700 obstacles at Omaha Beach – the highest density of any of the D-Day beaches.

At the high-water mark was a swathe of shingle, round stones the size of golf balls, sometimes backed by a sea wall. One or more rows of concertina wire or other barbed wire obstructions were placed immediately inland from this. Until the autumn of 1943 there were many small beach houses and other structures along the shoreline for vacationers and local residents. These were knocked down to deprive Allied infantry of cover. A few of the more substantial buildings along the shore were left intact, but were converted into infantry strong points. The beach area was heavily mined, though gaps that contained no mines were also marked with minefield warnings to confuse Allied troops.

In contrast to the other four Normandy beaches, which are relatively flat, Omaha Beach is characterized by bluffs rising up to 50m from the sea, most noticeably on its western side. The edges of these bluffs provide ideal defensive positions for infantry with clear fields of fire on the exposed troops below. On some of the cliffs on the eastern side of the beach, 24cm artillery shells were dangled over the cliff with trip-wires to serve as booby-traps for any infantry trying the climb. These were called 'roller-grenades' and they were spaced some 100m apart.

Ardenne Abbey, 8 June 1944. Gruppenführer Fritz Witt, commander of the 12th SS-Panzer Division *Hitlerjugend*, leaves the northern entrance of the headquarters of the 25th SS-Panzergrenadier Regiment in a motorcycle combination driven by the regimental commander Kurt Meyer. (Kevin Lyles © Osprey Publishing)

Access from the beach was limited to five gullies, called 'draws' by the US Army, and only two of these were readily passable by armoured vehicles or motor transport. These became the centre point of German defences at Omaha Beach. Since the tactical objective of the defence was to prevent the Allies from moving off the beach, all five draws were stiffly defended by establishing a fortified belt in and around them. Fourteen *Wiederstandnester* (strong points), numbered WN60 through WN73, were created along the beach. Most of the draws were covered by a strong point on the hilltops on either side of the draw. Two other strong points were constructed on the Pointe-et-Raz-de-la-Percée promontory on the eastern side of the beach to provide enfilading fire along the beach, and the three other strong points were constructed immediately behind the beach, covering the exits from the draws.

A StuG III in Normandy, swathed in foliage to camouflage it from Allied aircraft, which quickly asserted supremacy over Normandy in the summer of 1944. Although actual armour losses to air attack can be exaggerated, the air threat certainly prevented the effective and timely deployment of armour to the battlefront.

The configuration of each of these strong points differed due to terrain, and they were still being built when the Allies landed on 6 June 1944. Generally they consisted of small pillboxes, or concrete reinforced 'Tobruk' machine-gun pits, at the base of the bluff obstructing the entrances to the draws. The larger draws were also blocked by barrier walls, anti-tank ditches and anti-tank traps. One of the most effective defences was the *Bauform* 667 anti-tank gun bunkers built into the sides of the bluffs, with their guns pointed parallel to the beach. These bunkers had a defensive wall on the side facing the sea that made it very difficult for warships to engage them with gunfire. By careful positioning they prevented Allied tanks from entering the draw since they could hit the tanks on their vulnerable side armour from point-blank range and, furthermore, the guns were positioned to fire in defilade down the length of the beach. The bunkers often contained older anti-tank guns such as obsolete PaK 38s. However, such weapons were more than adequate to penetrate the side armour of the Sherman tank and they were also effective against landing craft. In total, there were eight anti-tank gun bunkers along Omaha Beach, including two 8.8cm guns.

Besides the fully enclosed anti-tank guns, there were three 5cm anti-tank guns on pedestal mounts in concrete pits, and ten other anti-tank guns and field guns in open pits in the various strong points. As an additional defensive installation, the turrets from obsolete French and German tanks were mounted over concrete bunkers. Around these fortifications, the German infantry dug out a series of trenches as a first step to creating a series of interlocking shelters and protected passages. However, the shortage of concrete in the spring of 1944 meant that only a small portion of these trench lines were concrete-reinforced. The construction of these defences was hampered by the haphazard priorities of the army, Luftwaffe and *Organization Todt*. The Luftwaffe, for example, built an elaborate concrete shelter for its radar station on the neighboring Pointe-et-Raz-de-la-Percée that was absolutely useless in protecting the radar from any form of attack. At the same time many key infantry trenches on the bluffs, lacking concrete reinforcement, flooded during spring rain and were rendered useless by the time of the attack.

Of all the defences near Omaha Beach, by far the most fortified was the Pointe-du-Hoc. The site was originally constructed to contain six 15.5cm guns in open gun emplacements, but at the time of the Normandy landings the defence was being reconstructed to protect each gun with a fully enclosed Bauform 671 ferro-concrete casemate. In addition, the site contained a fully enclosed artillery observation point on the seaward side of the promontory and fully protected crew shelters and ammunition bunkers.

FIELD DEFENCES

The German defences on the Western European coastline were naturally very different to the defences from which most of the German Army fought in World War II. The construction of individual or small-unit defensive positions had always been a part of Wehrmacht training, but from 1941 the skill became a matter of life or death for soldiers on all fronts. It also became something of a precision art, the construction of such positions being laid down with precise detail in manuals and training.

The basic rifleman's position, the *Schützenloch* (firing hole) was a two-man slit trench, analogous to a foxhole; it was also nicknamed a *Wolfgrabhügel* (wolf's barrow). While a one-man hole was used when necessary, the two-man was preferred – it offered soldiers moral support and allowed one to rest with the other on watch. Also, if a one-man position was knocked out, a wide gap was created in the defensive line, whereas in a two-man hole if one man was lost the other could still conduct the defence. The one-man rifleman's position, nicknamed a *Russenloch* (Russian hole), was a simple 70cm-wide, 60cm-deep hole – deep enough to allow a man to kneel in. Soil was piled in a crescent to the front to reduce the amount of digging required. As with other positions, the soil was meant to be removed, but often time constraints meant the parapet remained. In the absence of a parapet, the rifle was propped on a small mound of earth or a Y-shaped fork driven into the ground.

German field defences. The two trenches shown here would eventually have been linked up by a communications trench if the unit stayed for more than a few days. This meant that the men would not be exposed to observation or fire whilst moving about within the position. Further rearward trenches would also be dug leading to latrines, headquarters, ammunition reserves and to the field kitchen. (Elizabeth Sharp © Osprey Publishing)

The 'Russian hole' could be deepened to allow a standing position and could later be widened for two men. Initially, two-man positions (*Schützenloch für 2 Gewehrschützen*) were specified as a short straight trench, 80cm x 1.8m. A slightly curved trench was also approved and this became standard in 1944. This version had two firing steps with a deeper centre section, allowing the riflemen to sit on the firing steps with their legs in the centre hole during shelling and offering protection from overrunning tanks. *Panzerdeckungsloch* (armour protection trenches) used the same concept and they too were suitable as rifle positions. They could be V-, W- or U-shaped, or a shallow crescent. The firing steps were recommended to be 1.4m deep and the deeper central portion 1.8–2m. All of these positions were recommended to be 60–80cm wide at the top and

40cm at the bottom. The recommended distance between positions was 10m, but this varied depending on the unit's assigned frontage, the terrain and vegetation.

Anti-armour rifles were placed in two-man positions. No special positions were provided for *Panzerfauste*; they could be fired from any open position with a few considerations. This rocket launcher was normally fired held under the arm, but it could be fired from the shoulder from a dug-in position. In the latter case, the rear of the breech end had to be clear of any obstructions because of the 30m back-blast, meaning no rear parapet; nor could the breech-end be angled down too far. They could not be fired from within buildings unless from a very large room, such as a warehouse, with open doors and windows to relieve blast overpressure. The same restrictions applied to the 8.8cm *Panzerschreck*, but it had a greater back-blast. They were often employed in threes with two positioned forward and one to the rear, the distances dependent on terrain. This allowed the launchers to engage enemy tanks approaching from any direction, plus provided an in-depth defence: at least two of the launchers could engage a tank. A 2m-long, V-shaped slit trench without parapet was used, with the two ends of the 'V' oriented away from the enemy. The gunner would occupy the arm of the 'V' that offered the best engagement of the target tank, and the assistant would load and take shelter from the back-blast in the other arm.

The squad's *Schützenloch für leichte Maschine-gewehr* (two-man LMG position), or *Maschinegewehrloch oder nest* (machine-gun hole or nest), was a slightly curved, 1.4–1.6m trench with two short armour protection trenches angled to the rear. On the forward side was a 20cm-deep U-shaped platform for the bipod-mounted gun. The position could be placed anywhere within the squad line that provided it the best field of fire. Alternate positions were meant to be up to 50m from the primary position, but were often closer. The three-man *Schützenloch für s.MG.* (HMG position) was similar to the light one, but with armour protection trenches extending from the ends. The platform was still 20cm deep, requiring the long tripod legs to be dug in to lower the weapon's profile. The difference in design between the light and heavy positions was a weakness, as it allowed aerial photographic interpreters to differentiate between the types. A common design would have prevented this.

Expedient efforts and materials were used to construct positions. As the Soviets swept into East Prussia in late 1944, the Germans employed civilians to construct defensive positions and obstacles behind the field army, so that it could fall back on them. Two sections of 1.5m-diameter, 2m-long concrete culvert pipe were used to build 'Tobruk pit' machine-gun positions. A pit was dug and one section laid horizontally on the bottom with one end shored with sandbags or planks, creating the troop shelter. The second pipe was set vertically, with a U-shaped section cut out of one side of the bottom end to mate with the horizontal pipe. The top end of the vertical pipe was flush with the ground. It was quick to build and easily camouflaged.

OVERLEAF: German paratroopers man an MG 42 in the ruins of Monte Cassino. This epic battle ended in another German defeat, but it further secured the reputation of the *Fallschirmjäger* – the Allies called them 'Green Devils' after their splinter camouflage and their fighting prowess.

If a position was occupied for long enough, the rifle and machine-gun positions might be connected by trenches. Trench systems were widely used in the Western Desert campaigns, as they allowed concealed movement between firing positions in terrain otherwise devoid of cover. They were also used extensively within strong points. Trenches followed the terrain's contours, in contrast to the geometric patterns laid out in World War I-style that ignored the terrain. Trench systems were not necessarily

The *Machinegewehr-Schartenstand aus Rundholz* (log machine-gun bunker) was loosely based on larger concrete fortifications on the Westwall. The bunker's firing port (FP) was oriented perpendicular to the enemy's predicted line of advance in order to engage him from the flank. This allowed positions to have a thicker than normal wall on the enemy side, and to inflict a surprise attack from an unexpected direction: it also made it much easier to conceal the bunker. The interior included a *Kampf-Raum* (battle room; 1) for a machine gun, an adjacent *Munitions-Raum* (ammunition room; 2); and a *Vorraum* (entry alcove; 3). A communications trench (4) connected it to other positions. The double-log walls were filled with rock or packed earth (5). The roof was made of multiple layers of logs, clay, rocks and earth (6). The sides and roof were covered over with sods of turf and care was taken to ensure the bunker blended into the terrain. The large red arrow on the illustration indicates the direction towards the enemy; bunkers of this type were also built with the firing port oriented forward. (Ian Palmer © Osprey Publishing)

continuous. Some sections may have been covered with branches and saplings and perhaps a light covering of earth or snow.

Trench patterns were zig-zag with each section 10–15m in length: in this way, artillery or mortar rounds striking the trench would only inflict casualties in the section struck. The angled trench sections also prevented any enemy troops that gained the trench from firing down its full length. *Kriechgraben* (crawl trenches) were 60–80cm wide at the top (as specified for all trenches), 60cm deep and 60cm wide at the bottom. *Verbindungsgraben* (connecting trenches) or *Annäherungsgraben* (approach trenches) were 1.8–2m deep and 40cm wide at the bottom. *Kampfgraben* (battle trenches) were the same, but with firing steps (*Schützennische*) and ammunition niches cut into the sides. Some firing steps might be cut into the trench's rear side for all-round defence. Connecting trenches too might have firing steps, and adjoining armour protection trenches were recommended every 40–50m.

Two-man rifle and machine-gun positions were usually dug 2–3m forward of the battle trench and connected by *Stichgraben* (slit trenches). These were located at the points of trench angles and along the straight sections. *Unterschlupfe* (dugout shelters) protecting one to six men were situated in the trench's forward side at intervals, and nicknamed *Wohnbunker* (dwelling bunkers). These provided protection from sudden artillery and air

PzKpfw VI Tiger II (King Tiger) tanks hide in a Normandy forest, attempting to avoid the attentions of Allied ground-attack aircraft. The King Tiger's gun could kill any Allied tank, and its armour protection was formidable, but its combat influence was reduced by poor mobility (it weighed more than 69 tonnes) and mechanical problems.

attacks and tank overruns. They were built as small as possible and in a variety of manners. As the position developed, squad and half-squad bunkers were built off connecting trenches for both protection from artillery and as living quarters. In muddy and wet conditions plank *Lattenroste* (duckboards) might be placed in the trench's bottom over a central drainage gutter.

CREW-SERVED WEAPONS POSITIONS

Crew-served field fortifications were naturally more ambitious projects. The *Schützenloch für leicht Granatwerfer* (5cm mortar position) was a simple slit trench similar to a two-man rifle position, with a 70cm × 1m × 70cm step in the front for the mortar. Shallow rectangular pits were also dug as hasty positions with a U-shaped parapet open in the front. The position for the 8cm heavy mortar (*Nest für s. Gw.*) was a 1.6m-deep circular pit, 1.8m in diameter at the bottom. The top would be slightly larger, the degree of side slope depending on the stability of the soil. A 1m shelf was cut in the back for ammunition. On either side were armour protection trenches.

INFLUENTIAL TACTICAL MANUALS

The foundation of the German approach to infantry tactics was the pre-war service regulation HDV 300/1, the *Truppenführung* (Troop Leading). Punningly referred to as the *Tante Frieda* (Aunt Frieda), this was primarily the work of Generaloberst Ludwig Beck. The thinking outlined in its introduction underpinned all other tactical doctrine. Warfare, so it said, was 'an art', but one that rested on science and made the very highest demands upon individual character. Warfare was under constant development, and its changes had to be predicted and evaluated, its variety being limitless. Perhaps most importantly, it was a subject impossible to 'exhaustively summarize'; therefore it was the 'principles' of regulations which were important, applied according to circumstance. Also stressed was the role of the individual and the human factor: 'Despite technology, the value of the man is the deciding factor; scattered fighting has made it more significant. The emptiness of the battlefield demands those fighters who can think and act for themselves, those who exploit every situation in a considered, decisive, bold manner, those full of conviction that success is the responsibility of every man. Inurement to physical effort, to self regard, willpower, self confidence and daring enable the man to become master of the most serious situations.' Another inspirational publication was Erwin Rommel's *Infanterie Greift an* (The Infantry Attacks), a digest of tactical observations on battle in World War I that was first published in 1937. According to one source it was Hitler's reading of this volume which first prompted him to appoint Rommel to his headquarters the following year.

In 1943, the '8cm heavy mortar pit' was redesignated the *Feuerstellung für mittleren Granatwerfer* (firing position for medium mortar), as the new 12cm had been adopted as a heavy mortar. The latter's *Feuerstellung für s. Gw.* was simply an enlarged version of its 8cm counterpart, 2m deep and 2m in diameter. Since mortars were highly mobile and relatively small, they were often simply emplaced behind any available cover such as in gullies and ditches, or behind mounds, walls or rubble.

'Nests' for anti-armour and infantry guns too were redesignated 'firing positions' in 1943. Anti-armour gun positions were circular or oval, about 4m across (though this varied), and shallow (40cm for 3.7cm anti-armour guns, and slightly deeper for the 5cm and 7.5cm). Slots were sometimes dug for the wheels to lower the profile of these anti-armour guns. Infantry gun positions were similar, but deeper (3m in diameter, 50cm deep for the 7.5cm; 6m in diameter, 1.3m deep for the 15cm). Ramps dug in the position's rear allowed the gun to be emplaced and withdrawn. A low parapet was placed some 2m behind the ramp's upper end to protect the position's rear opening. If armour protection trenches were not cut on either side of the position, shallow slit trenches were dug inside the

This photograph of German infantry marching to the Italian Front provides a good frontal view of the *Heer* load-carrying system. The standard webbing system consisted of a set of black leather 'Y' straps supporting a backpack and a belt that carried ammo pouches, entrenching tool, gas mask case, bread bag and water bottle.

position immediately adjacent to the gun and in some instances beneath the gun, between the wheels. In fully developed positions, a downward angled ramp was sometimes dug, and the gun could be rolled down this to place it below ground level. The lower end of the ramp was sometimes provided with overhead cover known as an *Untersellraum*.

Infantry guns, being smaller and lighter than artillery pieces, were often emplaced in hastily built positions, like mortars. Anti-armour guns by necessity had to be in well-concealed positions to survive and inflict losses on enemy tanks. They also had to be able to relocate to other positions quickly once detected by the enemy. For this reason, while a gun's initial position may have been a fully prepared one, subsequent positions were often only partly prepared or simply a hastily selected site providing concealment and the necessary field of fire.

Luftwaffe 8.8cm Flak guns engage British armour around Cagny, France, 18 July 1944. The Luftwaffe commander of the guns was forced at gunpoint by a Panzer *Oberst* to move his unit and fire on the British tanks, which suffered many losses. The intervention of the 88s enabled the Germans to establish a more stubborn defence of Cagny. (Peter Dennis © Osprey Publishing)

The 2cm Flak guns, single and quad, were increasingly employed in forward positions in the ground fire role, especially on the Eastern Front. When deployed so, they were positioned on their own in the front line. The *Feuerstellung für 2cm Flak* (firing position for 2cm Flak) was circular, 5.5m in diameter and 45cm deep, and was lined with ammunition niches and compartments for gun equipment. The 2cm and 3.7cm guns were set on a slightly elevated triangular platform. The 8.8cm Flak gun, when used as an anti-tank weapon, was very large and had a high profile, making it hard to conceal and requiring a great deal of effort to dig in. Its large size and the need for a heavy prime mover made it difficult and slow to withdraw and reposition. When used in the anti-armour role, therefore, the '88' was hidden among buildings, or in wooded areas, or defiladed in gullies and road cuts.

Divisional field artillery pieces were provided with circular or roughly triangular firing positions known as *Geschützestellung*. These usually had substantial all-round parapets and were deeper than other more forward gun positions for protection from counter-battery fire. Ready ammunition niches might be dug into the forward side, armour protection trenches attached to the sides, a rear entry/exit ramp added, and separate ammunition niches and crew shelters located to the rear. A simple artillery firing position was prepared by digging a shallow pit and piling the earth to the front. Any existing cover might be used for this purpose.

Armour protection trenches or merely simple slit trenches were dug to either side of the gun to protect the crew from ground, artillery and air attack. As air attack became common, these slit trenches were placed further from the gun position. Several ammunition niches were dug to the rear. A battery's four gun positions were set 30–50m apart and could be placed in a straight or staggered line, a square or a diamond

ABOVE: A 2cm Flak gun position. Single and quad 2cm Flak 38 guns were found to be extremely effective against massed infantry attacks on the Eastern Front; they were also used against light armoured vehicles, as well as being used to engage ground-attack aircraft. (Ian Palmer © Osprey Publishing)

formation. The battery headquarters was to the rear of the positions, and the horse and ammunition wagon parking was well to the rear of the battery position (up to 200m) in a concealed area to protect it from artillery. Camouflage was essential for the battery to survive, and so positions were often covered with camouflage nets. Each battery had two LMGs for ground and air defence.

Slit trenches were dug in rear areas as *Luftschutzraum* (air raid shelters). These varied in form and dimension, but two typical examples were the straight trench (2m long, 40–60cm wide and 1.6m deep), and the three-leg zig-zag trench which had each leg with approximately the same dimensions as the straight trench. Trenches might be roofed over with earth-covered logs or bundled brushwood fascines. Interestingly, such shelters were dug in at distances as great as 40km behind the front.

A defining characteristic of the European theatre in 1943–44 was Germany's steady loss of air supremacy to the Allies. German camouflage (*Tarnung*) practices, therefore, attempted to blend fortifications into the surrounding terrain and vegetation to prevent detection from both the ground and air. Natural materials were used alongside camouflage nets, screens and pattern painting. German directives stated that cover and camouflage measures should not obstruct a weapon's field of fire.

DEFENSIVE POSITIONS IN ITALY

German theory of defensive positions is practically elucidated by examining the field fortifications constructed in the peculiar terrain of the Italian theatre. The theatre illustrated that while official doctrine was important, improvisation was key to creating a good defence in difficult or unusual terrain.

Italy itself aided defensive warfare. The Apennine Mountains run along almost the entire length of the Italian peninsula, while rivers running into the sea across the hilly coastal plains cross-compartmentalize the peninsula with narrow, flat valleys. The valleys were extremely muddy in the winter and spring, and a force fighting its way up through Italy was faced with repetitive ridges and steep-sided mountains. Citrus and olive groves and vineyards covered the terraced lower slopes and evergreen and scrub trees the upper. The roads were few and very restrictive, being limited to valleys with only infrequent passes, while the ground was extremely rocky. Villages were situated on naturally dominating terrain, making them ideal for defence as well as shelter from the harsh weather. The thick-walled buildings, most with cellars, were substantially constructed of stone and mortar and the towns irregularly arranged – they provided even better defensive positions when rubbled. Anti-armour and machine guns were often emplaced in cellars and the overhead floors reinforced by rubble. AFVs were limited to the easily blocked narrow roads and were extremely exposed when approaching towns.

OPPOSITE: A 7.5cm PaK 40 anti-tank gun, emplaced behind an improvised wall in Italy, 1944. The PaK 40 was developed to deal with the larger breeds of battle tanks taking to the field. As seen here, its low profile allowed it to stay hidden until the moment of attack.

While mutual support between fighting positions was desired, what Kesselring called a 'string of pearls', the terrain was often too rough and too many positions were required to block every avenue of approach. Anti-personnel mines were therefore used extensively and anti-tank mines and demolitions could easily block roads. While the mountains and ridges provided the defender with excellent long-range observation (clouds, fog, rain and snow permitting), fields of fire and observation in the immediate vicinity of defensive positions were usually limited. Surprise attacks and close-range fights were therefore common.

Abundantly available rock was the most commonly used construction material for pillboxes, bunkers and other positions. Cement was sometimes available for mortar, allowing some quite substantial structures to be built. Railroad ties and rails were also available. In the well-prepared, in-depth defensive lines, such as the Gustav Line spanning the peninsula south-east of Rome, concrete fortifications were built. Rock-built fortifications hidden among the scrub trees were easily blended into the surrounding terrain and difficult to detect from the ground or air.

Since digging was difficult to impossible in rocky, mountainous terrain, defenders made use of ravines, gullies, knolls and ground folds. Blasting was required to excavate many positions. There were usually enough nooks and crannies that could be covered over with logs and topped by rock for suitable fighting positions and shelters, if they were in the necessary location to cover approaches. Rock sangars were extensively used and these too were sometimes covered. Mortars proved to be especially effective in the short-range battles as they could respond quickly and their steep trajectory allowed them to reach into ravines and behind steep ridges.

The Germans in Italy were also adept at defending towns. Those in Italy were especially suitable for defence, with their heavily constructed stone and concrete multi-storey buildings with cellars. Combat in built-up areas was costly to both the defender and attacker. The Germans made the seizure of towns as punishing as possible for the Allies and took advantage of the cover and concealment urban landscapes provided from artillery and air and the time it bought.

To the Germans a town was a ready-built strong point and a deathtrap for enemy tanks. The main defence line was located well within the town to deny the enemy observation and direct artillery and tank fire on the defences. Outposts and observation posts were placed on the town's edge with others well outside the town to observe avenues of approach. Mines and other obstacles blocked roads, bridges were demolished, and mines and anti-armour ditches were emplaced across fields through which tanks could approach. Hills, clumps of woods and groups of buildings outside the town might be defended as all-round strong points or at least combat outposts to deny or delay the enemy use of them or to prevent the town from being enveloped.

RIGHT: In the mountainous terrain of Italy, a German artillery observer team relay fire directions back to an field gun unit. The team consists of a *Vorgeschobene Beobachter* (forward observer), here seen with the notepad, and a radio operator to transmit his colleague's instructions.

Engineers prepare a bridge for demolition in Italy in 1943. Being a country of mountains and passes, control of bridges became a matter of vital importance for both sides in the battle for Italy. The soldier sitting on the bridge wears an Iron Cross, an indicator of the engineers' frontline work.

The main defence line was laid out in an irregular pattern to make it more difficult to locate, and prevent outflanking if penetrated. Particularly strong or dominating buildings were fortified as strong points on the main roads through the town. Snipers, anti-armour teams with *Panzerfauste* and machine gunners were positioned in other buildings, as well as placed forward of the main defence line along with small strong points. These disorganised the attackers before they reached the main defences. Secondary lines were prepared along with switch lines to contain penetrations. Even if a defended town was incorporated into a main defence line, it was prepared for all-round defence in case the external lines were penetrated and the town encircled. Reserves were positioned well inside the town in stout buildings while others might be held outside the town.

RIGHT: Soldiers of the 10th SS-Panzer Division *Frundsberg*, in *Waffen-SS* uniforms of the 1943–44 period. They are (from left to right): an *SS-Brigadeführer* of armoured troops, 1944; an *SS-Grenadier*, 1943–44; and an *SS-Untersturmführer* of the 10th SS-*Sturmgeschütz* Battalion, 1944. (Stephen Andrew © Osprey Publishing)

Streets could be blocked with roadblocks built of rubble, wrecked vehicles and streetcars, and heavy logs buried vertically. These log walls could be formidable obstacles up to 3–4m high and braced with angled tree trunks, though these were more common in Germany. Rivers, streams and canals passing through towns were incorporated into the defence plan. Sometimes buildings were blown into streets blocking them with rubble. Mines were also used. Some streets were left unblocked to allow enemy tanks to move into close-range ambushes or tank-trapping cul-de-sacs. Side streets, conversely, were sometimes blocked to prevent tanks from turning off when engaged. These roadblocks were recessed back into side streets to prevent their detection until passed. Town squares and traffic circles were set up as killing zones.

Individual buildings were booby-trapped to inflict attrition upon enemy infantry, and in some cases they were prepared with explosions, to be detonated when the enemy occupied them. Doors and ground-floor windows were blocked with rubble and furniture, as were alleys. Other windows were left uncovered and open so that the enemy could not determine which windows were being fired from. Loopholes were knocked through walls and roof tiles and shingles removed. Many of these were unused, serving

Waffen-SS soldiers sprint quickly across a road in France, heading for their next point of cover. War crimes in France (particularly those committed by the *Das Reich* Division) and later in the Ardennes, bought the *Waffen-SS* the enmity of Allied forces, who had little incentive to take SS personnel prisoner.

BATTLE FOR ORTONA

Ortona was to be the first town in Italy in which the Germans conducted a major defensive and delaying effort. Ortona is on Italy's east-central coast opposite Rome and was the eastern anchor of the Gustav Line. The 10,000-population town was on level ground with the outskirts open, offering little cover. There were no natural terrain features to aid the defence, so the Allies had hoped that the Germans would abandon the town and defend further north. The northern old town had narrow, twisting streets, large squares and the buildings were more heavily constructed. The newer southern portion had wide straight streets. The buildings were stone and masonry, with many 3–5 stories high.

The Canadian Army experienced a tough fight on the southern approaches to Ortona. Two reinforced German paratroop battalions defended the town in depth, covering a 500m x 1,500m area. The Canadians launched their attack on 21 December 1943, and the Germans were gradually pushed back through the town, falling back on successive strong points. Both defenders' and attackers' tactics and techniques evolved through the battle with the Germans constantly introducing new methods. On the night of the 28th/29th the Germans withdrew after causing a nine-day delay to the Allied approach to the Gustav Line. Ortona was nicknamed 'Little Stalingrad' by the Canadians – they suffered more than 2,300 casualties taking the town, plus larger numbers suffering from combat fatigue. As a result, the 1st Canadian Division was temporarily combat ineffective.

only to mislead the enemy. Positions were set up using chimneys for cover. Lookouts and artillery observers did use church belfries as posts, but once the enemy closed on the town they would evacuate them, as they were obvious targets. Snipers avoided them, despite what is often depicted in motion pictures.

Attackers moved down streets hugging building walls, so defending riflemen and machine gunners took up positions on both sides of a street to cover the opposite side. Residences were mostly constructed as adjoining rows of houses. *Mauseloch* (mouse-holes) were knocked through interior walls to connect the buildings on different floors including cellars, and doors sometimes connected the cellars of buildings on the same block, allowing troops to reposition or reinforce without leaving cover. They were also used to reoccupy buildings that had been cleared by the enemy. Mouse-holes were sometimes concealed by furniture. Storm sewers were also used for movement between positions. Anti-armour and machine guns were positioned in cellars and other machine guns mounted in upper windows – tanks had limited gun elevation and could not engage higher floor firing positions. Rubble piles had firing positions hidden in them. *Panzerfauste* were fired from alleys and other hidden sites in the open

This plate shows a typical German bivouac in an olive grove in the foothills of the Apennine Mountains, where an off-duty section of *Fallschirmtruppen* is awaiting orders. It is only a temporary encampment, evidenced by the fact that the men's sole shelter against the heat of the sun during the day and the chill in the mountains at night is a collection of *Zeltbahn* tents. (Velimir Vuksic © Osprey Publishing)

as they could not be fired from within buildings. Tanks and assault guns were concealed in buildings to fire down streets.

The combination of new-found German defensive skills and the terrain of Italy itself combined to make the Italian campaign appallingly costly for the Allies. From their landings in Sicily to the final surrender of German forces in Italy in 1945, the Allies took about 340,000 casualties. The Germans, although heading for defeat, had ensured that the 'soft underbelly' was very hard indeed for those trying to break it.

MINES

Mines became an integral part of German defensive warfare, and were laid in their millions on all fronts. Mines could be laid in defined fields, with a tactical objective such as blocking an enemy advance, channelling him into 'killing grounds' or defending a specific locality. Anti-personnel mines could also be laid among, or even attached to, anti-tank mines, thus making the clearing of a passage for tanks highly dangerous. Otherwise they were scattered as 'nuisance' mining.

The main German anti-personnel mine at the outbreak of war was the small cylindrical *S-Mine* 35. This contained about 360 steel balls, and could be set off by means of a pressure igniter, a pull igniter used with a trip wire or an electrical command firing

An infantry unit displays various anti-tank weapons. They are: 1) 7.92mm PzB 39 *Panzerbüsche*; 2) *Nebelhandgranate* (NbHgr) 39 smoke hand grenades and smoke cylinders (*Rauchrohr* 39); 3) *Doppel-Ladung* (double charge), a pair of 1kg TNT blocks fastened to the ends of a short length of wire; 4) *Geballte-Ladung* (concentrated charge) of six *Stielhandgranate* (Stg) 24 stick grenade heads; 5) GG/P40 rifle grenade with a spigot-type discharger on his Kar 98k rifle. (Steve Noon © Osprey Publishing)

system. On its being activated, the inner casing was projected a yard or more into the air before the mine exploded into a cloud of fast-moving shrapnel – hence the American nickname 'Bouncing Betty'. The sobering reality of this weapon is contained in a British Infantry Training Memorandum of May 1944, which records:

> I had been given to understand that if you stepped on an anti-personnel mine, the only thing to do was to hold the foot down, lean well back, accept that the foot might be blown off, but hope that the mine would not explode above ground level. Eighth Army engineers who had a good deal of experience with S-mines told me that though this idea had been current for some time it was quite erroneous. The anti-personnel mine has a delay of three or four seconds. When you step on it there is a muffled click in the ground. Between three and four seconds after this click – that is, after the cap has fired – the cylinder blows four feet or five feet into the air. The cylinder seldom rises vertically on its axis, but generally takes a tilt one side or another. The splinters from the underside of the cylinder strike the ground about three yards from the position of the mine; those from the upper side fly in the air three or four feet clear of the ground. The base is usually blown downwards close to the original position of the mine...
>
> It is probably best to move three or four yards away from the mine and lie down. Even though three seconds is quite a long delay, and a man lying flat on the ground twenty yards away is not likely to be hit either by the splinters or the steel balls that fly out of the cylinder, running any distance is not to be recommended. The enemy has a habit of laying mines in clusters, and a man running from one mine is quite likely to step on another without knowing it, and may drop down beside it or even on top of it. He may, of course, do the same even if he moves away only a short distance from the first click, but the risk is preferable to leaving the foot on the mine. Sometimes, too, the Germans put down mines that have no delay action. These jump straight out of the ground and allow no time for any action to be taken.

By D-Day the *S-mine* was but one of a lethal family. Some German devices were made with the absolute minimum of metal so as to make detection by electronic means difficult. In the *Schü-Mine*, Types 1942 and 1943, the body of the mine was a wooden box, the pivoting lid of which depressed under the weight of the foot to activate a striker. An additional advantage was that the simple wooden boxes could be manufactured in schools and small workshops, thus saving on industrial capacity. In the 1943 *Glas-Mine*, the body was of thick glass, with a thinner shear plate that set off the mine when broken by downward pressure.

By the later part of the war, German mine warfare theory was highly developed. Major anti-tank minefields would be laid out in uniform patterns, with anti-personnel mines sprinkled around the forward fringes – often with anti-lifting devices or trip wires. In all instances minefields were at their most useful when covered by fire. German mine layers would keep track of the layout with a *Minenmessdraht* or mine measuring cord, made from old telephone wire. This was usually 24m long, with marks for measurements and mine positions on its length. Commonly, alternate rows would be staggered; optimum spacing for the S-mine was 2–4m apart, while *Schü-Minen* could be laid as closely as every 50cm. Belts of anti-personnel mines were anything up to 12 rows deep, producing densities of perhaps four per metre of front. Forward of the main fields would be scattered unmarked mines denying avenues of approach, covering supply dumps or disused defences.

A German non-metallic mine, used in Italy in 1944. Making a mine non-metallic reduced the chances of its detection by Allied mine-detection equipment. Such mines were often fitted with anti-handling devices, in case they were discovered and lifted.

THE ROLE OF THE PANZERS IN 1943–44

Although the German Army was forced onto the defensive from the summer of 1943, its leading principles of warfare remained unchanged; attack, or counterattack, was still the best way of achieving results against enemy forces. Facing more enemies and fighting on several fronts simultaneously, the German Army found in the Panzer divisions a suitable instrument for a makeshift solution: counterattacking enemy strikes when and where these took place. Until 1944 German doctrine envisaged a linear defence based on a main defence line, to be held at all costs regardless of enemy breakthroughs. Mobile forces, above all the Panzer divisions, were then ordered to counterattack, surround and eventually destroy the enemy forces and restore the situation. Such a system, which worked well on the Eastern Front until mid 1944, had several shortcomings, however; in order to face enemy attacks which threatened if not all at least good portions of the front, the Panzer divisions had to be scattered all along it because the lack of reserves and supplies did not permit the switching of units fast enough to face the impending crisis. This led to the exact opposite of one of the leading principles of German warfare: the concentration of forces. As a result, the Germans could still deal locally with enemy breakthroughs and restore the situation (though often with severe losses), but they were no longer able to regain the initiative and launch any major offensives.

Eventually, a lack of strength and resources led to the defence-in-depth concept. Since the enemy relied heavily on firepower, the forward defensive line was thinned down and comprised only a series of outposts intended to slow down the enemy attacking forces, while a main line of resistance was built in the rear. When the enemy attack came, the Panzer divisions had to contain their drives and eventually counterattack following the usual guidelines. Once again that led to a dispersion of forces and, as a result, no major offensive was possible – as witnessed in Normandy. A debate between Rommel and Von Rundstedt about the deployment of the Panzer divisions clearly reflects the situation; Rommel fully acknowledged Allied air superiority and its impact on the Panzer divisions' operational capabilities, while Von Rundstedt was seeking to regain the initiative through the concentration of forces and a major offensive. It is worth noting that both men were right in their view; as the Ardennes offensive of December 1944 was to show, only a concentration of forces that managed to seek out a *Schwerpunkt* against the weaker enemy positions could generate a breakthrough that might eventually lead to the surrounding and destruction of enemy forces and the regaining of the initiative.

LEFT: The German *S-mine*, known as the the *Schrapnellmine* 35 (S.Mi.35). When used as a booby trap it could be fitted with the S.Mi.Z. 35 pressure fuse (B1); Z.Z. 35 pull fuse (B2); a Y-shaped fitting holding two Z.Z. 35 pull fuses (B3); three-way adapter with an S.Mi.Z. 35 fuse in the centre between two Z.Z. 35 fuses (B4); or the Z.u.Z.Z. 35 pull-release fuse. Regardless of the means of activation, after a 3.9-second delay the inner case was projected 1–3m into the air to detonate, blasting 360 ball bearings to a radius of over 150m. The component parts illustrated are:

(5) Detonator well plug (x3)
(6) TNT detonating charge
(7) Steel ball bearings
(8) Detonating fuse well
(9) Filler plug
(10) Inner casing
(11) Detonator wells and detonators (x3)
(12) Outer canister
(13) 0.4- to 1.4-second delay pellets (x3)
(14) 4.5-second main delay pellet
(15) Black powder expelling charge
(Peter Dennis © Osprey Publishing)

DOCTRINE AND TRAINING

There was no major change in German armour doctrine in the closing years of the war, only adaptations to the terrain and to new weapons and equipment. In 1943 the Panzer regiment, or sometimes the Panzer battalion, was the leading unit around which the main battlegroup was built. In the closing stages of the war, many divisions were able to create fully armoured battlegroups that included elements of Panzer, Panzergrenadier, pioneer, *Panzerjäger*, artillery and other support units. It was employed like a miniature Panzer division, following the same rules of armoured doctrine; Panzer units led the way, breaking through theenemy defences, and were closely supported by self-propelled artillery, while follow-up infantry, supported by *Panzerjäger* and pioneer units, secured the area and defended the flanks of the armoured drive. Although it remained in use until 1945, this doctrine underwent several changes caused by new factors encountered on the battle front.

Looking eastwards, there were the new tactics of the Red Army, based on the creation of an anti-tank defence screen to meet German armoured counterattacks; since Panzer units could no longer afford huge losses, the infantry was now required to deal directly with the anti-tank screen while the Panzers manoeuvred against the enemy spearheads, often with the support of the Panzer reconnaissance battalion. This was now rarely used in its traditional reconnaissance role and, because of its organization, was instead used as a regular combat unit. Another decisive factor was Allied air superiority and firepower, which had a considerable impact on German armoured doctrine. While on the Eastern Front it was still possible to group large numbers of forces, in Italy (where Allied naval support was so deadly) and in North-West Europe this was no longer possible, since these large groups would have fallen prey to enemy air forces and artillery. Therefore, the Panzer units no longer spearheaded the leading battlegroup, but were rather split into smaller, company-sized units and used to support the Panzergrenadier and the Panzer reconnaissance units. The battlegroup became smaller, and doctrine returned to infiltration tactics, aimed at achieving modest breakthroughs followed by swift advances. The most logical consequence of this change was smaller, no longer decisive, breakthroughs that had little impact.

From 1943 onwards, both the Panzer corps and the Panzer army were armoured only in name. They turned into a mixture of armoured and non-armoured units which, though well-suited to defence, lacked the necessary make-up for major offensive actions. The need for closer co-operation between the Panzer divisions and the others, imposed by defensive needs, added further limitations to the former. The battle for Normandy offers a perfect example; in spite of the concentration of armoured forces achieved in the area, hardly any Panzer divisions were grouped together to launch a major counterattack; indeed, since the lack of forces led to their deployment on the front line, they were

OVERLEAF: The German vehicle in the background here is the *Elefant* tank-destroyer. Rushed into production in 1943, their performance at the battle of Kursk was unpromising, and many of the vehicles were sent to Italy, where they continued to suffer from breakdowns and a lack of spare parts.

The German defeat of the British airborne landings at Arnhem proved that the Wehrmacht and *Waffen-SS* were still forces to be reckoned with. Here British POWs hobble past a StuG III tank-destroyer of the 9th SS-Panzer Division *Hohenstaufen*.

denied the advantages of mobility and speed. Though still quite effective in defence, as the battles on the German border showed, the Panzer divisions had clearly lost the edge.

This was despite their increased firepower, which was greater than ever. Tiger tanks, discussed in more depth in the previous chapter, cost the Allies multiple AFVs for each Tiger destroyed. The new Panther tank, though slow to be delivered, provided Panzer units with a tank that greatly outmatched its Allied counterparts and dealt with the Soviet equivalents on a even footing. Even anti-tank defences were improved thanks to new hand-held anti-tank weapons like the *Panzerschreck* and the *Panzerfaust* and to the new *Jagdpanzer*, which replaced the old *Panzerjäger* with an all-round, heavily armoured gun carrier. The latter eventually brought about changes in German doctrine; turretless, self-propelled gun carriers like the *Sturmgeschütz* and the new *Jagdpanzer* became offensive weapons, though they now required closer co-operation with the infantry. However, due to enemy air superiority movement was now mainly confined to night-time or favourable weather, and anti-aircraft artillery (often self-propelled) was also required at every level – the presence of which further limited the divisions' speed and mobility.

Offsetting the improvements in Panzer firepower, however, was the fact that during the last two years of war the Panzer divisions also faced a major training crisis. The heavy personnel losses of the previous years, plus those suffered during the summer of 1944, could only partly be made good using newly recruited personnel, and when this did happen divisional and unit commanders discovered that replacements needed a lot of additional training before joining their experienced, battle-hardened comrades in arms. The *Feld Ersatz Bataillon* (the divisional field replacement battalion) allowed replacements to complete their training along with personnel from the division; this not only refined their skills (for example in the use of heavy weapons and of artillery), but also helped the recruits to acquaint themselves with battlefront conditions. Technical training required by Panzer, reconnaissance and pioneer units, on the other hand, meant that these units were sent back to Germany to refit and reorganize. Moreover, in 1944–45 the Germans faced serious problems due to a shortage of trained officers and NCOs, which could only be made good by promoting from the ranks. The situation became particularly troublesome

The scene here shows German paratroopers of the 3rd Parachute Regiment defending Cassino from within the ruins of the Continental Hotel. A PzKpfw IV tank was backed into the hotel's reception area and machine guns and mortars emplaced to cover every approach. The paratroopers here are manning an MG 34 machine gun, with an NCO acquiring targets through his binoculars. All of them are wearing the second pattern camouflaged jump smock with a silver Luftwaffe eagle on the right breast. (Howard Gerrard © Osprey Publishing)

THE PANTHER TANK

Design of the PzKpfw V Panther tank began in 1941, after the Germans had the shock of encountering the T-34 on the Eastern Front. Maschinenfabrik Augsburg-Nürnberg AG (MAN AG) sought to create a tank with battlefield superiority, and to a large extent they succeeded. Heavily armoured but with a max speed of 55km/h, the Panther was armed with a 7.5cm Rheinmetall-Borsig KwK 42 (L/70) gun that actually delivered more penetrative power than the Tiger's 8.8cm main armament. Its wide tracks gave it good performance across soft ground, and its slender hull shape made it a challenging target for enemy gunners to acquire. The Panther was, however, thrown into battle too early, and its appearance at the battle of Kursk in July 1943 was plagued by mechanical breakdowns and combat losses. A weak drive system was never entirely remedied, but steady improvements made it arguably the best tank of the war, of which about 6,000 were produced. Its ultimate undoing came more from Allied air superiority and the declining standards of Panzer crew training, rather than threats from enemy armour.

during the last, major reorganization in autumn 1944, in spite of the overall, dramatic, reduction in strength imposed by the new tables of organization.

All these problems notwithstanding, it is worth noting that even during the difficult last year of war the Panzer divisions performed well, often better than their *Waffen-SS* counterparts, and – as the Ardennes offensive was eventually to show – they still could achieve some decisive results.

PANZER ORGANIZATION, 1943–44

An order of the German OKH of 24 September 1943 introduced a common organization structure for all the Panzer divisions (with the exception of the 21st Panzer and Panzer Division *Norwegen*) which, minor variations apart, matched that already introduced in June for the Panzer divisions taking part in Operation *Zitadelle* on the Eastern Front. It was in practice a mere acknowledgement of the status quo, since no overall reorganization was possible due to the lack of men and equipment; nonetheless, on 1 November 1943 a new series of war establishment charts (KStN) were issued for the '1943 Panzer Division' organization. This was to have a total strength of 16,385 all ranks armed with 10,808 rifles, 1,818 submachine guns, 695 light and 103 heavy machine guns, 36 medium and 14 heavy mortars, 25 anti-tank guns plus 174 *Panzerschreck*, 25 field and four infantry guns and howitzers, eight 8.8cm and 38 2cm anti-aircraft guns (self-propelled ones not included), 771 cars, 1,946 lorries, 226 non-armoured half-tracks, 662 motorcycles, 215 tanks (of which 99 were Panther tanks and 98 PzKpfw IV), 45 *Panzerjäger* and 405 AFVs, including 37 self-propelled guns of all types, 39 half-track mounted Flak guns, almost 300 armoured half-tracks (233 SdKfz 251 and 64 SdKfz 250) and 32 armoured cars. In practice not a single division in the field matched its paper establishment, chiefly because most of the PzKpfw V Panther-equipped Panzer battalions were still forming.

Also foreseeing the availability of new weapons, on 1 April 1944 the new '1944 Panzer Division' organization was thus introduced, though the KStN were still being issued in July. In fact, between April and May 1944 several Panzer divisions were meant to be reorganized, but only a few of them actually completed the process before being committed to the front. On 3 August 1944, all divisions (except 21st Panzer and *Panzer Lehr* Division) were ordered to begin reorganizing using available equipment and personnel, while reporting on their status to allow for the issue of needed weapons and replacements.

Overall organization of the '1944 Panzer Division' still matched that of the 1943 version, and changes mainly took place at regimental and battalion level. First and foremost the new *freie Gliederung* (free organization) was introduced, which saw the creation for every battalion of a *Versorgungs Kompanie* (supply company) from the supply units and trains of every company. Since the commander of the supply company was also deputy battalion commander, the new organization enabled the latter to focus exclusively on combat duties, while the former took exclusive care of any logistical and administrative needs.

Other changes affected overall strength and equipment; most notably, infantry units lost their many anti-tank platoons, while heavy mortar and flamethrower platoons were introduced. The overall strength of the 1944 Panzer Division was 14,053 with 9,103 rifles, 1,637 SMGs, 768 light and 98 heavy MGs, 16 medium and 18 heavy mortars, 13 anti-tank guns and nine *Panzerschreck*, 25 field guns and howitzers, eight 8.8cm,

A PzKpfw IV heads towards the Normandy invasion beaches in June 1944. Note the spare track links and wheels on the front of the tank. Not only did these provide replacements for battle-damaged items, but they also added a layer of improvised armour to the front of the tank.

ABOVE: These figures are based on photographs of Wehrmacht troops fighting in central and northern Italy in 1944–45. They are: 1) *Obergefreiter*, 25th *Jäger* Regiment, Gothic Line, September 1944; 2) *Unteroffizier, Reichsgrenadier Regiment Hoch- und Deutschmeister* (High and German Leaders), Gustav Line, February 1944; 3) *Stabsfeldwebel*, 26th Panzer Reconnaissance Battalion, River Po, April 1945. (Stephen Andrew © Osprey Publishing)

36 2cm and six 3.7m Flak guns, 303 cars, 852 lorries, 95 half-tracks and 171 motorcycles plus 179 tanks (79 Panther, 81 PzKpfw IV, eight Flakpanzer and 11 command and recovery tanks), 31 *Panzerjäger* and 372 AFVs, including 16 half-track mounted Flak guns, 36 gun carriers, about 300 armoured half-tracks and 16 armoured cars, all heavy.

Even such a noticeable reduction failed to close the growing gap between availability and need, further exacerbated by the heavy losses suffered during the summer, and the overall lack of manpower and equipment. Therefore, on 1 November 1944 new KStN were issued, leading to the late 1944 Panzer division organization, which only affected Panzer and Panzergrenadier regiments plus the Panzer reconnaissance and *Panzerjäger* battalions. The overall strength now dropped to 13,067 with 8,719 rifles and 270 *Sturmgewehr* 44,

In North-West Europe, an American infantryman rushes a PzKw IV Ausf. H tank with a 20lb M1 satchel charge approaching from the direction of a blind spot. He would likely place the charge into the tracks, on the engine compartment or under the turret ring. (Steve Noon © Osprey Publishing)

On 12 September 1943, an elite force of German paratroopers rescued the deposed Italian dictator, Benito Mussolini, from a guarded hotel on the Gran Sasso mountain. The operation was dramatic and of great publicity value. This photograph shows two of the men involved.

1,527 SMGs, 574 light and 32 heavy machine guns, 12 medium and 18 heavy mortars, 13 anti-tank guns plus 96 *Panzerschreck*, 25 field howitzers and guns, eight 8.8cm plus 36 2cm and six 3.7cm Flak guns, 601 cars, 1,469 lorries, 201 half-tracks, 529 motorcycles, 160 tanks (including eight *Flakpanzer*, 67 Panther, 69 PzKpfw IV and nine recovery), 21 *Panzerjäger* and 366 AFVs, including 16 self-propelled Flak, 36 guns of all types, about 300 armoured half-tracks and 15 armoured cars.

PANZERGRENADIER ORGANIZATION 1943–44

In spite of the worsening situation, in 1943–44 Panzergrenadier units were better armed, motorized and equipped than ever before. According to the 1943 Panzer division establishment, a *Panzergrenadier Regiment gepanzert* (armoured infantry regiment) included an HQ and HQ company with a reconnaissance, a flamethrower, a *Panzerjäger* and a communications platoon, two Panzergrenadier battalions plus one regimental anti-aircraft company, one heavy infantry gun company, and one Panzergrenadier pioneer company.

Both Panzergrenadier battalions had considerable strength; in November 1943 an armoured Panzergrenadier battalion included three armoured companies plus a heavy company with two gun and one Panzerjäger platoons. A single Panzergrenadier company had three platoons and a fourth heavy platoon, the latter including two HMG groups and a rocket and a cannon group. The total strength of the Panzergrenadier battalion was 928 personnel, 552 rifles, 208 submachine guns (including those aboard the AFVs), 57 light and 12 heavy machine guns (excluding AFVs mounted ones), 39 *Panzerschreck*, two light infantry guns, three PaK anti-tank guns, 16 cars, 44 lorries, six non-armoured and 91 armoured half-tracks and 30 motorcycles. The motorized Panzergrenadier battalion, though stronger, was less mobile and had reduced firepower; it had just over 900 personnel, 579 rifles, 96 submachine guns, 59 light and 21 heavy machine guns, 39 *Panzerschreck*, three PAK, six 81mm and four 120mm mortars, 52 cars, 81 lorries, nine half-tracks and 24 motorcycles.

The striking differences between armoured and motorized Panzergrenadier battalions eventually supplied the Panzer divisions with two quite different infantry units,

GERMAN ASSAULT RIFLES

Germany had no equivalent for the American Garand M1 semi-automatic rifle, and seemed to have little interest in the development of an assault rifle until they met the Russian Tokarev in 1941. The first German equivalent to appear was the 41W/Gew 41/41 M range of weapons. The 41 W rifle (3a), designed by Walther, was a semi-automatic rifle that used the muzzle blast to operate the mechanism via a rod mounted on the top of the barrel. It was chambered for the standard German service calibre 7.92mm round, but was both heavy (4.65kg) and clumsy. The second design, the 41 M by Mauser, later became the *Gewehr* 43 or Kar 43 (3b). This weapon was again chambered for the full-size German service cartridge, but weighed only 4.03kg. It had a 10-round detachable magazine, and was very similar to the Russian Tokarev weapon – the design was good, although manufacture was crude. It could also be fitted with a telescopic sight for sniper use. The true assault rifle emerged in the MP 43 and MP 44 weapons, which were designed to fire the short 7.92 × 33mm intermediate military cartridge, rather than the more powerful 7.92 × 57mm fired by standard German infantry weapons. The short cartridge had the advantage that the weapon firing it, although having a reduced effective range, could be fired on full-auto but the user could maintain a controlled aim during such firing. Also known as the StG 44 (for *Sturmgewehr* – assault rifle), the MP 44 was a very effective short- to medium-range weapon, and the lighter cartridge meant that users could carry more ammunition, which was fed via 30-round pressed steel magazines. One disadvantage of the long magazine was that firing in the prone position was difficult. The rifle was, almost certainly, the precursor of the Kalashnikov AK47.

with the armoured Panzergrenadier regiment being stronger and also better suited to keeping up with the Panzer regiment. This would not last for long, however, since the new '1944 Panzer Division' organization brought some changes to both structure and strength. First of all, every heavy platoon of the Panzergrenadier company lost one HMG group, the remaining one being replaced by an anti-aircraft and machine-gun group; also, the heavy company was now down to the heavy rocket and cannon platoon. Total strength of the Panzergrenadier companies shrank to three officers, 36 NCOs, 151 other ranks, 94 rifles, 44 MPs, 18 LMGs, two cars, four motorcycles and a total of 23 SdKfz 251 of various kinds. The armoured Panzergrenadier battalion now had 841 personnel,

ABOVE: These soldiers represent patterns of uniforms worn during the campaign on the Western Front in 1944. The grenadier battalion commander (left) and Panzergrenadier (right) wear tops made from *Zeltbahn* 31 camouflage, while the anti-aircraft *Leutnant* (centre) has the M1940 summer field tunic. (Stephen Andrew © Osprey Publishing)

444 rifles, 173 SMGs, 58 light and nine heavy machine guns, four 120mm mortars, 17 cars, 30 lorries, 24 motorcycles and six non-armoured plus 101 armoured half-tracks.

Worst of all, a lack of weapons, vehicles and equipment greatly hampered the reorganization of those armoured Panzergrenadier units, and the creation of any new ones. Given also a widespread lack of motor vehicles, on 1 November 1944 a new organization was developed that not only reduced overall strength, but also envisaged the creation of the new bicycle-mounted (*Fahrrad bewegliche*) Panzergrenadier company which, though desperately lacking motorization (it only had one car and one motorcycle), was comparatively better armed since its first platoon was now turned into an assault platoon completely armed with the MP 44, the new assault rifle. Its strength was three officers, 17 NCOs and 120 other ranks, and it had 67 rifles plus 37 MP44s, 15 SMGs, 12 LMGs and three *Panzerschreck*.

Though lacking the mobility and firepower of the armoured version, the motorized Panzergrenadier regiment was a more common occurrence and also a kind of unit that would better suit the Panzer divisions' tactical needs when fighting in defence. Though overall organization matched that of its armoured parent, the heavy company

German troops occupy a series of shallow slit trenches around Arnhem in 1944. The defensive positions are mainly a series of *Schützenloch* (firing holes), relatively shallow two-man trenches, although a one-man *Russenloch* (Russian hole) is seen at the front.

of its Panzergrenadier battalion only had one *Panzerjäger* and one rocket platoon. Losses and overall lack of weapons, equipment and vehicles, however, also affected the organization of the these battalions; the '1944 Panzer Division' organization brought about, in the same manner as the armoured one, the disappearance of PaK units and to the creation of the supply company, plus an overall reduction in strength. The new organization of 1 November 1944 brought further changes, including the introduction of one assault platoon in every Panzergrenadier company, which now had three officers, 18 NCOs, 105 other ranks, 60 rifles plus 30 *Sturmgewehre*, 21 MPs, 12 light MGs, three *Panzerschreck*, one car, eight lorries and three motorcycles. As a consequence, the overall strength of the motorized Panzergrenadier battalion changed between 1 April and 1 November from 20 to 21 officers, 148 to 117 NCOs, 697 to 506 other ranks, 548 to 382 rifles (plus 90 MP 44 in November), 91 to 86 SMGs, 60 to 41 light machine guns, 12 to none heavy machine guns, none to 12 *Panzerschreck*, 50 to 24 cars, 75 to 62 lorries, 17 to 12 tracked or half-tracked vehicles, 25 to 21 motorcycles (the allowance of six towed 2cm Flak 38 and four heavy 12cm mortars was unchanged). In one year, the overall strength of the motorized Panzergrenadier regiment had dropped from 2,513 all ranks in November 1943 to 2,258 in April and eventually to 1,747 in November 1944, which clearly influenced the fighting power of the Panzer division.

ARTILLERY

The 1943 Panzer artillery regiment granted the Panzer divisions a greater allowance of firepower than when its 1st battalion was reorganized as a self-propelled, mixed light and heavy howitzer unit. The regimental HQ battery included, other than a communications platoon, a weapons maintenance and a medical section, while the HQ battery of every single battalion included a communications platoon, a light anti-aircraft troop with three towed 2cm Flak 38 guns, plus an artillery calibration detachment, supply and trains. Each battalion was made up of three batteries, each having either six (in the self-propelled units) or four guns in two *Geschütz Staffeln* (artillery squadrons); the second battalion was equipped entirely with the 10.5cm *leichte Feldhaubitze* 18 while the third one was equipped with four 10.5cm *Kanone* 18 in the first battery plus eight 15cm *schwere Feldhaubitze* 18 in the second and third. The first, self-propelled field howitzer battalion provided fully mobile, heavy firepower thanks to its 12 10.5cm armed *Wespe* (wasp) and its six 150mm *Hummel* (bumble bee) guns mounted either on PzKpfw II or IV chassis which, along with the accompanying *Befehl und Panzer Beobachtung* (command and armoured observation) tanks and AFVs, was perfectly capable not only of keeping up with all the armoured units of the division, but also of providing closer and more accurate fire support.

LEFT: German officers in Italy, 1944. The German campaign in Italy cost the Allies about 320,000 casualties in total, a severe price. On balance, however, German casualties were twice that figure, and included about 50,000 dead, largely the product of the Allies' superiority in artillery and air power.

German soldiers get to grips with the French 3.7cm Pateux gun. The Wehrmacht utilized huge numbers of captured foreign weapons. Although this sounds like common sense, in fact it complicated an already overworked system of logistics, particularly in terms of supplying all the various calibres in the field.

The reorganization that followed the introduction of the '1944 Panzer Division' organization brought some strengths reduction and a few changes; the first artillery battalion shrank from 135 to 129 NCOs and from 413 to 365 other ranks. The second battalion, though maintaining its 12 *leichte Feldhaubitze* 18, was reorganized into two six-gun batteries, thus resulting in an even greater reduction of personnel; its 17 officers shrank to 15, its 107 NCOs to 89 and its 361 other ranks to 267. The third battalion, on the other hand, only saw a reduction to its other ranks, down to 344 in 1944. All in all, the Panzer artillery regiment was one of the few units to suffer less from the reorganization, as is shown by its vehicle allowance which mainly saw a reduction in the number of lorries from 227 to 167, while half-tracked, non-combat vehicles reduced from 31 to 28. There was no further reorganization in November 1944.

ANTI-TANK WARFARE

By June 1944, the Wehrmacht was faced with fighting enemies who could field far more tanks and AFVs than Germany could possibly produce. As already noted, therefore, anti-tank warfare became increasingly important in the defensive duties of the German Army. During the later years of the war, furthermore, the Wehrmacht utilized a new range of hand-held anti-weapons that cumulatively had a significant battlefield effect.

The *Panzerwurfmine* 1 (Anti-armour Thrown Mine type 1), for example, was a 1.35kg hand-thrown hollow-charge mine issued in 1944. It consisted of a hemispherical-nosed warhead with a long tailboom and four folding cloth vanes. When it was thrown, the igniter was armed and vanes opened like an umbrella to stabilize the mine. Its range was about 20m and it was considered to be quite effective – penetrating 80–100mm of armour – but somewhat unsafe to handle.

The 8.8cm *Raketenwerfer* 43 (Rocket Launcher 1943) or *Püppchen* ('Dolly'), by contrast, looked like a small artillery piece, a breech-loading tube on two wheels. Its high-explosive anti-tank rocket was effective to 200m against moving targets and up to 350m for stationary targets, to penetrate 160mm. The weapon was not recoilless and there was no back-blast. It was expensive to make, and insufficiently portable for infantrymen, its 149kg weight being broken down into seven sections for man-packing.

Captured American 2.36in M1 bazookas led to a new design, the 8.8cm *Raketenpanzerbüchse* 43 (RPzB 43; Rocket Tank Rifle), also known as the *Panzerschreck* (armour terror) or *Ofenrohr* (stovepipe). This electrically fired shoulder weapon was 1638mm long and weighed 9.5kg; it used the same 8.8cm warhead as the *Püppchen*, but with a redesigned motor, and had a range of about 150m. The *Panzerschreck* was highly portable, low cost, and could be produced rapidly in large numbers. The almost identical RPzB 54 was produced in 1944; this weighed 11kg because an added shield protected the gunner from muzzle blow-back. Only a small number were produced before the RPzB 54/1 appeared, and with its weight reduced to the former 9.5kg it could fire an improved rocket to around 165m. This was the most common model of the almost 290,000 models produced. (The RPzB 43 could not fire the new rocket, and was reissued to second-line units.) Regimental anti-tank gun companies were replaced by *Panzerzerstörer* (armour destroyer) companies with up to 54 *Panzerschreck* in three platoons, each with 18 launchers in three squads. Some companies retained a platoon with three 7.5cm guns.

The *Panzerfaust* is the best known of the new German anti-armour weapons, and was genuinely revolutionary. The 'Faust' was actually a single-shot recoilless gun launching a fin-stabilized shaped charge warhead with a propellant cartridge. It consisted of a steel tube, just under a metre long and of 44mm bore. An over-calibre shaped-charge warhead was fitted to the muzzle. It was held under the arm or over the shoulder, and fired by a percussion igniter, which was exposed to the rocking trigger when the gunner flipped up a folding sight on top of the tube. Looking through one of three apertures in the latter, he lined up a barleycorn sight on the top edge of the warhead with the target. Once fired, the non-reloadable tube was discarded.

The first *Panzerfaust klein* model, issued in July 1943 (aka *Panzerfaust* 1, or *Gretchen* – 'Peggy'), had a 100mm diameter warhead, weighed 1.5kg and penetrated 140mm of armour

at 30m. The *Panzerfaust 30 gross* followed immediately; it had the same range, but it and subsequent models employed a 3kg 150mm warhead capable of penetrating 200mm at an impact angle of 30 degrees. The *gross* weighed 5.22kg in total. This and subsequent models were designated by their effective range in metres, and had progressively larger propellant charges. The 6.6kg *Panzerfaust 60* was introduced in the summer of 1944; with the same warhead and twice the range, it saw the widest use. In September 1944 the *Panzerfaust 100* appeared, weighing the same as the 60. More advanced models were under development when the war ended.

More than eight million *Panzerfauste* of all models were produced. While short-ranged, they were effective weapons, mainly because of the sheer numbers available. They had no specialist crews, but were issued to individuals just like grenades; indeed, in the closing months of the war German propaganda made much of the fact that Hitler Youth teenagers, old *Volkssturm* home guardsmen, and even housewives could be trained to use them. Allocation to infantry divisions was 36 per rifle and pioneer company, 18 per anti-tank company and other company-size units and 12 per artillery battery.

Although such weapons were not capable in themselves of stopping the armoured forces of the Soviet Union and United States, combined with other anti-tank weapons and sound doctrine they did make life hard for the advancing Allies. German anti-armour doctrine called for all units including rear services to prepare for tank defence by emplacing anti-tank weapons to cover likely avenues of approach, to tie tank-proof terrain into the defensive plan and to provide for early warning – a function of reconnaissance units and infantry outposts. Terrain was classified as *Panzerschier* (armour-proof) – impassable to AFVs; *Panzergefährdet* (armour-risk) – difficult for AFVs; or *Panzermöglich* (armour-feasible) – passable to armour. This determination was made by map and ground reconnaissance. Armour-proof terrain included dense forest, swampland, deep mud, numerous large rocks and gullies, steep slopes, railroad embankments or cuttings.

Anti-tank guns were well dug in and concealed, positioned in twos and threes, and emplaced in depth throughout the regimental defensive sector. Selected single guns might begin picking off tanks at maximum range, but most held their fire until the target was within 300 to 150m range. Close-combat teams attacked tanks that reached the German battle positions. Once a tank attack was repulsed the guns moved to alternative positions.

The Germans learned that the massive effort expended in laying vast minefields was wasted, since they were so easily breached. They mainly laid small delaying minefields on routes and within their positions to knock out marauding tanks. Anti-tank ditches were no longer dug well forward of the frontline because they provided enemy infantry with jump-off cover; they were now dug immediately in front of fighting positions. The *Panzerabwehrgeschutz* (armour defence centre of resistance) was established on the suspected tank approach route, where weapons were concentrated.

LEFT: A US soldier inspects a captured 8.8cm *Raketenwerfer* 43 – also known as the *Püppchen* (Dolly) – recoilless anti-tank rocket launcher. The *Raketenwerfer* fired a fin-stabilized, shaped-charge missile over a range of about 350m. Only about 3,000 were manufactured.

Panzerjagdgruppe (tank-hunter teams) consisted of an NCO and at least three men well trained in anti-tank close-combat techniques and equipped with weapons to 'blind, halt and destroy'. Such teams were employed only as a last resort, when there were no

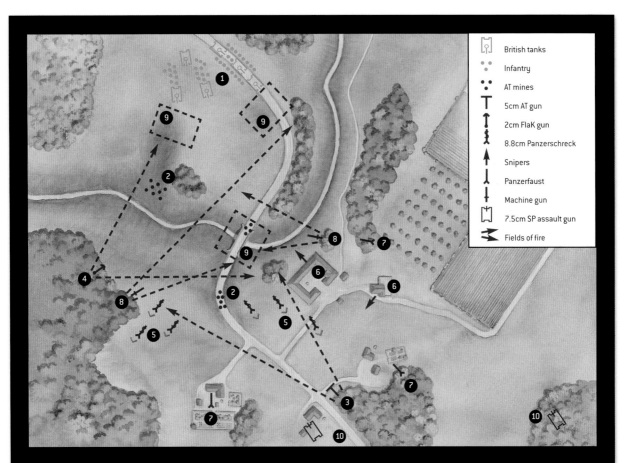

British tanks	
Infantry	
AT mines	
5cm AT gun	
2cm FlaK gun	
8.8cm Panzerschreck	
Snipers	
Panzerfaust	
Machine gun	
7.5cm SP assault gun	
Fields of fire	

German *Panzerkampfgruppe* in a covering position, 1944–45. The mission of this small armour battlegroup is to delay the approach of British tanks (1) on a secondary route into a defended village. Point anti-tank minefields were laid at chokepoints (2), intermingled with anti-personnel mines. The few anti-tank guns available at this date were often employed singly, like this 5cm PaK 38 (3), rather than in larger groups; 2cm FlaK guns were positioned on flanks (4) to help make up for the lack of anti-tank guns. A single squad with six 8.8cm RP54 *Panzerschreck* have taken up positions in a typical pattern (5). While there are farm buildings in the area, only a few snipers occupy them (6); buildings attracted suppressive fire and allowed the enemy to pinpoint German positions quickly. Scattered pairs of grenadiers hide on tank routes armed with a few *Panzerfauste*, ready to engage tanks that might slip through (7). With rifle strength reduced in many grenadier units, higher allocations of MG 34 and MG 42 machine guns (8) were made to increase firepower. As the enemy approached the position, 8cm and 12cm mortars from the main battle position would fire on pre-registered barrage areas (9). Assault guns (10) might be positioned to the rear, usually dug-in or hidden in buildings to further deter the advance. (Steve Noon © Osprey Publishing)

A *Waffen-SS* soldier armed with a *Panzerfaust* anti-tank weapon keeps watch for Allied aircraft on the Western Front. The limited range of the *Panzerfaust* – about 30m – meant that it required a good deal of courage to use effectively, especially if enemy infantry were present.

anti-tank guns operational or a position had been overrun. Machine guns and mortars concentrated on separating enemy infantry from their tanks. Small-arms were directed against tank vision ports, and the team moved under cover of smoke grenades. If possible they would lie in wait for the tank to come within 20m before attacking. After *Panzerfauste* became available, they were the preferred method of attack, fired in barrages from multiple directions. Tank-hunter teams would move in close and attack from the rear or sides. Close-range ambushes were set up in woodland and built-up areas. Riflemen covering the close-in attacker would cease fire if it hampered him, but be prepared to fire if the crew opened a hatch to defend the tank. Once a tank was disabled and captured, its gun breechblocks would be removed and the tank set on fire.

In 1943, the Germans in Russia developed the *Pakfront* (armour defence gun front). This was an extension of the idea of emplacing anti-tank guns behind the forward positions to engage tanks after they broke through, when their fighting formations were less organized and they might be separated from their supporting infantry; Soviet tanks often broke through in large numbers. The concept was for the divisional anti-tank battalion (corps and army level battalions were also employed) to position six to ten or more well dug-in and concealed 7.5cm guns under a single commander, on favourable terrain blocking the main tank routes. Their towing vehicles were hidden close by, ready to relocate or withdraw the guns quickly. In effect, the *Pakfront* ambushed tanks at short range, with all guns opening fire simultaneously. Artillery and rocket projectors supported the *Pakfront* while available reserves and armour moved into a counterattack.

In spite of its ever-growing importance, the anti-tank unit was to suffer the most from the reorganizations of the Panzer divisions in 1943–44. In November 1943 it was still organized as earlier in the same year, with three self-propelled *Panzerjäger* companies equipped with a total of 45 Marder II or III tank destroyers supported by three self-propelled 2cm anti-aircraft guns in the light anti-aircraft platoon, attached to the HQ company. Following the introduction of the '1944 Panzer Division' organization, the *Panzerjäger* battalion was left with only two self-propelled *Panzerjäger* companies while the third one reverted to the old *motorisiert Zugkraftwagen* (motor towed) organization, leaving it with 31 self-propelled tank-hunter AFVs plus 12 towed 7.5cm PaK guns. In the meantime, all the PaK guns had been withdrawn from every other divisional unit, which produced an imbalance of a dozen anti-tank guns within the division, with the total shrinking from 24 to 12, the latter all in the *Panzerjäger* battalions. Since the new KStN did not list the availability of *Panzerschreck* (they were back with those from 1 November 1944, bringing the total from 174 in November 1943 to the actual figure of 93), apparently the Panzer division lost a good deal of its anti-tank capability, which could only be partly made good by the widespread diffusion of the portable *Panzerfaust*. The situation worsened in November 1944, since not only was one *Panzerjäger* dropped from every platoon, but also the HQ, no longer with an HQ company, was reduced down to a single one, thus bringing the grand total to 21 self-propelled guns. Such reorganizations did not help an army fighting for its survival against heavily armoured forces.

An 15cm howitzer opens up at Monte Cassino in March 1944, fired when the gunner pulls on the visible lanyard. Such guns formed the heavy end of German Army divisional artillery. High artillery observation positions around Cassino allowed the Germans to put down highly accurate fire on the Allies.

ORGANIZATION TODT

As we shall see in the following chapter, in the final days of the Third Reich the Wehrmacht came to rely increasingly on various civilian and paramilitary support units to fulfil a variety of tasks from engineering work through to actual combat duties. One significant organization, dating back to before the war, was the *Organization Todt* (OT), which had a particularly integral relationship to the German defences on the Western Front.

On 28 May 1938 Hitler ordered Fritz Todt, since June 1933 the Inspector-General of German Roads, to build a line of 5,000 concrete blockhouses along the border with the Netherlands, Belgium, Luxembourg and France – the Westwall. Completion date was to be 1 October 1938, in time to repel a French attack in response to Hitler's planned invasion of Czechoslovakia. From 22 June 1938, Todt mobilized 1,000 private construction firms, and organized them in 22 brigade-status *Oberbauleitungen* formations. In a speech on 18 July, Hitler christened them *Organization Todt.*

The French attack never materialized; and by late November 340,000 OT personnel, 90,000 Army engineers and 300 *Reichsarbeitsdienst* (RAD; Reich Labour Service) companies were engaged on the Westwall, with 9,000 railway waggons, 96,000 lorries and 4,100 Postal Service buses transporting workers and materials (the project used 51 per cent of the cement industry's annual production), co-ordinated from the OT HQ in Wiesbaden. Work continued until the French surrender in June 1940.

On 9 December 1938, Todt was appointed Commissioner-General of Construction Industries, and on 4 September 1939 he declared that the OT would function in wartime as a fortress construction organization, employing building firms organized on military lines, with Xaver Dorsch as operational commander. Some 40,000 OT personnel served in Poland in *Strassenbautrupps* (road construction troops) and *Brückenbautrupps* (bridge construction companies), repairing and upgrading communications damaged in the fighting. The OT also cleared sites and built administrative and living quarters for the German occupation forces, using Jewish battalions recruited by Polish Jewish Councils.

On 7 March 1940, Todt gained more power by being appointed Reichsminister for Armament and Munitions. For the seven-week Western campaign, *Westwall Oberbauleitungen* were reformed as *Frontoberbauleitungen* (mobile front units) and assigned to Field Army Engineer Staffs. The 13,500 *Frontarbeiter* (front workers) in the eight units under Army Group A built 324 bridges and repaired 3,000km of roads in northern France, hiring 1,600 French labourers (at three Reichsmarks a day). The 8,650 personnel in the five units under Army Group C in eastern France built 157 bridges, often under fire from guns on the Maginot Line, and replaced road signs destroyed by retreating French troops.

The OT was mainly active in the occupied territories, responsible for all construction projects behind the front line, and, from August 1943, also in combat zones. Members

A coastal artillery battery of the Atlantic Wall, manned by the *Organization Todt* personnel. German coastal guns went from diminutive 3.7cm anti-aircraft weapons up to massive 40.6cm monsters mounted in concrete casemates, and with ranges in excess of 54km.

were designated 'armed forces auxiliaries' until November 1942 when they were granted full armed forces status.

On 8 February 1942, Todt died mysteriously in a flying accident; and the architect and confidant of Hitler, Albert Speer, assumed Todt's duties. He made the OT directly responsible to Hitler, thus avoiding a take-over by the state trade union, the *Deutsche Arbeitsfront* (German Labour Front). On 19 August 1943, *Bautruppen* (army construction troops) were transferred to the engineers as *Baupioniere* (construction engineers) to avoid transfer to the OT; but Speer insisted that Field Army and army group staffs included an OT *Generalingenieur* (engineer-general), usually the local OT corps commander, to co-ordinate all construction projects.

OT organization remained very flexible; but in 1943 the largest unit was the corps-status *Einsatzgruppe*, under a *Leutnant* or *Generalmajor* controlling brigade-status *Oberbauleitungen*, 5,000–15,000 strong, each under an *Oberst* or *Oberstleutnant*, sometimes grouped into division-status *Einsatze*. An *Oberbauleitung* comprised regimental-status *Bauleitungen*, 3,000 strong, each under a *Oberstleutnant* or *Major*, with battalion status *Baustellen* (building sites) or *Lager* (camps) with about 1,000 men under a subaltern, sometimes grouped into *Abschnittsbauleitungen* (ABL). A *Baustelle* was divided into company-size troops, 150 strong, under a subaltern or later a senior NCO, with *Kameradschaften* (platoons) and *Rotten* (sections) under junior NCOs.

OT comprised German volunteer and conscript personnel plus civilian workers – employees of private companies on OT contracts. As men were drafted into the armed forces, the OT accepted older recruits; in March 1942 these were mainly 35–55-year-olds, from mid 1943 43–58-year-olds, from April 1944, 45-year-olds and above. To make good the deficiency in available manpower, ethnic Germans (mainly from Romania, Yugoslavia and Hungary), military detention camp inmates and civilian petty and political criminals

ABOVE: Three *Organization Todt* (OT) soldiers, seen in the typical uniforms issued between 1940 and 1944. From June 1938 OT personnel often wore civilian clothes, but in September 1939 NCOs and privates were issued with a brown uniform to indicate their military status. (Simon McCouaig © Osprey Publishing)

were conscripted; from mid 1943, women volunteers were accepted for signals and secretarial posts; and from April 1944, men with part-Jewish ancestry were also taken.

Foreigners joined the OT as volunteers, often to avoid deportation to Germany, service in army penal units, or, especially for Jews, imprisonment and death in a concentration camp. Employees of firms under OT contract, and from 1941 forced labourers, and from 1943 some Allied POWs, were transferred to OT command. Men of the 'Germanic nations' – Dutch, Danes, Flemish, Walloons, Finns, Norwegians and ethnic Germans – received German pay and conditions. Eastern Europeans were also used in large numbers, with Russians comprising the largest foreign group. In September 1942 Hitler decreed that menial tasks, such as carrying cement bags and breaking stones, should be carried out by foreigners, and indeed by 1944 most Germans in the OT were in supervisory positions.

OT strength reached its maximum in November 1944, with 1,360,000 members – 44,500 German and 12,800 foreign personnel, 4,000 German women, 313,000 Germans and 680,700 foreigners in contracted firms, 165,000 POWs, and 140,000 'petty criminals' (including Jews). Its duties had taken it to every theatre in the war, building fortifications, airfields, roads and *Atlantikwall* (Atlantic Wall) fortifications, laying railway lines, repairing bomb damage, and performing no end of engineer and labour projects. Often working under the shadow of the front line, this auxiliary Wehrmacht force contributed significantly to the offensive and defensive capabilities of the Wehrmacht.

The OT is an example of the extent to which the entire German population, and many foreign groups, became mobilized, serving the Third Reich. Yet regardless of how much the Wehrmacht reorganized its units and formations, or relied upon ad hoc manpower resources, by late 1944 the writing was on the wall. Hitler, beginning his final retreat into a fantasy world in which victory was still possible, commanded an army whose knees were buckling. And yet, as our last chapter will show, the German Army would still prove to be a stubborn foe for the Allies, fighting on even to the streets of Berlin itself.

LEFT: At Anzio/Nettuno, German artillery forces prepare to open fire on the Allied beachhead in 1944. The artillery piece is the 21cm Möres 18, a howitzer issued from 1936. It had an excellent dual recoil system that made it steady to fire, and it was accurate to 16km.

THE FINAL DEFEATS: RETREAT TO THE FATHERLAND, 1943–45

THE LAST TWO YEARS OF FIGHTING IN WORLD WAR II BROUGHT SCENES OF unimaginable trauma to Europe. As the Third Reich imploded, the Wehrmacht faced what had been unthinkable just a few years previously – fighting on the soil of Germany itself. On the Eastern Front in particular, the combat was frenzied, as the Germans strained to stop a vengeful Soviet Army descending on its towns and cities. Yet by this time locked in a two-front, with the equally powerful Allied forces bearing down from the West, the battle could only end in defeat.

The story of Hitler's forces during this period is one of collapse, destruction and eventual defeat. By late 1944 and 1945 the Wehrmacht no longer resembled the army of 1939 or 1940. The quality of German infantry formations had steadily declined as the war had progressed, due to the number of casualties suffered and the speed with which replacements were required. From 1943 onwards, an increasing proportion of the infantry were being recruited from the fringes of Germany itself, from people known as *Volksdeutsche*, or ethnic Germans. Many senior commanders were worried as to the fighting qualities of these troops, as even units raised within Germany itself contained increasing numbers of Alsatians, Poles and other ethnic minorities who might not be overly enthusiastic about dying for the Third Reich.

The German Panzer formations did not really suffer these problems to the same extent, but they were facing their own challenges with mobility, as there was an ever-growing shortage of fuel, made worse by the eventual loss of access to the Romanian and Hungarian oilfields. This also led to reductions in training, which would have an increasingly detrimental effect on the quality of the Panzer troops. While German troops were still, on the whole, better than their Soviet equivalents, the large qualitative advantage the Germans had enjoyed in the opening phases of the Russo-German conflict had been significantly eroded.

German tank production had increased significantly during 1943 and 1944, but it still lagged behind Soviet industrial output. Its war industry had remained one of Germany's major weaknesses, despite Albert Speer's 1943 reforms. Germany had certainly out-performed the Soviet Union in heavy industrial output before the war, the victories of 1939 and 1940 had brought a great deal of Europe's industrial capacity under German control and the 1941 invasion had deprived the Soviet Union of much of its industrial potential. Even so, Germany had failed to keep pace with the Soviet Union, partly due to the effects of the Allied bombing offensive, but also because most of the leadership did not fully understand the importance of the economy in fighting a modern industrialized war. Germany had not mobilized her industries for full war production until very late on. The huge attrition of manpower in World War I had given way to the equally huge attrition of material in this conflict, a challenge the Germans could not meet. This strategic blunder had become painfully obvious once

RIGHT: A PzKpfw V Panther rolls through the Ardennes forest during the German offensive there in the winter of 1944/45. Some 400 Panthers were assigned to the offensive, although not all were operational, but by 15 January only 98 remained in combat. Just under 200 in total were lost altogether.

the industrial powerhouse of the United States joined the conflict, and as the war had approached its closing stages.

As ever, though, the German forces proved obdurate to the last, and were still inflicting thousands of casualties on the Allies until the last shots were fired in Berlin. They were also capable of springing some surprises, as the offensive in the Ardennes proved in the winter of 1944/45. The story of the German Army's downfall, therefore, is one of many small victories within a massive overall defeat.

EASTERN FRONT

The turning point had come on 2 February 1943, when the Stalingrad garrison surrendered. From June 1941 to December 1941, and then from June to November 1942 in the Caucasus, the German army groups had advanced into the Soviet Union, employing the Panzer divisions and Luftwaffe bombers to penetrate Soviet lines and attack enemy command centres with *Blitzkrieg* tactics, and Panzer and infantry divisions to destroy the resultant pockets of by-passed Soviet troops in the 'decisive manoeuvre' tactic. This twin-track strategy required well-equipped, well-armed and well-supplied mobile forces enjoying tactical independence and room for manoeuvre; but by February 1943 all these advantages had been lost. Thereafter German divisions were defending fixed positions from which they were gradually dislodged by overwhelming Soviet superiority in weapons and manpower.

German advances in 1941–42 had been paid for by huge casualties, and by February 1943 the three-million-strong army had already been reduced to 2,300,000. Hitler insisted on reraising destroyed units, developing new types of divisions, and creating *Waffen-SS* and Luftwaffe formations, all of which competed for resources. The result was that the number of field divisions actually increased, but potential frontline troops were diverted into support units to complete divisional tables of organization, leaving existing divisions seriously under strength but still expected to accomplish their original missions. Regiments, nominally 3,000 strong, often fought at less than 30 per cent strength; huge losses of junior officers meant that the company, a *Hauptmann*'s command, was routinely led by an inexperienced *Oberleutnant* or *Leutnant*, and sometimes by an *Oberfeldwebel* or *Feldwebel* – who often survived only a few days in the role before being wounded or killed. Losses in tanks had been equally huge, and AFV production was easily outstripped by the vast Soviet industrial capability. German

LEFT: Eastern Front infantry of 1943/44. The greatcoat, snow camouflage suit and padded and reversible camouflage jacket seen on these figures are all of the M1942 pattern. The *Leutnant* on the left also carries a 3kg anti-tank assault charge. (Stephen Andrew © Osprey Publishing)

Panzer forces at the battle of Kursk in 1943. By this point of the war, Soviet anti-tank weapons and tactics were much improved, the former including guns such as the 76.2mm ZiS-3, nicknamed *Ratch-boom* (crash-boom) by the Germans on account of its high velocity, which left a barely discernable interval between firing and impact.

armour, as we have seen, was now often deployed in infantry support, mimicking the earlier disastrous tactics of Polish, French and British forces, and allowing the Red Army the initiative to adopt *Blitzkrieg* tactics. Increased issue of automatic weapons gave individual units greater firepower, but this was not enough to compensate for the shortage of manpower and heavy weapons.

As we saw at the beginning of this work, a German division had traditionally recruited from a specific military district, fostering a close regional identity which gave it great cohesion and high morale. By 1943 this system had broken down under the mounting losses, and soldiers were drafted into units in most need, destroying critical unit cohesion. Increasingly strident Nazi propaganda on the paramount need to 'defend German civilization from the Bolshevik hordes', and a growing fear of eventual revenge by the Red Army for widely tolerated German atrocities against the Russian civilian population, went some way to stiffening fighting spirit. However, this desperation could not replace the high morale of the 1939–41 period, and incidents of desertion and indiscipline increased. As the Eastern Front moved inexorably towards the German heartland, the under-strength divisions fought ferociously and with great individual heroism, but by spring 1945, with the war clearly lost, increasing numbers of troops attempted to retreat to the Western frontline in order to surrender to the Western Allies, from whom they could expect reasonable treatment in captivity. It was a picture of an army unravelling.

LEFT: German Army troops man a defensive trench network at an unknown location, and wait for the inevitable enemy attack. Note the zig-zig configuration of the trench – this prevented enemies from delivering enfilading fire along a long, straight trench, and it also helped minimize casualties from artillery strikes.

ZITADELLE

An overview of developments on the Eastern Front following the Stalingrad defeat gives an insight of the German disintegration, as much due to Soviet strengths as German weaknesses. Following the Stalingrad debacle, a counteroffensive by Manstein, launched on 15 February, achieved complete surprise, recovering much of the lost territory, including Kharkov, and forcing a Soviet withdrawal to the Northern Donets river. The spring thaw then imposed a lull.

The Soviet withdrawals created a huge salient, centred on the town of Kursk, and Hitler's plan for summer 1943 was to destroy the two Soviet fronts (Central and Voronezh) defending it. His desire for as many as possible of the new Tiger heavy and Panther medium tanks and Ferdinand self-propelled guns for the offensive, codenamed *Zitadelle*, led him to postpone it several times, finally settling on 5 July. Hitler's interference in war planning was now becoming a central problem for the Wehrmacht, and *Zitadelle* received a mixed reception from the generals designated to implement it when they met in Munich on 4 May. Model questioned the adequacy of the resources allotted while Kluge and Manstein wanted it launched sooner than July, before Red Army strength built up even further. Guderian, now Mobile Forces' Inspector-General, totally opposed any offensive in the East. Axis forces in North Africa were only nine days away from surrender; an Anglo-American invasion of Europe was inevitable, and perhaps imminent. Guderian wanted to husband tanks for that, not squander them on the steppes. Hitler satisfied nobody. Model got only part of the extra resources he wanted, while Kluge and Manstein did not get quick action because Hitler waited until more tanks arrived. Guderian would see most of the tanks he wanted destroyed at Prokhorovka on 12 July. Furthermore, the Soviets reinforced the sector – Central and Voronezh Fronts totalled 1,272,700 men, on a front of almost 560km, with 3,306 tanks and assault guns, 19,300 guns and mortars and 920 of the multiple rocket launchers known to the Red Army as 'Katyushas', and to the Germans as 'Stalin Organs'. In reserve behind them was Steppe Front, with 400,000 men and another tank army. These greatly outnumbered the 900,000 men, 2,700 tanks and 10,000 guns of Army Groups Centre and South.

The main assault began at 5.30am on 5 July, spearheaded by three Panzer divisions, with five infantry divisions in support. Model's troops advanced about 10km that day on a 32km front; but Rokossovsky had merely pulled back to the second defensive belt. The Germans gained little more ground, suffered heavy losses in men and tanks, and within two days were stopped.

LEFT: A Panzer crewman (left) and two infantryman on the Eastern Front in the summer of 1943. The fusilier in the centre has the unpopular Walther 7.92mm *Gewehr* 41W semi-automatic rifle in addition to the *Panzerfaust*. Note also the tankman's M1942 Panzer jacket without pink collar piping but with M1934 pink-piped skull collar patches and shoulder straps. (Stephen Andrew © Osprey Publishing)

Army Group South initially fared no better. Heavy rain during the night and most of next day made it hard to bridge streams and rivers, slowing both tanks and infantry. However, 48th Panzer and 2nd SS Panzer Corps penetrated the first line of Soviet defences, and by nightfall on the second day had advanced about 11km.

A *Waffen-SS* soldier of the *Das Reich* Division in action at Kursk in 1943, armed with an MP 40 submachine gun. The protrusion beneath the muzzle was intended for hooking onto the rim of armoured vehicle apertures to provide more stable shooting.

ABOVE: The weaponry of these three infantrymen, deployed for the battle of Berlin in 1945, reflects late-war shortages and issue problems. The soldier in the centre is armed with the *Panzerfaust*, while the man on the left has a *Panzerwurfmine* anti-tank grenade. The Panzergrenadier on the right has a captured Soviet 7.62mm PPS 43 submachine gun. (Stephen Andrew © Osprey Publishing)

On 12 July, the Soviet 5th Guards Tank Army, with about 850 tanks and self-propelled guns, confronted 2nd SS-Panzer Corps with about 600 AFVs near the village of Prokhorovka in the largest tank battle of the war. Losses on both sides were heavy, but the Germans withdrew, and thenceforth the Soviet tank generals had the upper hand.

The battle of Kursk degenerated into a sprawling battle of attrition that eventually the Wehrmacht had to break off, and by late August it was on the retreat again. The Wehrmacht's net manpower loss, 448,000, was almost double the 226,000 of Stalingrad. The Kursk campaign was in fact more decisive than Stalingrad. It was the Red Army's first major summer offensive, and the Germans' last. After Stalingrad Manstein had mounted a successful large-scale counteroffensive; after Kursk no German general could. From now on the Red Army had overwhelming superiority in men, tanks, guns and aircraft, and would lunge from river to river, Dnieper to Vistula to Oder to Elbe, to meet the British and Americans.

The first Soviet 'lunge' was to the Dnieper. Central, Voronezh and Steppe Fronts launched huge resources against Army Group South, which had only 37 infantry and 17 Panzer or Panzergrenadier divisions. All were severely below strength, and the Panzer/Panzergrenadier divisions had only 257 tanks and 220 assault guns between them, an average of only 15 tanks and 13 assault guns per division. A Soviet offensive in early November took Kiev, and the Soviet advance continued, though with local setbacks, until 26 November, when the autumn rains and mud temporarily immobilized both sides.

BAGRATION

The German struggle to hold the Dnieper was futile, notwithstanding localized offensives that made short-lived but valiant headway. A Soviet offensive in late December contained 188 divisions, 19 corps, 13 brigades and 2,406,100 men in the five fronts that had not much less than the Wehrmacht's total Eastern Front strength (195 divisions, 2,850,000 men). In tanks and guns they outnumbered the Germans by over three to one, and their growing superiority was marked by the breadth of their assault, on a front of over 1,300km.

The Soviet advance in the south continued for 116 days. When it ended, on 17 April 1944, the front line had moved up to 480km west since December. Despite the transfer of 34 German divisions from western Europe, the Red Army had reached the eastern Carpathians, and taken the war into enemy territory by crossing into Romania. On 14 January, with the advance in the south in full swing, another Soviet offensive was launched, this time against Army Group North. It lasted until 1 March, ended the siege of Leningrad, and drove the Germans back up to 280km on a 595km front, and took Soviet

troops into Estonia for the first time since 1941. German defensive skills were nevertheless proficient enough to inflict 76,686 casualties on the attackers.

Army Group Centre was left holding a bulge that the Russians christened the 'Belorussian balcony'. In February, the Soviet General Staff began planning to eliminate it and as many as possible of the German defenders. The Soviet plan, codenamed *Bagration*, was to be the funeral of Army Group Centre. On 19 June, Soviet partisans began a seven-day rampage in Belorussia against the army group's communications and supply lines. They blew up almost 1,100 rail and road bridges, derailed many trains, and destroyed or damaged thousands of locomotives and goods wagons. On 21 June, Red Air Force bombers joined in the destruction, and on the 23rd the infantry advanced behind rolling artillery barrages from 31,000 guns, ranged almost wheel-to-wheel at an average 270 guns or Katyushas per mile (1.6 km) of front.

Against 168 divisions, 12 tank corps and 20 brigades, Army Group Centre, with only two Panzer and 36 infantry divisions, could expect hard times. Hitler made them even harder, by ordering numerous towns and cities to be made *Festungen*, breakwaters against the Soviet tide. But the tide simply bypassed them, and all Hitler achieved was to make potentially

Waffen-SS infantrymen and the crew of a Tiger pause during the battle of Kursk in 1943. Between them the Wehrmacht and *Waffen-SS* took nearly 3,000 armoured fighting vehicles into action at Kursk.

ABOVE: Flanked by two Panzergrenadier soldiers, the *Generalmajor* of the 454th Security Division in the centre is wearing the general officers' uniform virtually unchanged from 1939, including the M1935 officers' field tunic and M1935 stone-grey breeches with general officers' piping and stripes. (Stephen Andrew © Osprey Publishing)

mobile forces static. An example of this was the 3rd Panzer Army. Despite its title it had no tanks, only a brigade of assault guns and a battalion of 'Hornet' 8.8cm tank-destroyers, plus 11 infantry divisions. This was little enough to face a tank corps and 24 infantry divisions of the 1st Baltic Front, and another tank corps and 11 infantry divisions from the 3rd Belorussian. Yet Hitler ordered four divisions committed to the 'fortress' of Vitebsk.

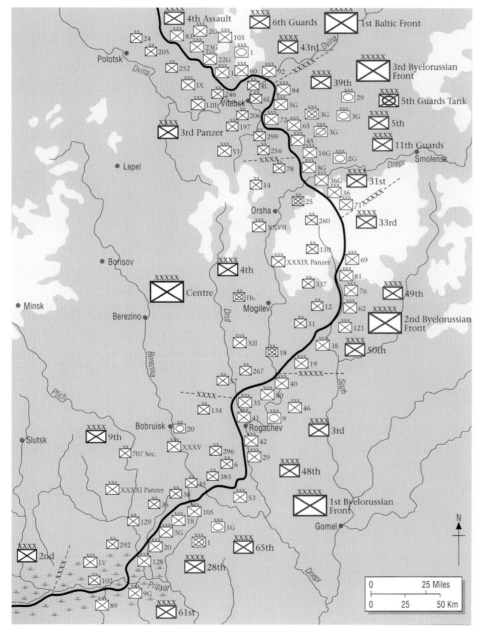

Opposing Forces, *Bagration*, 23 June 1944

The Soviet juggernaut was unstoppable. The Red Army took Vitebsk on 27 June, Mogilev on 28 June, Bobruisk on 29 June and Minsk on 4 July, inflicting 300,000 casualties and virtually annihilating the army group. By mid July the Red Army had cleared Belorussia and advanced into eastern Lithuania, taking Vilna on 12 July and Kaunas on the 30th. They rolled on into eastern Poland, capturing Brest-Litovsk, Bialystok and eastern Warsaw by the end of July. The Soviet armies then halted on the Vistula and shamefully allowed German suppression of the Warsaw Uprising (1 August–2 October 1944). Generaloberst Georg-Hans Reinhardt took over command of the shattered Army Group Centre in August 1944.

THE COLLAPSE IN THE EAST

The lull following completion of *Bagration* on 29 August was very brief. With Anglo-American forces approaching Germany's western borders, advancing in Italy and, on 15 June, landing in southern France, Germany was now fighting on four fronts. On 31 July, Army Group North was briefly isolated when 1st Baltic Front reached the Gulf of Riga, but after Hitler dismissed its commander his successor, Ferdinand Schörner, mounted a counteroffensive that by 21 August had reopened a corridor to Army Group Centre. It was, however, only 19km wide, and the Soviets made its closure high priority in a campaign to isolate and if possible destroy Army Group North. Troops from the

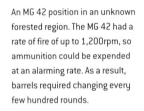

An MG 42 position in an unknown forested region. The MG 42 had a rate of fire of up to 1,200rpm, so ammunition could be expended at an alarming rate. As a result, barrels required changing every few hundred rounds.

Baltic Fleet and the five fronts took part. With 1,546,400 men in 156 divisions and 11 brigades, they outnumbered Army Group North by about three to one in manpower and more than that in weapons.

The offensive began on 14 September, only 16 days after the end of Operation *Bagration*. In the first three days, the men of the 1st Baltic Front advanced 48km, to within 26km of Riga, but strong German defence made the progress of soldiers from the 2nd and 3rd Baltic Fronts painfully slow. However, the troops of the Leningrad Front joined in on 17 September, capturing Tallin on the 22nd, then turning south on to the flanks of the 16th and 18th Armies, which were preparing to withdraw from Narva to positions north of Riga. Also on the 22nd, men from the 2nd and 3rd Baltic Fronts broke through, and by the 27th they were north-east of Riga, up against the northern section of the Sigulda Line, which ran in a semicircle around Riga at 40–48km from it. The 31 German divisions manning the line beat off attempts to break through, so the two fronts regrouped for a set-piece assault. An attempt by troops of the 1st Baltic Front to break through from the south also failed, and Stavka ordered them instead to head for Memel. They moved on 5 October, and reached the coast at Palanga, north of Memel, five days later.

Memel would not fall until January 1945, but by the end of October men from the 1st Baltic Front had isolated most of Army Group North in the Kurland peninsula. The men of the 3rd Baltic Front had also reached the coast, south of Memel, and were in East Prussia, only 100km from its capital, Königsberg. Troops from the Leningrad and 3rd Baltic Fronts swept the Germans out of Estonia, and men from all five fronts, except 3rd Belorussian, were along the Sigulda Line by the beginning of October.

Schörner, although appointed to 'stand fast,' soon realized that Army Group North would be cut off if it did not withdraw into East Prussia. In early September he sought Hitler's permission to do so, but by the time Hitler gave it, in mid-September, the Red Army had made it impossible.

In all campaigns from September 1944 onward, German mobility was very low due to the lack of fuel. Loss of the Ploesti oilfields, and Anglo-American air attacks on the hydrogenation plants that manufactured oil from coal, reduced German petrol production in September to only 8 per cent of its April level. In 1941 the Wehrmacht had been more mobile than the Red Army, but by 1944 the situation had reversed. The Red Army, with its indigenous oil supplies and fleets of US-made trucks, could move and supply its troops far faster than the German Army – and do so in safety, as fuel shortages kept most of the Luftwaffe on the ground.

Coincident with the Baltic operation (14 September–24 November) were Soviet offensives in the eastern Carpathians (8 September–28 October), Yugoslavia (28 September–20 October) and Hungary (29 October–13 February 1945). The forces involved in the simultaneous September–October 1944 offensives were 295 divisions and 26 brigades, more than Germany's entire Western and Eastern Front forces, nominally 276 divisions, but many now divisions only in name.

Hungary was the next German ally to come under the Soviet sledgehammer. Its ruler, Admiral Horthy, sent emissaries to Moscow on 1 October to seek an armistice, but the Germans learned of this and seized all Hungary's main communications centres. On 15 October, Horthy broadcast that Hungary's war was over, but a German-supported coup installed a pro-Nazi government. It ordered the armed forces to fight on, but in Hungary, as elsewhere, enthusiasm to die for a lost cause was waning, and mass desertions began.

About the only reason to continue fighting was knowledge of the atrocities committed by Soviet troops on captured territory. Fear of what lay in store prompted Axis forces to fight on desperately in the East, while the will to do so in the west began to evaporate. Guderian even proposed making peace with the Anglo-Americans while continuing to fight the Soviets, but Hitler would not hear of it. His riposte was instead to try to repeat the decisive breakthrough of 1940 in the Ardennes, demanding at the same time house-by-house defence of Budapest and an offensive in the Lake Balaton area of Hungary, west of the Danube.

At the start of 1945, Germany's Eastern Front comprised five Army Groups, from north to south:

North (16th and 18th Armies) – isolated in Kurland.
Centre (3rd Panzer, 4th and 2nd Armies) – eastern Prussia and northern Poland.
A (9th and 4th Panzer, 7th and 1st Panzer Armies) – southern Poland–northern
    Carpathians.
South (6th and 8th German, 1st, 2nd and 3rd Hungarian) – Hungary.
F (2nd Panzer) – Hungary and Yugoslavia.

On 26 January, Army Group North was renamed Army Group Kurland, Centre was renamed North, and A became Centre.

The largest Soviet offensive, against the renamed Army Groups Centre (Reinhardt) and North (Schörner), would set the stage for the final advance to Berlin. It was launched from three bridgeheads across the Vistula, and was to advance to the Oder and seize bridgeheads across it, only about 100km from Berlin. Of the two offensives launched on 13 January, the East Prussian was much the larger, involving 1.67 million men,

RIGHT: Men of the 1st SS-Panzergrenadier Regiment rest during the Ardennes offensive. They utilize captured US rations and cigarettes, and the soldier on the right has also appropriated a US M1 carbine firearm. (James R. Arnold © Osprey Publishing)

Camouflage-clad SS soldiers watch as a half-track pulling a PaK 40 anti-tank gun rolls past. The SdKfw 251 half-track was produced in a large number of variants, but in its basic armoured personnel carrier format it could carry a total contingent of 12 soldiers.

in 157 divisions and ten brigades. Army Group North, however, resisted much more determinedly than Army Group Centre; the German rate of retreat over the operation's 103 days averaged only about 2km a day, and they inflicted 126,464 casualties on the Soviet forces in the sector. The retreat was constant, however, and by early February the Soviets were on the Oder.

A new opponent for the Soviets in the Vistula–Oder offensive was the recently created Army Group Vistula, of 2nd and 9th Armies, both agglomerations of units and parts of units, and a re-formed 11th Army, which lacked most of the necessities for fighting. They were commanded not by a professional soldier (Hitler increasingly distrusted them for recommending withdrawals, or even surrender), but by Heinrich Himmler. Army Group Vistula was inserted north of Army Group Centre, and these two were to cover Germany's eastern approaches, while Army Group South in Hungary, the forces in Italy and Army Group E (withdrawn from Greece to Yugoslavia) covered the south and south-east. Hitler and Himmler were now so divorced from reality as to expect a counteroffensive by Army Group Vistula to decide the entire war in Germany's favour.

It began on 16 February, and pushed 1st Belorussian Front back about 11km – a remarkable achievement in itself – but by the 20th it had been stopped, and the six divisions that conducted it were counterattacked on 1 March by six armies. Some units held out until the war ended, but others fled in panic, and as an organized entity Army Group Vistula ceased to exist. A competent professional, Generaloberst Gotthard Heinrici, replaced Himmler on 20 March, but there was little left for him to command. Gdynia fell on 28 March and Danzig on the 30th. The Soviets claimed 91,000 prisoners; the operation removed any risk of a flank attack on the 1st Belorussian Front's planned drive to Berlin, and freed 10 more armies for that drive.

Hitler's grasp of strategic realities was now gone. While men from the 1st Belorussian and 1st Ukrainian Fronts were gathering for the final lunge to Berlin, he ordered an offensive in Hungary, aimed at recapturing Budapest and safeguarding the minor oil-producing districts in Hungary and Austria. The 6th SS-Panzer Army, attacking from east of Lake Balaton, was to spearhead it, while the 6th Army and a Hungarian corps pushed south on its left, 2nd Panzer Army attacked due east between Balaton and the Drava River and Army Group E attacked the 1st Bulgarian and 3rd Yugoslav Armies, guarding the 3rd Ukrainian Front's left flank.

Waffen-SS soldiers stay low during house-to-house fighting. In the retreat to the Reich, German forces developed urban warfare skills to an advanced level, covering streets with interlocking fields of fire and demonstrating ingenuity in the application of booby traps.

PREVIOUS PAGE: Troops on the retreat through the wreckage of the Greater German Reich, 1945. Note how most still have their gas mask containers – by this time the metal drums were more commonly used to store personal items rather than gas masks.

Army Group E and the 2nd Panzer Army attacked on the night of 5 March. The main assault, by the 6th-SS Panzer and 6th Armies, went in the next morning, and made good distance in four days, but it was then halted by the 3rd Ukrainian's massed artillery and infantry. Casualties on both sides were heavy, but by 15 March the offensive had clearly lost its impetus, and a Soviet counteroffensive started on the 16th.

Expulsion of the Germans from Hungary forced Army Group E to begin withdrawing from Yugoslavia. Soviet forces, advancing into eastern Austria and southern Czechoslovakia, took Vienna on 13 April. The operation formally concluded on 15 April, and on the next day three Soviet fronts and two Polish armies began the final push to Berlin.

WESTERN FRONT

A German defensive position on the Saar, centred around a light cannon, with one soldier looking out for the Allied advance from the West. The earth from the trench has been piled up in front to provide additional protection from small arms fire and artillery shell fragments.

As we have seen, Hitler's belief in the power of the offensive did not wane even in the very last days of the war. On the Western Front, as on the Eastern Front, this perspective would ultimately lead to futile disaster for tens of thousands of German troops. Nevertheless, these localized offensives still illustrate many of the ingredients that had brought major German victories in 1939–42. The Ardennes offensive is a prime example.

FUEL SUPPLIES IN THE ARDENNES OFFENSIVE

Fuel would be a constant problem in the Ardennes Offensive. At the outset of the campaign, the divisions carried enough fuel with them to travel 100km under normal conditions. But in the move from staging areas to the front in the days before the attack, the divisions found that the terrain and the drivers' inexperience led to such high consumption that only 50–60km could be covered with the remaining fuel. A resupply of another 100km-worth was brought up on the morning of 16 December 1944. Although a significant stockpile of fuel had been built up for the offensive, it was far behind the front lines and difficult to move forward. The fuel situation was exacerbated by the use of tanks such as the Panther and King Tiger, which respectively consumed 350 and 500 litres of fuel per 100km of road travel. By comparison, the PzKpfw IV consumed only 200 to 210 litres of fuel – between 40 and 60 per cent of a Panther's or King Tiger's consumption.

FROM THE BULGE TO REMAGEN

As early as 16 September 1944, Hitler had decided to stage a counteroffensive in the West that would seize the strategic initiative and decisively alter the course of the war. Hitler hoped to seize the key port of Antwerp by a surprise strike through the Ardennes, despite the unfavourable battlefield situation. Well aware that Allied aerial superiority hampered their mobility, however, the Germans decided to attack only during a predicted period of lengthy bad weather that would ground the powerful Allied tactical air forces.

During October and November the Germans prepared frantically for the attack – now planned to begin in mid December – while covering their activities with sophisticated deceptions. These preparations included rebuilding seven shattered Panzer divisions slated to spearhead the operation, as well as augmenting German infantry strength with 12 *Volksgrenadier* divisions, recently mobilized by throwing together ex-naval recruits, air force ground crew and convalescents.

The Germans earmarked the three armies of Model's Army Group B for the offensive, with Oberstgruppenführer Josef Dietrich's 6th Panzer Army and General Hasso von Manteuffel's 5th Panzer Army spearheading the operation in the northern and central sectors, respectively; the weaker Seventh Army was merely to secure the southern flank. Excluding reserves, this force amounted to eight mechanized and 14 infantry divisions with 950 AFVs.

The intended German battle-zone was the hilly, stream-bisected and forested terrain of the Ardennes, since this region's apparent unsuitability for armoured warfare had led the Americans to defend it with just four divisions. Consequently, the Ardennes offered the German attack the prospect of local success, despite its unsuitable terrain. Hitler,

Panther tanks arrive by train to participate in the Ardennes offensive. In open terrain, the Panther proved itself superior to almost all Allied main battle tanks, particularly in its long-range gunnery standards.

however, gambled on an ambitious strategic victory by seeking to capture Antwerp, 153km away, to cut off Montgomery's British command from the American forces deployed to his south.

Despite the frenetic German preparations, the attack's objective was too ambitious relative to the modest force assembled and the vast resources the Western Allies could call upon. Indeed, many German commanders argued that their forces were too weak to seize Antwerp, but Hitler remained obdurate. The greatest flaw in the Germans' plan was that their logistical base remained utterly inadequate to support such a grandiose attack. The German forces remained short of fuel, and some commanders planned to utilize captured Allied fuel stocks to sustain the offensive. At Hitler's insistence – and contrary to his senior commanders' professional advice – the *Westheer* risked its last precious armoured reserves on the triumph that might be achieved by a barely sustainable surprise blow against this Allied weak spot. Hitler failed to consider the consequences that would accrue if the gamble failed.

Before dawn on 16 December 1944, the Volksgrenadiers of 6th Panzer Army broke into the Allied defences before I SS-Panzer Corps struck west toward the Meuse bridges south of Liège. Obersturmbannführer Joachim Peiper's armoured battlegroup spearheaded the corps advance with a mixed force of Panzer IV and Panther tanks, plus 30 lumbering King Tigers that did their best to keep up. Peiper's mission was to exploit ruthlessly any success with a rapid drive toward Antwerp before the Allies could react. Given Peiper's mission and the terrain, his King Tigers played only a minor role in the offensive – contrary to popular perception, which regards this operation as being dominated by these leviathans.

Kampfgruppe Böhm races to the Meuse in the days before Christmas 1944. This battlegroup was based around the 2nd Panzer Division's reconnaissance battalion, but its combat power was reinforced by a few Panther tanks from the division's Panzer regiment. This bolstering was necessary as its reconnaissance battalion had been only partially refitted prior to the Ardennes operation. (Peter Dennis © Osprey Publishing)

A Panther tank lies abandoned in a village in Luxembourg in 1945, having simply run out of fuel. The Allied strategic bombing campaign, plus the loss of the Romanian Ploesti oilfields in 1944, meant that Germany had to rely on synthetic oil production, but the volumes could never keep pace with demands.

On 18–19 December, Peiper's force stalled at Stoumont because the Americans had destroyed the few available river bridges in the area, and flanking forces had failed to protect Peiper's supply lines. By 22 December, Allied counterstrikes – supported by fighter-bombers after the mist that had kept them grounded over the previous six days lifted – had surrounded Peiper's forces at La Gleize. On the night of 23–24 December, Peiper's doomed unit – now out of fuel and munitions – destroyed its vehicles, and the remaining 800 unwounded soldiers exfiltrated on foot back to the German lines.

The destruction of Peiper's group forced Dietrich on 22 December to commit II SS-Panzer Corps to rescue the collapsing northern thrust, but by 26 December this too had stalled near Manhay. Overall, the thrust undertaken by Dietrich's army had proved a costly failure. On 16 December, to Dietrich's south, the 5th Panzer Army also struck the unsuspecting Allied front. Although fierce American resistance at St Vith slowed Von Manteuffel's infantry thrusts during 16–17 December, further south his two spearhead Panzer corps advanced 32km toward Houffalize and Bastogne. During 18–22 December, these corps surrounded the American 101st Airborne Division at Bastogne and pushed further west to within just 6.4km of the vital Meuse bridges. When the Germans invited the commander of the surrounded Bastogne garrison to surrender, he tersely replied:

'Nuts!' After this rebuff the initiative slowly slipped out of the Germans' grasp thanks to fierce American resistance, rapid commitment of substantial Allied reserves, and severe German logistic shortages.

The Americans commenced their counterattacks on 23 December, driving north-east to relieve Bastogne on 26 December, and forcing back the German spearheads near the Meuse. Even though Von Rundstedt, *Oberbefehlshaber West* (Commander-in-Chief West), now concluded that the operation had failed, the Führer nevertheless insisted that one more effort be made to penetrate the Allied defences. Consequently, on New Year's Day 1945, Von Manteuffel's army initiated new attacks near Bastogne. To help this last-gasp attempt to snatch success from the jaws of defeat, the *Westheer* initiated a diversionary attack, Operation *Northwind*, in Alsace-Lorraine on New Year's Eve 1944. The Germans intended that a thrust north from the Colmar pocket – the German-held salient that jutted west over the Rhine into France – would link up at Strasbourg with a six-division attack south from the Saar. Although Hitler hoped that the attack would divert enemy reinforcements away from the Ardennes, in reality *Northwind* incurred heavy losses, yet only secured modest success and sucked few forces away from the Ardennes.

Consequently, the renewed German Ardennes attack soon stalled in the face of increasing Allied strength. Finally, on 3 January 1945, Allied forces struck the northern and

German soldiers strip anything valuable from the bodies of US soldiers killed during the fighting of the 'Battle of the Bulge' in late 1944. By this stage of the war, US kit and certain uniform items were superior to much of the equipment and clothing provided by the war-ravaged German economy.

southern flanks of the German salient to squeeze it into extinction. Over the next 13 days, instead of immediately retreating, the *Westheer* – at Hitler's insistence – conducted a costly fighting withdrawal back to its original position.

During the four-week 'Battle of the Bulge', Model's command lost 120,000 troops and 600 precious AFVs. By mid January 1945, therefore, only weak German forces now stood between the Allies and a successful advance across the Rhine into the Reich. With hindsight, the Ardennes counterstrike represented one of Hitler's gravest strategic errors. It was a futile, costly and strategically disastrous gamble that tossed away Germany's last armoured reserves. Moreover, the Germans managed to assemble sufficient forces for the counterstrike only by starving the Eastern Front of much-needed reinforcements. Consequently, when the Soviets resumed their offensives in mid January 1945, they

Attack in the Ardennes – *Kampfgruppe Peiper*, 17 December 1944. Probably the most vivid image to have emerged from the 'Battle of the Bulge' was the sight of the massive King Tiger tanks advancing through the snowy pine forests of the Ardennes, immortalized by a series of photographs taken by a German combat cameraman on the morning of 17 December near the German/Belgian border. That moment is recreated here in a battlescene painting. (Howard Gerrard © Osprey Publishing)

A King Tiger drives past US prisoners, mostly from the 99th Division, captured during the fighting on December 17. The village of Merlscheid lies in the background and the King Tiger is on its way towards Lanzerath, the start point for *Kampgruppe Peiper*. (NARA)

easily smashed through the German front in Poland. By late January, therefore, these German defeats on both the Eastern and Western Fronts ensured that it would only be a matter of months before the Nazi Reich succumbed.

Further offensives pushed back German forces until by mid March the Allies had closed up to the entire length of the Rhine. Overall, these hard-fought actions to clear the west bank of the Rhine, conducted by five Allied armies between 10 February and 23 March 1945, had secured 280,000 German prisoners, for the cost of 96,000 Allied casualties.

From north to south, the eastern bank of the Rhine was defended by Army Group H, Army Group B and Army Group G. Despite the rapidity of the US 1st Army's advance toward the Rhine, the Germans nevertheless managed to demolish all of the Rhine bridges in this sector – except the Ludendorff railway bridge at Remagen, between Cologne and Koblenz. In a fatal blow to Hitler's hopes, on 7 March, Hodges' forces captured the badly damaged – but still intact – Remagen bridge. Recognizing the opportunity that this good fortune offered, Hodges daringly pushed reinforcements across the river to enlarge the bridgehead before the Germans could throw in whatever reserves they had available.

Hitler reacted furiously to the loss of the Remagen bridge: he ordered that five German officers be executed, and sacked Von Rundstedt as Commander-in-Chief West. In his place, the Führer appointed Albert Kesselring, transferred from the Italian

front. Yet Kesselring could not close the flood gates. By the end of March the Allied Rhine crossings had pushed into Germany from Nijmegen in the north to Mannheim in the south.

Model, the commander of Army Group B, guessed that his cautious enemy would swing inwards to clear the Ruhr (which remained a German-held pocket) before driving deeper into the Reich. Consequently, he organized his depleted regular ground forces – now reinforced with *Volkssturm* units and Luftwaffe Flak troops – to fight a protracted urban battle for the Ruhr that would inflict the horrific German experience of Stalingrad onto the Americans. The latter recognized the likely heavy costs involved in such an attritional struggle in the ruins of the Ruhr's cities, and instead sought to encircle the region in a deep pocket. On 29 March, however, Model discerned Bradley's intent, and in desperation flung whatever meagre reserves he possessed in a local riposte at Paderborn. Despite fanatical resistance, these scratch forces failed to stop the 1st and 9th US Armies linking up at Lippstadt on 1 April 1945 to encircle 350,000 troops in the Ruhr – a larger force than that trapped at Stalingrad.

Hitler forbade Model from breaking out and promised a miracle relief operation mounted by the 11th and 12th Armies, then being raised from Germany's last part-trained recruits as, in sheer desperation, the Germans closed their remaining training schools and flung these troops into the fray. Model, however, remained unimpressed by such Hitlerian fantasies, and so on April 15 – to avoid being the second German field marshal in history to be captured alive (after Von Paulus at Stalingrad) – Model dissolved his army group and committed suicide. By 18 April, when German resistance in the Ruhr ended,

THE REMAGEN BRIDGE

At Remagen on 6 March 1945, with the Americans rapidly approaching the Ludendorff bridge, the German garrison commander understandably was anxious. If the enemy captured the bridge, he faced execution; if he blew up the bridge too soon, trapping German forces on the west bank, he faced execution. The commander decided not to blow up the structure until the next morning to allow friendly forces to cross, but unexpectedly American armour – spearheaded by the powerful new Pershing tank – appeared and stormed the bridge. The Germans triggered their demolition charges, which failed to explode, and then ignited the back-up charges, which exploded but only damaged the bridge instead of destroying it. Within hours, substantial American forces had crossed the river and established a bridgehead on the eastern bank. The elusive intact Rhine bridge had fallen into Patton's hands, and the *Westheer*'s hopes of stopping the Western Allies at the Rhine had been shattered.

LEFT: German motorcyclists attempt to negotiate the treacherous landscape of the Ardennes during the offensive of late 1944. Experience on the Eastern Front meant that the Wehrmacht was well-placed to deal with the challenges of cold and mud, but the confines of the Ardennes still limited progress.

A US soldier stares thoughtfully at the Ludendorff Bridge at Remagen. Hitler was furious at the failure of the German garrison to destroy the bridge over the Rhine, and allow it to fall into Allied hands. Four officers were arrested and executed, and one was sentenced to death *in absentia*.

316,000 troops had entered captivity. The Western Allies had torn a hole right through the centre of the Western Front, while to the north and south, the *Westheer* was now rapidly disintegrating.

Hitler reacted to the catastrophic setbacks recently suffered on all fronts, as well as to growing signs of defeatism, by increasing the already draconian discipline under which German soldiers toiled. On 2 April, for example, Hitler ordered the summary execution of any soldier who displayed defeatism by advocating surrender or retreat. Even Kesselring now reminded his soldiers that it was a German soldier's duty to die well. Although these strictures did foster continuing resistance, the main motivation behind such efforts remained the intense professionalism displayed by many German troops – qualities that kept frontline units cohesive despite appalling battlefield losses. Yet now Hitler again displayed his contempt for the army's professional officer corps by placing control of the *Volkssturm's* defence of German cities in the hands of Nazi Party officials, despite their lack of military experience.

In desperation, Hitler committed Germany to a 'total war' against the Allies by exhorting the entire population to wage a 'Werewolf' guerrilla struggle in enemy-occupied German territory. Despite extensive propaganda, in reality only a few hundred well-trained Nazi fanatics undertook Werewolf operations, which not surprisingly achieved little. Nazi propaganda also sought to boost German defensive resilience by publicizing the establishment of a strong defensive position – termed the 'National Redoubt' by the Allies – in the mountains of south-eastern Bavaria and western Austria. In reality, this fortified region existed only on paper and when on 22 April Hitler decided to remain in Berlin to face his fate, any inclination to defend this mythical fortress ebbed away. Thankfully for the Allies, there would be no protracted fanatical Nazi last stand in the mountains.

ABOVE: Soldiers of the Reich defence, Western Front, 1945. From left to right: *Oberleutnant*, 2106th Panzergrenadier Battalion, Cologne, March 1945; *Gefreiter*, 48th Grenadier Regiment, Ruhr Pocket, April 1945; Panzergrenadier, 156th Panzergrenadier Regiment, Reichswald Forest, February 1945. (Stephen Andrew © Osprey Publishing)

As history now knows, it was left to the Soviets to take the final stronghold of the Third Reich – Berlin itself. The Western Allies nevertheless pushed the front line to about 100km from Berlin and Prague, the German forces collapsing like decks of cards during late April. Hitler's Wehrmacht was now set to enter its final hours.

BERLIN

The final battle for the Reich took place within the context of the complete disintegration of the Hitler-centric command structure. In contrast to the tight system of centralized control that characterized the Soviet chain of command, the Wehrmacht's equivalent had become chaotic and frightened. Adolf Hitler had vested in himself absolute control over military operations, but had moved between desolately located command bunkers, gradually becoming divorced from reality. His immediate subordinates fought behind-the-scenes battles for power and influence and did nothing to try and inject a sense of reality about what was happening.

Hitler had finally installed himself in the Führerbunker under the *Reichskanzlei* (Reich Chancellery) on 16 January 1945. This facility suffered from a chronic lack of communications equipment and had not been set up to the same standard as the other headquarters that had been used around Europe during the war. It came with a one-man switchboard, a single radio transmitter and a radio telephone, which was dependent on having its aerial raised by means of a balloon.

Tiger II tanks form up on the Sennelager training ground. Set on the edge of the Teutoburger Wald (Teutoburger forest), the Sennelager was used by German forces for training from the late 19th century, and was particularly suited to armoured vehicle exercises.

The fate of many German soldiers during the battle of Berlin in 1945 was that of this officer here. It is extremely difficult to arrive at accurate casualty figures for this battle, but total German casualties could be anywhere from 100,000 to close to a million (including prisoners).

Hitler's state of mind was not helped by stress, overwork, the attempted assassination the previous July or his failing health. He had taken over command of both the armed forces and the army in December 1941, and had complicated the command structure even more by directing operations on the Eastern Front exclusively through the OKH, while its responsibilities for other theatres had been passed to OKW, forcing the two to compete for scarce resources for their respective areas of responsibility. Additionally, Hitler's attitude to the General Staff was a major source of friction, as his system of unquestioning obedience to orders clashed with their system of mutual trust and exchanges of ideas.

Hitler's system of command was reflected in the state and composition of the German armed forces by 1945. One confusing practice was the use of corps and army headquarters that had been taken out of the line and placed in reserve to control formations that had been rebuilt or newly raised, regardless of what branch of service they came from or their primary function. For example, V SS-Mountain Corps disposed only one *Waffen-SS* division and no mountain troops, while XI SS-Panzer Corps consisted mainly of ordinary infantry units.

Soviet forces assault the Seelow Heights, east of Berlin, on 16 April 1945. The attack started with a staggering artillery barrage, but the first waves of Soviet tanks and infantry had difficulty moving over the river valley as the area had been deliberately flooded by the Germans. (Peter Dennis © Osprey Publishing)

The German ground forces were still primarily composed of army formations, although the abortive coup in July 1944 had led to a great purge of army officers, with political officers being appointed to formation headquarters to ensure the appropriate Nazi spirit. Himmler had taken over control of the Reserve or Home Army, a position of considerable influence, and all new recruits had been assigned to the newly formed *Volkswehr* (People's Army) of *Volksgrenadier* and *Volks* artillery units. They were considered to have greater political reliability and therefore had priority in men and equipment.

LEFT: A *Fallschirmjäger Leutnant* from the Ardennes campaign, seen with personal kit and some late-war weaponry: the FG 42 assault rifle and the *Panzerfaust* and *Panzerschreck* (right) anti-tank weapons. (Velimir Vuksic © Osprey Publishing)

After the army, the main organization that fielded ground units was the *Waffen-SS*, also under Himmler. These, too, received priority of equipment over the army and had their own sources of supply, chiefly the slave labour camps. Unable to compete with the Wehrmacht with regard to the conscription laws, they turned to other sources of manpower and as a result, resembled the French Foreign Legion in composition. By 1945, the faith of even the *Waffen-SS* generals in Hitler was wavering and they no longer believed in final victory.

Finally, there was the Berlin Garrison, which had its headquarters located opposite the *Zeughaus* (Arsenal) on the Unter-den-Linden. This command administered a motley collection of units, including military police, regular garrison troops, thousands of POWs and slave-labourers, penal units, an engineer battalion and the *Grossdeutschland* Guard Regiment. The garrison formed part of *Wehrkreis* III that had been administered by the headquarters of III Corps during peacetime. When III Corps went off to war, a deputy headquarters remained, which came under the Reserve or Home Army.

The Luftwaffe contributed not only Generaloberst Ritter von Greim's *Luftflotte* VI (6th Air Fleet), but three types of ground formation. The first were the *Fallschirmjäger*, Germany's elite paratroopers. Many of the earlier replacements were from the non-flying branches of the service, but were trained and indoctrinated into the elitist traditions of the service as these units were often used as shock troops alongside army formations. Later replacements, however, including redundant aircrew, did not have the benefit of such training. The second type of formation was the anti-aircraft artillery branch of the service

LUFTWAFFE FIELD DIVISIONS

The Luftwaffe field divisions had their origins in 1942, as the Wehrmacht began to look around for new sources of manpower to fuel the war on the Eastern Front. They also emerged from Hermann Göring's attempt to extend his influence within the war, by sharing in the ground campaign. At first regiments, and eventually entire divisions, were formed by Luftwaffe personnel pulled from a variety of sources, such as ground crew, police units, air force administration staff and airfield construction units. In total, 22 Luftwaffe field divisions were raised during the war, the numbers of men increasing as the war made various aspects of the Luftwaffe, such as the bomber arm virtually redundant by 1944. Divisional strength could range from anything between 4,000 and 12,000 men (the core fighting element consisted of just two rifle regiments), and the divisions were grouped into corps numbered I–IV. On the whole, the Luftwaffe field divisions were of questionable value, and these frequently poorly trained men often fared badly under Soviet attacks.

that provided around 90 per cent of all German anti-aircraft defence personnel and was attached to all army formations down to divisional level. This branch of the Luftwaffe had started as an elite formation and remained so throughout the war, with batteries often acting as mobile artillery and fighting courageously until they were overrun.

Up until the beginning of 1945, the main defence of Berlin had centred on its anti-aircraft capabilities in relation to the Allied bombing campaign. This defence was manned by the 1st 'Berlin' Flak Division and concentrated around three enormous Flak towers that had been built in the parks at Friedrichshain, Humboldthain and the Zoo, each being a fortress with walls some 2m thick and steel doors over every aperture. There were also another dozen or so permanent anti-aircraft positions around the city, usually on the flat roofs of large well-built buildings. All of these could be expected to provide valuable support during the land battle, and could serve either as command posts or defensive positions, too. Third, there were the Luftwaffe Field Divisions that had been initially raised in 1942 from personnel skimmed from training organizations, Flak and other ground service organizations, and committed as infantry.

An artilleryman loads 15cm rockets into a *Wurfgranate* 41. Originally the launcher used a six-tube mount, but by the later part of the war a ten-tube half-track mounted version was in operation. The rockets could be ripple-fired to deliver an impressive area bombardment to ranges of around 7,000m.

For the battle of Berlin, the Germans had a variety of tanks, self-propelled guns and *Jagdpanzer* available, but the desperate situation they found themselves in meant that units were raised and equipped with anything that was available. The German armoured force was also severely handicapped by the lack of fuel, the production of which was a major target of the Allied bombing campaign.

The residual talents of the Wehrmacht were demonstrated by the ferocity of the battle of Berlin. Launched on 16 April 1945, it became one of history's largest urban battles. Men from three Soviet fronts drove into the city, behind awe-inspiring volumes of artillery fire, and thereafter fought for almost every street and house. Despite 300,000 Germans facing 2.5 million Soviet troops, and vast amounts of Soviet artillery and armour, the defenders still managed to kill more than 70,000 Soviet troops before the inevitable happened. Following Hitler's suicide on 30 April, by the end of the first week of May Wehrmacht forces had surrendered in their entirety.

This scene depicts the chaos of urban warfare in Berlin in April 1945. Soviet tanks proceeding in column were excellent targets for small teams armed with *Panzerfaust* or *Panzerschreck* anti-tank weapons; the teams would knock out the first and last tanks, especially when they had been stopped by barricades constructed by local volunteers. (Peter Dennis © Osprey Publishing)

STRUCTURAL DEVELOPMENTS

As we can see from the above narrative, in the last months of the war the Wehrmacht was a mix of collapse and competence. One of the main continuing strengths of the German Army lay in its tactical skills, the flexibility of its command system and its ability to reorganize quickly, particularly in the defence. German field headquarters were kept small and well forward to maintain close contact with their subordinate commands. Officers were highly trained and able to make quick decisions.

An interesting document, worth quoting at length, was a training circular, based on combat experience on the Eastern Front, that was published in a simple cartoon format. It laid down 30 rules and was aimed primarily at junior officer level. What follows is not an exact translation, but a summary of the salient points, and it illustrates perfectly how the Wehrmacht retained and distributed tactical knowledge until the very end:

1   Acquaint yourself with the terrain, and share this information with subordinates.
2   Always put subordinates 'in the picture' about the tactical situation, the mission and any other relevant information.

An evocative image of soldiers from the *Waffen-SS Wiking* Division (PzKpfw IIIs move in the background) at the battle of the Korsun-Cherkassy Pocket in January–February 1944. About two-thirds of the Germans trapped in the pocket managed to escape. These troops wear full winter uniforms, and the man in the foreground has a *Panzerfaust* over his shoulder.

During the mid afternoon of 11 February 1945, the 53rd Welsh Division made their attack on this German machine-gun post in the Reichswald Forest. The defenders had been in action continuously for three days, but fought to delay the Allied advance as long as possible. (Tony Bryan © Osprey Publishing)

3   Protect your flanks as well as your front.

4   Always make constant appreciation of the changing situation.

5   Maintain strict radio discipline.

6   Lead with strength! At least two Panzers forward. The more firepower that is laid down in the first minute, the faster the enemy will be defeated.

7   When breaking from cover do so quickly and in unison. The more targets the enemy is faced with at one time, the more difficult it will be for him to control his fire, and you will have all the more firepower available to strike him.

8   During an attack, move as fast as possible. You are much more likely to be hit at slow speed. There are only two speeds – slow for firing, and full speed ahead.

9   When facing anti-tank weapons at long or medium distance, first return fire before moving against them. First, halt to return fire effectively, then commit the bulk of the company to move against them whilst leaving one platoon to give supporting fire.

10 If anti-tank weapons are encountered at close range, it is suicide to stop! Only immediate aggressive attack at full speed and with all guns firing can be successful and reduce losses.

11 In action against anti-tank guns, never allow a single platoon to attack alone, even with strong covering fire. Anti-tank guns are not deployed singly. Remember, lone tanks in Russia are lost!

12 Keep a good distance between vehicles. This divides the enemy's defensive fire. Avoid narrow gaps between vehicles at all costs.

13 If an impassable obstacle such as a minefield or ditch is met, withdraw into cover immediately. Standing still in the open will cost you losses. Make your deliberations from the safety of cover.

14 If passing potential enemy tank positions, either pass so close that you are within their minimum range, or so far as to be outside their maximum range.

15 Do not attack enemy tanks directly, they will then know your strength and respond before you can kill them. Wait until you are in a favourable position and attack from the flanks or the rear. Pursue all retreating enemy vigorously.

16 An enemy strong point should be attacked from different directions simultaneously if possible. Defensive fire will be split and the true source and direction of your attack concealed. Your breakthrough will be easier and your casualties fewer.

17 Always prepare dug-in positions and camouflage against air or artillery attacks. There is no excuse for losses suffered through these causes.

18 In decisive moments, do not try to conserve ammunition. At such times it is acceptable to expend ammunition at exceptionally high rates to minimise casualties.

19 Never deploy your company in such a manner that the two parts cannot support each other. If there are two objectives, attack each in turn with your full strength.

OVERLEAF: Werhmacht troops, possibly in the Netherlands, take a break from the fighting in October 1944. By this stage of the war, army formations were increasingly filled with poorly trained or rear-echelon troops, as the Army High Command combed Germany for all available manpower to sustain a defence.

20 Make use of supporting artillery or dive-bomber attacks immediately. Do not wait until such attacks cease. They only have suppressive, not destructive effect. It is better to risk friendly fire than rush into an active anti-tank defence.

21 Do not misuse attached arms. For instance do not use engineer troops as infantry, armoured infantry in place of tanks.

22 Protect any non-armoured or lightly armoured units attached to you from unnecessary losses until they are needed for the task for which they were attached.

23 Attached units are not your servants but your guests. Supply them with their needs and share with them. Do not just use them for guard duties!

24 In combined operations, work closely together and help each other. Your battle cry will be 'Protect the Infantry!' and theirs will be 'Protect the Panzers!'

25 Always concentrate on your mission and do not be diverted into attacking enemy flanking positions unless they threaten accomplishment of your mission.

26 After a victory, always be prepared for a counterattack.

27 In defensive positions, leave only a few Panzers in static firing positions. Keep the remainder mobile so that they can be brought into play quickly and effectively. Tanks should defend aggressively.

28 In meeting exceptionally strong resistance, break off the attack. Continuing only costs more casualties. It is better to hold the enemy with minimal forces whilst you mass your strength for a surprise attack from another quarter.

29 Never forget. Your soldiers are not yours, but Germany's. Glory hunting only rarely succeeds but always costs blood. Temper your courage with judgement and cunning. Use your instincts and tactical ability. You will then earn the loyalty and respect of your soldiers.

30 The Panzer division is the modern equivalent of the cavalry. Panzer officers must carry on the cavalry traditions and its aggressive spirit. Remember the motto of Marshal Blücher: 'Forwards and through' (but sensibly).

Most of the points have tactical relevance to infantry even today, and such core guidelines helped German soldiers keep a semblance of defence even in the last week of the war.

Yet as entire formations disintegrated on the front lines, structural changes were inevitable and often rapid. Looking at the big picture, the army on the Eastern Front in 1943–45 was organized into four, later five army groups, with a sixth covering the Balkans; these comprised nine infantry and four Panzer armies, and an independent mountain army on the Arctic Front. Each army controlled two to five infantry, Panzer, mountain, cavalry, reserve corps or army formations, each with a varying number of German and allied divisions. In autumn 1944, three armoured corps –XXIV, *Grossdeutschland* and *Feldherrnhalle* – were organized as powerful integrated attack formations on the *Waffen-SS* model, each with two divisions and supporting arms, fighting in eastern Germany in 1945.

RIGHT: German sappers prepare a bridge for demolition outside Grodno in Belorussia. Such attempts to delay the Soviet advance across Belorussia were largely futile, and the Red Army's Operation *Bagration*, launched in June 1944, not only cleared German forces from White Russia but also almost entirely destroyed Army Group Centre in the process.

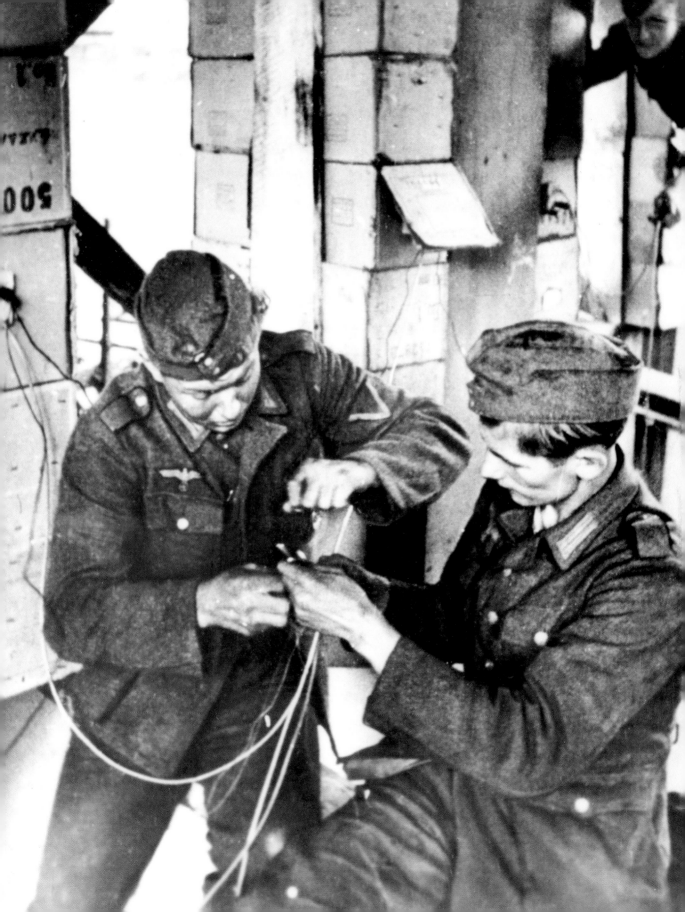

The infantry division remained the backbone of the German Army, accounting for about 82 per cent of the divisions. On 10 December 1944, all infantry divisions were ordered formed as 'M1945 Divisions', each with 11,211 German troops and 698 *Hilfswillige*, with divisional services reorganized as a supply regiment with a motor transport company, two horsedrawn transport companies, an ordnance company, a mechanical repair platoon, an administration company, medical company, veterinary company and field post office. In March 1945, manpower was further reduced to 10,728 Germans and 642 *Hilfswillige*.

On 25 January 1945, Hitler had ordered all available units to be reorganized as infantry divisions in an attempt to stem the relentless Red Army advance. Reserve, training and replacement divisions became general numbered divisions of the Replacement Army. In February 1945 'named' infantry and Panzer divisions were raised from local schools and garrisons. Twelve town garrisons, manned by army and *Volkssturm* personnel were reorganized as fortress units for last-ditch defence. Breslau became a fortress corps; Danzig, Frankfurt an der Oder, Gotenhafen, Stettin, Swinemünde and Warschau became fortress divisions; Kolberg, Küstrin, Posen, Scheidemühl and Garlitz became 'fortresses'. (After May 1945 all these towns, except Frankfurt an der Oder, became part of Poland.)

A *Jagdtiger* tank is parked on a street corner in Germany in April 1945, a potent weapon in a collapsing regime. The *Jagdtiger* was a tank-destroyer variant of the Tiger II tank, and it was armed with a powerful 12.8cm PaK 44 anti-tank gun plus a secondary MG 34 machine gun.

By 1945 the Panzer forces of the Wehrmacht were also undergoing yet another shake-up. The worsening situation did not prevent the revision and updating of the organization of the Panzer divisions, though often that simply meant further reductions in strength, weapons, vehicles and equipment. On 22 January 1945, the divisional lorry allowance fell to about 1,200 vehicles, with the divisional supply and services units now down to only 279 lorries. Furthermore, on 25 March 1945 an order was issued to reorganize all the Panzer and Panzergrenadier divisions (minus the 232nd Panzer Division) according to the new 1945 establishment. In its general outline this included a Panzer regiment now made up of a single Panzer battalion and with the second battalion replaced by the armoured Panzergrenadier battalion, plus two motorized (on paper, since only heavy units were intended to have motor transport) Panzergrenadier regiments, the Panzer reconnaissance and *Panzerjäger* battalions, the Panzer artillery regiment, the anti-aircraft battalion and the pioneer battalion, the intelligence battalion and the field replacement battalion. Overall strength was set at 11,422 all ranks and the division was to have 54 Panzers, 90 armoured personnel carriers, 16 armoured cars, 22 *Panzerjäger*, the same allowance of artillery guns and 2,171 vehicles (of which 1,080 were lorries).

German troops and Panzers, plus Hungarian infantry, retreat from Budapest. Four German divisions were trapped inside the city by a Soviet offensive in December 1944, and Hitler declared the city a 'fortress' to be defended at all costs. This the Germans did, although it cost Hitler's forces about 150,000 casualties.

Those units that, because of their current status, could not be modified following these outlines had to reorganize instead according to the '1945 Battlegroup Panzer Division' tables of organization, which saw a Panzer division's combat group being made up of an escort company, the mixed Panzer regiment, one single motorized Panzergrenadier regiment, a Panzer reconnaissance battalion down to two companies, the *Panzerjäger* battalion, the Panzer artillery regiment only with its first and third battalion, the anti-aircraft battalion, the Panzer pioneer battalion and one single intelligence company, plus the field replacement battalion and supply and services units. The total strength of the battlegroup was set at 8,602, though vehicle (including combat vehicle) allowance was the same as for the '1945 Panzer Division'. In theory, all commands had

Here we see two Panther tanks in 1945, caught in a joint Allied air and artillery strike. One tank has received a direct hit and has been totally destroyed. The second vehicle has been hit in the engine compartment and caught fire. The surviving crew will either be killed by the blaze, or by enemy small-arms fire as they try to escape. (Velimir Vuksic © Osprey Publishing)

An artillery observer looks out for potential targets. He is using the SF14Z scissor periscope, which had a magnification of x10 and used stereoscopic principles to provide an extremely clear view of the battlefield, with an impressive depth of field.

to report about the status of their subordinate units by 1 May, though presumably none ever did. It appears that only some, not all, divisional units could actually be reorganized according to the new establishment.

Although the regular armed forces still made up the bulk of Hitler's shattered army in 1945, it became increasingly clear that additional manpower was needed to stem the tide of the Allied advances. For these reasons, Hitler turned to other sources for his combat strength. Both the young and the old would be dragged into the final conflagration.

THE HITLER YOUTH

The *Hitlerjugend* (HJ; Hitler Youth) was one repository for Hitler's last stand. It was not in essence a military organization. From its origins as the youth department of the brown-shirted SA, the HJ expanded to become an all-encompassing institution of the Nazi state. Its purpose was to indoctrinate German children in Nazi ideology, and prepare them physically and ideologically for lives of service to the *Volksgemeinschaft* (national community).

By the outbreak of war in 1939, membership in the various Nazi youth organizations dominated the lives of all German children between the ages of 10 and 18. For boys this meant the *Deutsches Jungvolk* (DJV; German Youth) for ages 10–14 and the *Hitlerjugend* (HJ; Hitler Youth) for 14–18-year-olds. The equivalent girls' organization were the *Jungmädelbund* (JM; Young Girls' League) and the *Bund Deutscher Mädel* (BDM; League of German Girls). For the boys, on turning 18 compulsory labour service in the RAD took over, followed by conscription into the Wehrmacht or *Waffen-SS*.

Nazi ideology venerated the soldier as the epitome of the masculine ideal, and it is not surprising that the HJ was decidedly paramilitary in tone from the beginning. Young German men inducted into the Wehrmacht from the HJ brought with them the skills and attitudes they had learnt there.

Following the disaster at Stalingrad, Joseph Goebbels gave his famous speech at the *Berlin Sportpalast* on 18 February 1943, in which he called upon the German people to embrace 'total war'. For young German children, 'total war' meant that they found themselves increasingly mobilized for actual participation in combat. From February 1943,

A group of Hitler Youth soldiers look nervously at their US captors. They were the lucky ones – thousands were killed in the fighting, particularly on the Eastern Front, where many committed suicide rather than fall into Soviet hands.

15- and 16-year-olds came to bear the brunt of manning the air defences of the Reich as *Luftwaffenhelfer* (air force auxiliaries). The year 1943 also saw the creation of the *Hitlerjugend* Division, under the aegis of the *Waffen-SS*, but recruited from senior members and recent graduates of the Hitler Youth. As the 12th SS-Panzer Division, this unit fought savagely against British and Canadian troops around Caen after the D-Day landings, and was largely destroyed in the process.

From late 1944, units of HJ were directly used in combat as part of the people's militia, the *Volkssturm* (see below). In the final months of the war, therefore, Allied soldiers regularly encountered armed children in battle, including boys as young as ten and girls from the BDM.

The boy or girl newly inducted into the HJ became a member of a unit organized along military lines. Membership in a particular group was determined geographically, with boys or girls from the same area or street being grouped together, rather than by

A young man signs a statement to say that he is racially 'pure', and thereby able to serve within the Hitler Youth organization. Depending on his age and the year of the war, he would likely find himself on an actual battlefront soon in the future.

school classes. On joining the HJ, a boy was assigned to a *Kameradschaft* with nine other boys. (Translations are here omitted, as literal translations often do not adequately evoke the sense of the German.) Four *Kameradschaften* made up a *Schar*, four *Scharen* a *Gefolgschaft*. Between three and five *Gefolgschaften* made up a *Stamm*, the administrative control area of which was called an *Unterbann*. Four or five *Unterbanne* together formed a *Bann,* with around 40 *Banne* belonging to a *Gebiet*, an administrative area corresponding to a *Gau* of the NSDAP. The triangular patch worn by all members of the HJ on their upper left shoulder identified the *Gebiet* to which they belonged. This appeared under the name of one of the six *Obergebiete* in the Greater German Reich – *Nord, Süd, West, Ost, Mitte* and *Südost* after the *Anschluss* with Austria in 1938. All four branches of the HJ were organized along similar lines, although the names of units varied.

At the outbreak of World War II, there were probably no other teenagers in the world as well prepared for military service as the youth of Germany. German society during the 1930s intensively socialized them for their future role as soldiers. Hitler laid down his ideal for the youth of Germany in a speech at the Nuremberg Party Rally in September 1935: 'In our eyes the German youth of the future must be slim and slender, swift as the greyhound, tough as leather, and hard as Krupp steel.'

In line with this ideal, hard physical games and competitive activities were the main focus of the HJ, even for the 10-year-olds. The emphasis on competitive physical challenges continued throughout a boy's experience of the HJ. Sports such as athletics, football, discus and especially combative sports such as boxing were undertaken by all boys, and were organized into annual competitions at local and regional levels. Hiking and camping were also widely practised. One insidious result of the focus on aggressive competition in the HJ was that any weakness was actively despised. Those who could not reach the exacting physical standards required were often treated brutally. For example, non-swimmers were sometimes 'taught' to swim by being thrown into a deep pool, and only rescued when on the point of drowning. Atrocities committed against prisoners by the German armed forces, such as the execution of Canadian prisoners by elements of the *Hitlerjugend* Division in Normandy, owed much to the brutalizing effect of such training.

LEFT: A HJ member leads a *Gefolgschaft* of 150 boys in exercises with an 'Indian club', which strongly resembled the German hand grenade. He wears the standard summer HJ uniform of brown shirt with black shorts and scarf. His rank as a *Gefolgschaftsführer* is shown by the three silver pips on his shoulder strap, and his leadership function by the lanyard. Also shown is a detail of the HJ belt buckle (1) and dagger (2) – this was designed to resemble an army bayonet, and bore the inscription 'Blood and Honour'. The boy wears a proficiency badge (3) and marksmanship badge (4). Proficiency badges awarded to the DJV incorporated the formation's Sig rune (5). Two other patches are shown: one from the BDM, which used white lettering (6), and a *Traditionsarmdreieck* with gold bar (silver for the BDM) (7). This showed that the wearer's *Bann* had been formed prior to 1933. (Elizabeth Sharp © Osprey Publishing)

In addition to the emphasis on physical training, special units of the HJ were formed to offer training specific to different branches of the armed forces. In 1933 the *Motor-HJ* had been formed, which catered to members of the HJ with particular interests in motor vehicles. With the increasing focus on military training after 1937, this trend towards specialization within the HJ continued. The *Flieger-HJ* was formed in 1937 to provide training for future Luftwaffe cadets. Its members learnt the rudiments of practical flying in gliders, as well as skills such as navigation. Close links were often formed between the boys of *Flieger-HJ* units and the personnel of nearby Luftwaffe airfields. The *Marine-HJ* offered maritime training as preparation for the navy, while other smaller specialized units of the DJV and HJ focused on military skills such as horsemanship, signalling and air-raid defence.

After conscription was reintroduced on 16 March 1935, overt military training became a more pronounced aspect of life in the HJ. Drill and marksmanship with air rifles and small-calibre firearms had been among the activities since the late 1920s. However, from 1935 the Wehrmacht and SS began to furnish the HJ with resources and instructors to provide pre-military training, and sought to secure the best recruits for their formations. In 1937, Rommel played a leading role in establishing formal liaison between the army and the HJ, although his attempts to bring the HJ under army control were strenuously resisted by Baldur von Schirach, the head of the HJ. Members of the HJ were now able to make use of expert army instructors to teach marksmanship and field craft, and experience interesting visits to army facilities. Throughout Germany, the result of this relationship between the army and the HJ was reflected in the rising standard of marksmanship within the youth organization. By early 1939, 1.5 million boys were training regularly on rifle ranges under Wehrmacht supervision, and 51,500 boys had won the prestigious HJ marksmanship medal.

TERRAIN GAMES

Of particular use as pre-military training in the HJ were the popular 'terrain games'. A typical game involved a *Kameradschaft* of about ten boys spending a day in a forest attempting to locate the headquarters of a rival group. When they discovered it, their goal was to remove their opponents' flag. Each of the boys wore woollen threads around their arms, indicating their 'lives'. When they inevitably clashed with the boys from the 'enemy' group, the day of creeping through the forest climaxed in a free-for-all scuffle, they had to tear off the 'lives' of their opponents. Through these games, German boys from a young age learned skills of field craft, map reading and camouflage, as well as attitudes of aggression, which would prove useful to many of them in the Wehrmacht.

Realizing the potential recruitment opportunities, Himmler also began furnishing the HJ with trainers drawn from the ranks of the SS from 1936. The relationship between the SS and the Hitler Youth was encouraged as early as 1934 by the creation of the *HJ-Streifendienst* (Patrol Service), the security wing of the HJ, which formed close ties with the SS and Gestapo. Former members of the *Streifendienst* were obvious candidates for recruitment into the Gestapo and the *SS-Totenkopfverbände* (Death's Head Units), the formations that furnished the guards for concentration camps. By the end of 1938, the SS were also actively recruiting from the *HJ-Landdienst* (Land Service), as part of a programme envisaged by Himmler to create soldier-farmers for the colonization of conquered territories in Eastern Europe.

An even more direct challenge to the Wehrmacht's prerogative in recruiting the cream of the HJ was posed by the creation of the SS-VT with the reintroduction of conscription in March 1935. Service in the *Waffen-SS*, as the SS-VT units were generally known by spring 1940, was attractive to many HJ in the early stages of the war, drawn by the sense that they were joining an elite brotherhood. Others found the high standards of the SS intimidating, or were repelled by the hostility towards church affiliation that was typical of its members. It also became widely known that the formidable reputation the *Waffen-SS* won in battle was achieved at the cost of significantly higher casualties than were suffered in other units.

After the outbreak of war, the role of the Hitler Youth in providing pre-military training for the armed forces became even more apparent. By 1940, members of the HJ were expected to spend four hours every week in 'defence readiness' activities such as marksmanship and field exercises based on those in the infantry training manual, with an additional six hours every month to be devoted to sports. In an ominous development, the leadership of the HJ changed the name of its 'Office for Physical Education' to that of 'Military Training' in January 1941, in an attempt to co-ordinate the pre-military instruction more effectively.

During the war the HJ war sought to revive in German children the sense of urgent duty that had characterized the movement prior to 1933. Once again, German youth were living through a 'time of struggle', and their duty was to prepare themselves for the important work to which the Führer was calling them. For German boys, this of course meant the work of soldiers, and the leadership of the HJ spent considerable resources in glamorizing the armed forces as an exciting life to be keenly anticipated. One example of this was the 'Front soldiers speak to the HJ' programme, which organized exciting talks by soldiers who were on home leave or recuperating from wounds.

KRIEGSEINSATZ

At the outbreak of war in September 1939, Schirach called upon the Hitler Youth to make its own contribution to victory. As a result, increasingly heavy demands were placed upon its members to engage in *Kriegseinsatz* (war employment). Some tasks, such as involvement in the *Landdienst* (consisting of unpaid work on farms) and collecting money for the Winter Relief appeal, were already part of HJ before 1939. However, the outbreak of the war saw the whole emphasis of the HJ shift away from ideological instruction and sport towards their use in the war economy, which would culminate in the boys at least being viewed as soldiers by 1945.

Members of the HJ were called on to fulfil a range of duties, over which their parents and schools had little control. Boys would go around houses collecting material for the war effort, knocking on house doors to ask whether the household had any clothing, scrap paper or scrap metal that it could spare. They even collected old bones, which were used to manufacture explosives. Girls from the JM and the BDM were mobilized to scour forests and fields for mushrooms, herbs and flowers for the production of teas and pharmaceuticals.

Boys and girls of the HJ were also called upon to take over jobs previously held by adults. Members of the HJ and BDM performed a myriad of roles in order to free up

men for the front, including tram conductors, road workers, postmen, telephonists and clerks. For example, during the first year of the war 64,000 BDM girls worked for the German Red Cross, 60,000 more were caring for the wounded in military hospitals, 11,000 were engaged in clerical duties for the police, 1,500 were working for emergency fire departments, and up to 100,000 were working in railway stations.

Another way in which young Germans found themselves entrusted with heavy responsibilities was through the *Kinderlandverschickung* (KLV) programme. The KLV was originally conceived in 1934 as a way of allowing urban children in poor health to spend time in the healthy air of the countryside. In 1941, the scheme was transformed into an evacuation programme, under Schirach's direction, to enable children aged 10–16 to escape cities threatened with air attack. This was particularly appealing to some within the leadership of the HJ, as it provided the opportunity to gain complete control over the education of the children, separated as they were from parental and school supervision. Many parents recognized this fact, but their reluctance to allow their children to come under the control of the KLV was balanced against the danger of their staying in the cities, and the fact that whole schools were evacuated at the same time. Children who stayed behind were left without their friends or access to education.

Fallschirmjäger troops take cover behind a Tiger tank during fighting on the Eastern Front in 1944. Note the *Zimmerit* coating applied to the tank's body; this was designed to prevent enemy soldiers attaching magnetic mines to the tank's hull.

By 1944, there were 3,500 KLV camps throughout the Greater German Reich, and 800,000 children had passed through them. Many of the leadership duties within these camps fell to senior members of the HJ and BDM. For example, it was not unheard of for a girl of 16 to be the director of a camp holding 130 girls between the ages of 10 and 13. This was part of a general trend within the Hitler Youth as a whole, in which younger and younger members held leadership positions during the war, as older members were conscripted to military duties. Having been indoctrinated with HJ values, such as contempt for weakness, from an early age, the young leaders at KLV camps instituted regimes that were often severe. Children who wet their beds, for example, were often harshly 'disciplined', with beatings or other punishments. In one camp, minor misdemeanours were corrected by locking the child in a smoke house used for curing ham until they passed out. The young leaders of such KLV camps were also often faced with the problem of dealing with a hostile local population around the camp. As with the *Landdienst*, KLV camps were often located in conquered territories as a form of colonization. It was not unknown for children staying in the camps to be attacked, especially in the face of the looming German defeat in 1944–45.

THE *WEHRERTÜCHTIGUNGSLAGER*

By the beginning of 1942, the rigours of war on the Eastern Front were felt to require the expansion of training facilities for the HJ. A decree from Hitler on 13 March 1942

Hitler receives a warm welcome from a group of *Bund Deutscher Mädel* (League of German Girls) members. Hitler's attitude to women was patriarchal and traditional, although that did not prevent thousands of German girls serving in harm's way as Germany slid into defeat in 1944–45.

authorized the establishment of *Wehrertüchtigungslager der Hitlerjugend* throughout the Reich. The purpose of the *Wehrertüchtigungslager* (military service competency camps) was to provide 16–18-year-old members of the HJ with a concentrated infantry training course over three weeks. The boys were expected to use their annual holidays from school or work to attend the training. By the end of 1943, 226 of these camps had been set up, servicing 515,000 HJ members. The camps were run by HJ leaders who held Wehrmacht officer ranks, working in conjunction with training personnel drawn from the Wehrmacht or the *Waffen-SS*. Predictably, the *Waffen-SS* saw the *Wehrertüchtigungslager* as presenting a golden opportunity to poach the best recruits, and used their good relationship with Reichsjugendführer Artur Axmann to have as high a profile in the camps as possible. By 1943, no fewer than 42 of the camps were staffed by *Waffen-SS* instructors, an impressive achievement given that the *Waffen-SS* only comprised about 5 per cent of the total manpower of the armed forces.

Training at the camps was dominated by slogans such as 'We Fight', 'We Sacrifice' and 'We Triumph'. The boys received a great deal of ideological training revolving around such slogans, the point of which was to portray violent struggle as their natural and glorious contribution to the destiny of the German *Volk*. While at the *Wehrertüchtigungslager*, they were also trained in the use of high-powered weapons such as the Mauser 98K carbine, the MG 42, grenades and the *Panzerfaust*. It was the *Panzerfaust* above all that offered the leadership of the HJ the opportunity to deploy often extremely young children in combat in 1944 and 1945. Being recoilless, even a ten-year-old could use one, whereas the recoil of a rifle or machine gun would knock him flat.

The training of the *Hitlerjugend* Division was distinct from that of other Wehrmacht and *Waffen-SS* formations, and reflected many of the core values of the HJ. In particular, the idea that youth must be led by youth was reflected in the relatively young age of the cadre of former HJ members who provided many of the officers and NCOs of the division. The youth of the division as a whole was reflected in the fact that its members were issued with a ration of sweets instead of cigarettes, much to their disgust. Although he had few qualms about throwing German children into battle, Himmler remained concerned to the end that they not learn the habit of smoking.

Despite all the efforts made by the leadership of the Third Reich to ensure that young men received the maximum pre-military training possible, the endemic factionalism of the Nazi bureaucracy meant that this was done in a deeply inefficient manner. In the HJ, the *Wehrertüchtigungslager*, the RAD and finally the armed forces, young recruits were taught and re-taught drill with no attempt to co-ordinate this instruction between the different services. This was often extremely frustrating for HJ leaders who had taught drill sometimes to hundreds of younger boys, only to have their skills treated with contempt by instructors in the RAD and Wehrmacht.

RECRUITMENT AGE

Competition was fierce between the *Waffen-SS* and the Wehrmacht for the best recruits from the HJ, and, as the war progressed, for any recruits at all. With the successive drop in the age of conscription during the war, recruits increasingly moved from the HJ straight into the armed forces, bypassing the RAD. The call-up age in 1940 was 19, dropping to 17 in 1943. In autumn 1944, a major attempt was made to recruit voluntarily those boys born in 1928, the remainder of whom were conscripted in February 1945. Finally, those born in 1929 were conscripted by a directive of 5 March 1945. Hitler responded with 'pride and joy' in a proclamation of 7 October 1944 to the registration of the class of 1928 as *Kriegsfreiwillige* (war volunteers), citing their 'unshakeable will to victory' that had been already demonstrated in combat.

It is also important to note that many of the avenues intended to provide members of the HJ with training were overstretched to the point of collapse by the end of the war. Many young boys were thrown into combat with inadequate training. *Luftwaffenhelfer*, for example, provided an obvious reservoir of 'manpower' to be used in ground combat once they were no longer needed in the Flak defences, but most of them had never gone through even the basic infantry training of the *Wehrertüchtigungslager*. Instead, they might be rushed through a mere four days of weapons training at a *Wehrertüchtigungslager* before being thrown into battle against US or Soviet troops, usually to be killed, wounded or taken prisoner.

THE *FLAKHELFER*

Although 15-year-olds were officially conscripted into the armed forces in 1945, many other German boys of the same age, as noted above, had been engaged in frequent and harrowing combat experiences from spring 1943 as anti-aircraft auxiliaries. As with the formation of the *Hitlerjugend* Division, the enlistment of members of the HJ and later BDM into the anti-aircraft defences was a response to the catastrophic defeat at Stalingrad. In early 1943, Göring obtained the reluctant permission of Bernhard Rust, the Reichs Education Minister, to allow the Luftwaffe to conscript auxiliaries from German schools. Under the provisions of this law, whole classes of schoolboys aged between 15 and 17 were enlisted in the Luftwaffe. Flak auxiliaries were liable to indefinite service, theoretically proceeding into the RAD and the Wehrmacht when they turned 18. Despite initial assurances that the boys would be stationed close to their homes, they were often moved about in response to the changing military

LEFT: Panther tanks of the *Hitlerjugend* Division. The principal variant of the Panther tank deployed in Normandy was the Ausf. A. Note the highly sloped turret armour, which gave improved resistance to anti-tank shells.

situation, with most being sent to Berlin, Hamburg, the Ruhr or the Baltic Coast. By the end of the war, about 200,000 German teenagers had served in this way. The auxiliaries called up in this manner were officially known as *Luftwaffenhelfer-Hitlerjugend* (LwH-HJ), which was shortened to *Luftwaffenhelfer*, or *Luftwaffenhelferin* in the case of women. Although the name was unofficial, *Luftwaffenhelfer* were ubiquitously referred to as *Flakhelfer* (Anti-Aircraft Auxiliary).

The boys drafted into the Flak defences found themselves living a strange pseudo-adulthood. Officially, they remained members of the HJ, and were supposed to continue receiving school instruction. Gymnasium students were supposed to receive 18 hours of lessons each week, half their normal school load. Lessons were to be taught by the boys' regular teachers, who were expected to travel to the Flak positions and give instruction to their students at the site. HJ service also remained an expectation placed

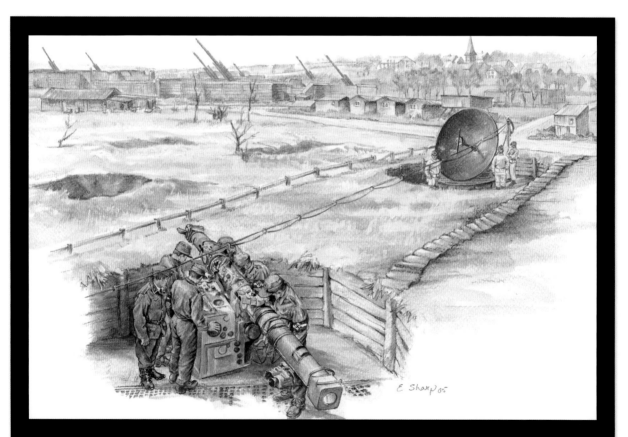

Luftwaffenhelfer at a Flak installation, March 1944. The 'brain' of the battery was its fire-control system, known as 'B1'. This was usually positioned about 100m from the guns themselves. When visibility allowed, crewmen used the long Em 4m R40 stereoscopic range-finder to find out a target aircraft's altitude, speed and course. (Elizabeth Sharp © Osprey Publishing)

upon the young *Flakhelfer*. As late as September 1944, the leadership of the HJ urged regional leaders to make a greater effort to visit the boys at their emplacements, and to ensure that normal HJ activities such as drill, sports and marksmanship training were still being done.

Shown here is a 150cm *Flakscheinwerfer* 34 in action outside Berlin in autumn 1944. Two members of the crew are 17-year-old volunteers from the BDM. Unlike their male equivalents in the HJ, girls from the BDM were not officially supposed to be serving as anti-aircraft auxiliaries, and had no uniform of their own. (Elizabeth Sharp © Osprey Publishing)

These expectations were completely unrealistic, and stemmed from the fiction the Nazi leadership sought to maintain that *Luftwaffenhelfer* were auxiliaries or cadets rather than actual combatants. Under the pressure of attacks by the RAF at night and the USAAF during the day, maintaining any pretence of school lessons usually fell by the wayside. Even when an attack was not imminent, the boys were often exhausted and in shock after combating the RAF until the small hours of the morning, and in no mood for Latin or Geography. Their teachers were also often unable or unwilling to make the sometimes-dangerous journey to the Flak emplacements, especially since most of them by 1943 were old men called out of retirement to replace those conscripted for the front.

The attempts by the HJ to maintain control over the *Flakhelfer* were also unsuccessful. The ambiguous position *Flakhelfer* occupied between the HJ and the Wehrmacht – and between childhood and adulthood – often resulted in them holding a distinct sense of their own identity. Boys who were continually putting their lives at risk and operating powerful weaponry saw themselves as soldiers, not as members of the HJ. *Flakhelfer* usually resisted attempts by local HJ leaders to reassert their authority over them, often with the support of their Luftwaffe commanders.

Nazi ideology emphasized the life of the soldier as the natural destiny of a man. In contrast, the idea of women bearing arms was abhorrent to Hitler personally, and totally counter to the value the Nazis placed on women as passive child bearers and housewives. Nevertheless, from 1940 women were called up to serve in auxiliary contexts such as clerical posts and communications. Senior graduates of the BDM and RAD were conscripted as *Helferinnen* (assistants) into the army, Kriegsmarine, Luftwaffe and SS. By 1945, there were approximately half a million *Wehrmachtshelferinnen*. Although they were officially forbidden to take part in combat, this prohibition was often unrealistic given the contexts in which *Wehrmachtshelferinnnen* served. For example, service in the occupied territories left them open to partisan attack.

Members of the BDM were never officially conscripted into serving in the Flak defences in the way that members of the HJ were. Nevertheless, by 1944 it was not unusual for detachments of *Luftwaffenhelferinnen* to be augmented by 17- and 18-year-old girls drawn from the RAD, or 16- and 17-year-olds from the BDM. Usually, these young women were responsible for crewing searchlights, fire control and sound detection equipment. However, by the end of the war *Luftwaffenhelferinnen* could be found crewing the Flak guns themselves. In any case, Nazi ideology never reconciled itself to the employment of women in such martial roles. For example, training for *Luftwaffenhelferinnen* encouraged young women to think of their barracks as a home, thus maintaining the official position that the role of women belonged in the domestic sphere. Similarly, when some young women were trained in the use of Flak artillery in 1945, this was not officially acknowledged.

RIGHT: Troopers of the 12th SS-Panzer Division *Hitlerjugend* in Normandy in 1944. This division gained a reputation for fanatical resistance. More than 8,500 members of the division were killed, wounded or reported missing between June and September 1944 on the Western Front.

From 1942, HJ members in general were employed in a variety of *Luftschutz* (air defence) roles. For example, many major cities had fire-fighting squads made up of members of the HJ. As a boy in Hamburg in 1943, one former Hitler Youth acted as a messenger stationed at an air-raid bunker. In the case of the telephone system being knocked out, his job was to run messages from one shelter to another, even during air raids. He performed this duty in addition to the six hours every day he spent at school, his HJ service twice a week, and afternoons spent collecting scrap. Along with many of his peers, he was brought face to face with the horror of war from a young age, being required to help with the stacking of bodies after raids. Girls from the DJM and BDM were also often employed in *Katastropheneinsatz* (disaster action) duties, feeding and assisting the homeless and shocked after air raids. In such ways, Germany's young people sustained the defence of the Reich, while becoming intimately acquainted with the horrors of war.

WEREWOLF

A final way in which children of the HJ became combatants at the end of the war was as 'Werewolves'. The Werewolf organization was originally envisaged by Himmler in November 1944 as a guerrilla force, charged with sabotage and raids behind the lines of the advancing Allies. *Gauleiters* (NSDAP district leaders) were to suggest suitable recruits, who were trained at secret locations in the Rhineland and Berlin. The most important training centre in the west was at Hülchrath castle, near the Rhenish town of Erkelenz, which in early 1945 was training around 200 recruits. Most of these were drawn from the HJ.

The most famous achievement of the Werewolves was the assassination of Dr Franz Oppenhoff, whom the US Army had installed as the mayor of occupied Aachen. A Werewolf commando of five men and one woman was dropped by parachute from a captured US B-17 behind Allied lines on 20 March 1945. The youngest of them was a 16-year-old boy named Erich Morgenschweiss. The Werewolves achieved their aim on 25 March, gunning down Oppenhoff outside his home. Numerous other acts of sabotage and murder were undertaken by small groups of SS-trained Werewolves as late as July 1945. However, Goebbels used the assassination of Oppenhoff as propaganda for wholesale resistance against the Allies in occupied Germany. Many sporadic acts of resistance were carried out by members of the HJ and others who considered themselves to be Werewolves, in line with Goebbels' propaganda, but who had nothing to do with the actual Werewolf organization. For example, in the face of imminent capture by US troops, one German officer commanding a unit of HJ asked for volunteers to fight on with him as Werewolves. When only one boy stepped forward, the officer decided that he might as well surrender after all.

UNIFORMS AND APPEARANCE

The members of the newly created youth arm of the NSDAP after 1922 modelled their appearance on that of the SA. This was a source of some friction between the two organizations. After Kurt Gruber was appointed *Reichsführer* of youth in July 1926, a concerted effort was made to standardize the uniforms of the HJ, and to differentiate them from those of the SA.

The basic uniform for boys of the HJ changed little between the mid 1930s and the end of the war. The summer uniform theoretically consisted of a brown shirt, black shorts and long brown or grey socks. A black scarf was worn around the neck, and a black belt with regulation HJ buckle. Headgear consisted of a brown side cap, replacing an earlier peaked cap, which bore a diamond-shaped HJ badge at the front. The M37 winter uniform consisted of very dark blue-black trousers and waist-length blouse, worn over a brown shirt with black scarf. The blue-black peaked M35 field service cap was worn with the winter uniform. The same insignia was worn with both the summer and winter uniform, the most striking feature of which was the swastika armband, worn on the upper left arm. In deliberate contrast to the armband of the SA, this featured a black swastika within a white diamond, the red armband divided in two by a white stripe.

Girls of the JM and BDM wore a white blouse with a navy blue skirt. On transferring to the BDM, the 14-year-old girl was given a black scarf, worn under the collar and fastened with a plaited leather woggle. In cooler months, a brown imitation suede jacket with four pockets was worn over this basic uniform, nicknamed an *Affenhaut* (monkey skin). A diamond-shaped Hitler Youth patch was worn on the left sleeve. The popular uniform was completed with black shoes, white ankle socks and a navy-blue cap or black beret. Both boys and girls were expected to supply their own uniforms, which could have embarrassing consequences. For example, one former member of the BDM remembers having to wear a navy skirt made by her mother, which was not nearly as smart as the ones bought in shops.

Uniforms worn by the 10–14-year-old boys of the DJV were similar to those of the HJ, with some distinctive differences. For example, *Pimpfen* often wore shorts with their winter uniforms. Most notably, members of the DJV did not wear the HJ armband, instead wearing a circular black patch on their upper left arm, which bore a single Sig rune. This distinctive insignia was a reminder of the fact that the DJV had a separate origin to that of the HJ, originating amongst Austrian and Sudeten Germans, before it was absorbed into the HJ during the early 1930s.

Above the armband, Sig rune insignia or diamond-shaped patch of the BDM, all members of the Hitler Youth wore the triangular cloth patch that identified the *Gebiet* and *Obergebiet* to which they belonged. Blue-black or black shoulder straps were in theory worn with both summer and winter uniforms, although these often appear in brown on the summer uniform. The shoulder straps were piped with colours identifying the branch of the HJ to which the member belonged. For example, those of the *Allgemeine* or 'general' HJ were piped in bright artillery red, while the *Flieger-HJ* had blue, the *Motor-HJ* pink and the *Marine-HJ* yellow. Arabic numerals on the shoulder straps identified the boy's *Gefolgschaft* and *Bann*, and Roman numerals, if carried, his *Unterbann*. Rank was denoted by a system of pips, bars and oak leaves on the shoulder straps. For example, one pip indicated a *Kameradschaftsführer*, two pips a *Scharführer*, and three a *Gefolgsschaftsführer*, leading 10, 40 and 160 boys respectively. Different coloured lanyards indicated leadership responsibilities, as distinct from rank. A patch on the upper right arm, bearing a system of chevrons and pips, indicated rank in the DJ. The addition of a narrow red cord on the shoulder straps of the HJ identified its wearer as a *Kriegsfreiwilliger* (war volunteer).

Specialist formations of the HJ also had their own distinctive uniforms. For example, the *Marine-HJ* wore uniforms modelled on those of naval cadets, with the addition of HJ insignia. Uniform distinctions such as cuff titles identified those belonging to other special formations such as the *HJ-Streifendienst* (Patrol Service).

During the early years of the war, a field training uniform was introduced for the HJ. This consisted of a waist-length jacket with two breast pockets and lay-down collar, trousers, black ankle boots with leggings and a side cap. There was considerable variation in the colour of this uniform, from brown to olive-green to field grey. The only insignia normally worn with this uniform was the HJ armband, and an HJ badge on the cap. Another specialist uniform that proved popular as a combat uniform in the last months of the war was the M42 *HJ-Feurwehr* (fire protection) uniform. This practical and sturdy uniform included a four-pocketed tunic, and was coloured olive-brown.

The only specifically combat uniform to be introduced for the HJ was that introduced for the *Flakhelfer* after February 1943. This was similar in cut to the M37 HJ winter uniform, consisting of long trousers and a waist-length blouse with two breast pockets. Headgear consisted of either a peaked cap similar to the M1943 fieldcap worn by the infantry or a side cap, and a distinctive greatcoat with two breast pockets was also provided. The uniform was coloured Luftwaffe-grey. The HJ armband and cap insignia were supposed to be worn with this uniform, although many *Flakhelfer* omitted to wear these whenever possible. Instead, many caps unofficially bore a Luftwaffe eagle. A distinctive triangular patch bearing a Luftwaffe eagle was also worn on the right breast, surmounted by the letters 'LH' (*Luftwaffenhelfer*) in Gothic script. Members of the BDM pressed into service as *Flakhelferinnen* towards the end of the war had no uniform of their own, as they were officially not supposed to be performing these duties. Those who did serve probably wore the same uniform that *Flakhelferinnen* over the age of 18 were issued with.

In the final months of the war, many *Luftwaffenhelfer* found themselves pressed into action as ground troops, and generally fought in their distinctive uniforms. Other members of the HJ and DJV were drawn into active combat roles wearing a bewildering variety of uniforms. Mostly, they saw combat as members of the *Volkssturm*, after its creation on 25 September 1944. The *Volkssturm* did not have its own uniform, requiring its members to provide themselves with military or party uniforms. The distinguishing insignia of the *Volkssturm* was nothing more than an armband worn on the left arm, seen in a variety of styles, and bearing the legend 'Deutscher *Volkssturm* – Wehrmacht' in two lines.

Since members of the Hitler Youth did possess their own uniforms, they often presented a more standardized appearance than older members of the *Volkssturm*, who could be seen wearing a motley collection of civilian clothes, SA or RAD uniforms, and military uniforms of World War I vintage. The greater uniformity of the HJ within the *Volkssturm* was heightened by the tendency to create separate companies within *Volkssturm* battalions consisting solely of members of the HJ. Many members of these simply wore their HJ uniforms, or some combination of HJ uniform items. The blue-black M37 winter uniform was often worn, although its colour did not make it the most practical uniform to wear in combat. More suitable were the M42 *Feurwehr* uniform or the field service *Arbeitanzug*. When supplies were available, some HJ units were issued with army uniforms. For example, one *HJ-Nahkampfbrigade* (close fighting brigade) formed at Rothenburg was equipped with stocks of surplus desert uniforms. In practice, members of the HJ, DJV and BDM often equipped themselves as best they could, and variety was the rule. Some eyewitnesses even recall seeing members of the DJV fighting in Berlin wearing shorts, a sight that would have been laughable were it not so tragic.

VOLKSSTURM

The HJ were just some of the unfortunates caught up in the final collapse of the Third Reich. For those who became combatants in the *Volkssturm*, they stood at the young end of a scale that incorporated thousands of individuals who had no place facing the combined might of the Allied armies.

On 25 July 1944, having just escaped assassination in the 20 July bomb plot and with Allied forces massing on Germany's western and eastern borders, Hitler issued a 'Decree for Total War'. He announced on 25 September that all Germans aged 16–60 who were not Jews, gypsies, criminals or members of French, Polish or Slovene minorities, and who were not already in the armed forces or RAD, would join the new 'People's Militia', the *Deutscher Volkssturm*. The six-million-strong force would have about 10,180 battalions – limited staff personnel and rear-echelon facilities, and lack of weapons standardization, made the battalion the largest tactical unit – divided into four *Aufgebote* (levies):

The *Hitlerjugend* Division counterattacks near Caen, June 1944. The men wear the M1943 SS pattern camouflage smock over the field-grey uniform. The heady success of the division's first attack was not to last, and the formation was ground down over the following weeks in vicious defensive fighting without relief. (Elizabeth Sharp © Osprey Publishing)

1st Levy: 1.2 million men in 1,850 battalions (400 in frontier districts); all physically fit 20–60-year-olds without essential war work exemption, assigned to frontline battalions, quartered in barracks, liable for service outside their home district, and including all available NSDAP political officials, *Allgemeine-SS*, SA, NSKK and NSFK (Nazi Air Corps).

2nd Levy: 2.8 million men in 4,860 battalions (1,050 in frontier districts); all physically fit 20–60-year-olds with essential war work exemption, usually organized in factory battalions, quartered at home, liable for service within their home county.

3rd Levy: 600,000 16–19-year-olds, plus some 15-year-old volunteers, in about 1,040 battalions; mostly 16-year-old Hitler Youths trained in the *Wehrertüchtigungslager*.

ABOVE: A *Volkssturm Panzerjäger* cycles into action with multiple *Panzerfaust* anti-tank weapons at the ready. Shown at top left are the cartoon instructions for operation of the weapon. (Seán Ó Brógáin © Osprey Publishing)

Soldiers of the *Volkssturm* man a trench system in the late months of the war, armed mainly with World War I-vintage rifles. The price paid by the *Volkssturm* for their last-ditch defence of the Reich is unclear, but the number of those killed or captured would potentially reach 175,000.

4th Levy: 1.4 million 20–60-year-olds unfit for active service, plus volunteers over 60 in about 2,430 battalions, for guard duty, including guarding concentration camps. The *NS-Frauenschaft* (Nazi Women's League) provided rear-echelon support, and on 23 March 1945 were issued with firearms.

Not all planned battalions were formed, but at least 700 did see combat, the vast majority of these recruited from the frontier districts in the East, who, along with recruits from the South East, found themselves facing the Soviet forces. Troops recruited from the West were faced with the Western Allies.

Reichsleiter Martin Bormann, Nazi Head Office Chief and Hitler's deputy, commanded the militia on the Führer's behalf. He was assisted by two chiefs of staff: Oberbefehlsleiter Helmut Friedrichs, responsible for organization and political affairs, and Gottlob Berger, SS Main Office Chief, representing the SS and Replacement Army commander, Heinrich Himmler. A staff of army officers, under Colonel Hans Kissel, was responsible for equipment, weapons and training.

Each of Germany's 42 districts formed a *Volkssturmabschnitt* (*Volkssturm* District) under a NSDAP *Gauleiter* assisted by an SA general or senior NSDAP official. A district contained on average 21 *Kreise* (counties), each under a NSDAP *Kreisleiter* assisted by a

Kreisstabsführer, and required to raise about 12 battalions. Berger and Friedrichs achieved a good working relationship, but Bormann and Himmler frequently clashed for control of the *Volkssturm*, a situation exacerbated by a confused chain of command, leaving NSDAP officials and SA officers resentful of the SS' upper hand.

Given the nature of the recruits, the *Volkssturm* was given an ambitious range of missions: surround and contain large seaborne and airborne landings; eliminate agents and small sabotage groups; guard bridges, streets and key buildings; reinforce depleted army units; plug gaps in the front after enemy breakthroughs, and to man quiet sectors; and crush feared uprisings by the estimated 10 million POWs and foreign workers in Germany.

A 649-man 1st Levy Battalion had a 27-man staff; companies 1–3, each with three or four platoons, containing three or four ten-man sections; and a 4th infantry howitzer company. Other levy battalions had 576 men. Each company was supposed to have three five-man *Panzernahbekämpfungstrupps* (Tank Close Combat Squads), each with ten *Panzerfauste* anti-tank weapons, often manned by HJ volunteers. Each battalion received a consecutive number within its district, e.g. *Bataillon* 25/97 = 97th Battalion (HQ Königsberg) in District 25 (East Prussia).

During 1945, *Volkssturm* units helped form army *Gneisenau* formations within the Replacement Army. In January, 26 '*Baden*' battalions joined Upper Rhine Infantry Regiments 1–15, later grouped into the 805th and 905th Divisions and 1005th Brigade of the 19th Army – nicknamed the '19th *Volkssturm* Army'. The 303rd, 309th, 324th, 325th and 328th and '*Barwalde*' Divisions contained *Volkssturm* battalions, as

Volkssturm recruits undergo some basic rifle training. Because labour requirements still took priority in the Third Reich, *Volkssturm* training was limited to a few hours every Sunday.

ABOVE: Hitler's citizen army in the last months of the war covered all manner of duties. Here we see a *Panzerfaust*-armed *Volkssturm* combatant (left), an Army Female Signals Auxiliary soldier (centre) and a member of the *HJ-Streifendienst* (Hitler Youth Patrol Service), the latter assisting security services to 'keep order'. (Malcolm McGregor © Osprey Publishing)

did the *Volksgrenadierdivisionen* established by Himmler. Other *Volkssturm* recipients included 16 grenadier regiments and SS-Grenadier Regiment '*Becker*', later part of the *Waffen-SS 30. Januar* Division. Also in 1945, the army formed *Festungs* units from *Volkssturm* companies with army staffs, with the unforgiving job of manning defensive lines in the East.

Volkssturm recruits, many already working a 72-hour war-emergency working week, were given a 48-hour training programme by armed forces instructors, and were expected to master the rifle, *Panzerfaust*, the grenade-launcher, hand grenade and *Panzerschreck*, and in emergency the pistol, SMG and land mine. In fact there were scarcely enough weapons for the 1st and 2nd Levies, and many militiamen were sent into

A *Volkssturm* squad defence of a roadblock in Isselburg. To conceal roadblocks from enemy detection, the Germans often located them as illustrated, around a bend in the road between two buildings. (Seán Ó Brógáin © Osprey Publishing)

Hitler Youth wait to board a train. Their thorough pre-war training would mean that they would play a valuable role in the home defense of the Reich.

battle unarmed. The 3rd Levy was not issued weapons, and the 4th Levy were expected to use hunting-rifles or captured firearms. Troops were often only issued a trench-spade for self-defence.

The *Gauleiters* on the eastern border began to establish a series of defensive lines during the pause in the fighting after July 1944. Thousands of local men and women, Hitler Youth, RAD conscripts, POWS and foreign forced labourers built tank-traps, artillery and anti-tank positions, protected by earthworks and linked by trenches. Eight lines skirted the East Prussian frontier, three in Wartheland and two in Upper Silesia. Other lines faced the Czech border. By December 1944, these lines were manned by armed forces and *Volkssturm* units, many organized from January 1945 into fortress battalions.

In combat, the *Volkssturm* paid heavily for its role as last-ditch infantry. Driven from East Prussia by the Soviet offensives of autumn 1944, they became escorts to the three million refugees heading westwards along congested snow-swept roads, harassed by Polish guerrillas. About 750,000 people died from exposure, were killed by overtaking Soviet or Polish forces, drowned on evacuation ships in the Baltic sunk by Soviet air or submarine attacks, or caught in the Dresden air raid of 13/14 February 1945. Some *Volkssturm* soldiers, aware of the Soviet writer Ilya Ehrenburg's encouragement to Red Army troops to butcher all Germans, still stood their ground to buy time for the escape of the refugees. Others, afraid of being shot as guerrillas if captured, joined the mass retreat.

The *Volkssturm's* final, epic defence was in the German capital itself. The last Soviet offensive began on 16 April 1945. The Oder Line was breached, and by the 25th Berlin defenders included 24,000 *Volkssturm* (18,000 of whom were 'Clausewitz Levy' troops of the 2nd Levy, on six hours' standby). The fighting was desperate. Those *Volkssturm* who could find the courage – bolstered by the threat of SS police squads hanging them for cowardice – would assault Soviet tanks at close range with *Panzerfauste*, utilizing their knowledge of the city's layout. If they secured a good hit, they might knock out the tank, but the blistering Soviet response frequently resulted in their deaths. Nevertheless, many individual *Volkssturm* rose to the occasion, and defended their city with a passion. In the battle for Berlin, and that of Breslau (with 45,000 defenders including 25,000 *Volkssturm* in 38 battalions) Battalion 21/41 and two Hitler Youth 3rd Levy battalions distinguished themselves in the fighting.

On 8 February 1945, the Western Allies, in three army groups, began their advance into western Germany. On the 12th the local *Volkssturm* was mobilized and sent to man the Westwall, but they showed none of the desperate determination of their comrades in the East. Many ignored the call-up; others surrendered at the first opportunity, or threw away their armbands and hid in the woods or returned home. The Westwall was quickly breached and on 7 May the Western Allies met Soviet forces in central Germany.

Hitler deceived himself into believing that a huge civilian army, led by militarily inexperienced Nazi officials, could stave off Germany's defeat. The *Volkssturm's* ultimate failure, however, should not blind us to the bravery of many of its members who, though unfit, untrained and underequipped, fought not to preserve their state, but to save fellow Germans from a Red Army eager to exact vengeance for the brutal German occupation of the Soviet Union.

CONCLUSION

LEFT: Hitler and his generals pour over a map of the Eastern Front. Hitler's interference in both the strategy and tactics of war ultimately had a disastrous effect on the Wehrmacht, leading to hundreds of thousands more casualties than might have been incurred if more competent hands were in control.

THE KEY EVENT THAT MADE POSSIBLE THE END OF WORLD WAR II IN EUROPE occurred at 0300hrs on 30 April 1945. At that moment, the German *Führer*, Adolf Hitler, committed suicide in his bunker beneath the Reich Chancellery in Berlin, as above ground the triumphant Soviet forces advanced to within a few hundred metres of this installation. Back on 22 April, as Soviet spearheads began to encircle the German capital, Hitler had abandoned his notion of escaping to lead Germany's war from Berchtesgarden in Bavaria, and instead decided to remain in Berlin to meet his fate.

Even into the last hours of his life, Hitler remained determined that the Wehrmacht would continue its desperate resistance against the Allied advance, if necessary to the last man and last round, irrespective of the destruction that this would inflict on the German nation. With his death, so passed away this iron resolve to prosecute a war that almost every German now recognized as already lost. The war ground on in many localities for a few more days yet, but on 8 May Generalfeldmarschal Keitel signed the confirmatory German instrument of surrender. By 15 May, all remaining German forces in the East had capitulated, laying down their arms after the Wehrmacht's epic six-year war.

Since the war, historians have attempted to unpack the complex reasons for the defeat of German forces. This question is complicated by the fact that at a tactical level the German Army and *Waffen-SS* remained formidable right up to the very last days of fighting, despite an evident decline in manpower and training from 1943. Defeating the Nazi military force was therefore never going to be easy or quick. The German defenders had the benefit of considerable combat experience, and a realistic, proven doctrine and tactics refined through years of war. Operating under a totalitarian regime, the military potentially had all the resources of the state at its disposal. Moreover, the Germans were a martial people with a long and proud military history.

Nevertheless, the Nazi war machine was by no means invincible; nor were its soldiers the 'supermen' that racist Nazi propaganda extolled them to be. In reality, the German military fought under severe constraints. Brutal attrition in the East had already torn the heart out of the Wehrmacht and it was scraping the manpower and resources barrels by 1944. But its biggest deficiencies were logistical. Constant combat ensured that the Germans lacked the supplies necessary for victory, and throughout the later campaigns on the Eastern, Western and Italian Fronts they operated on a logistical shoestring, particularly in terms of liquid fuels. Moreover, the German war economy had long been inefficient and poorly managed. While dramatic increases in production were eventually realized by ruthless rationalization, the German war economy was from 1943 subject to punishing Allied heavy bomber attacks and was unable to meet the needs of a three-front war.

Consequently, the German military remained perennially short of the means of conducting modern operations. It was eventually rarely able to contest Allied aerial supremacy, which hindered all German ground operations and denied them information

about the enemy. German commanders remained woefully ignorant of enemy actions and intentions, which hampered German countermeasures. Attrition had also badly denuded German ground forces of vehicles, reducing the strategic mobility that had hitherto allowed German forces to evade annihilation by a numerically superior enemy. This dwindling mobility progressively increased the vulnerability of German formations to encirclement and destruction by a far more mobile enemy. These deficiencies ensured that the German military was unable to mount the combined-arms defence necessary to prevail, and that instead it would slowly be driven back in grim attritional warfare.

Nonetheless, the determination of German troops and commanders, their professionalism, as well as their realistic doctrine, tactics and training allowed them to offer sustained, stubborn resistance that cost the Allies dearly. Influenced by Nazi racism and propaganda, as well as the instinct for self-preservation, German troops continued to fight to protect their families at home from the vengeance that they feared the Allies would exact for the horrible measures the Nazis had taken to keep Europe under control. The Germans could be expected to fight long and hard. And even if they could not win, they could at least postpone the inevitable for as long as possible and increase the price of the enemy's victory. In summary, therefore, Hitler's forces were defeated by poor strategic decisions made by their *Führer*, the realities of war production and the overwhelming force of powerful Allies. Although the regime they served was abhorrent, however, their achievements on the battlefield have never failed to command respect.

Generalfeldmarschall Wilhelm Keitel, the commander-in-chief of the Wehrmacht, signs the ratified surrender terms for the German Army on 8 May 1945, officially bringing war in Europe to an end. Keitel was subsequently arrested, put on trial and later executed for war crimes.

FURTHER READING

This book was drawn from information and artwork included within the following Osprey Publishing titles. For a complete list of our books on the German Army during World War II, please visit our website, www.ospreypublishing.com.

BATTLE ORDERS SERIES

BTO 15 *German Airborne Divisions: Mediterranean Theatre 1942–45*, Bruce Quarrie (2005)

BTO 20 *Rommel's Afrika Korps: Tobruk to El Alamein*, Pier Paolo Battistelli (2006)

BTO 23 *Desert Raiders: Allied and Axis Special Forces*, Andrea Molinari (2007)

BTO 32 *Panzer Divisions: The Blitzkrieg Years 1939–40*, Pier Paolo Battistelli (2007)

BTO 35 *Panzer Divisions: The Eastern Front 1942–43*, Pier Paolo Battistelli (2008)

BTO 38 *Panzer Divisions: 1944–45*, Pier Paolo Battistelli (2009)

CAMPAIGN SERIES

CAM 3 *France 1940*, Alan Shepperd (1990)

CAM 5 *Ardennes 1944*, James Arnold (1990)

CAM 42 *Bagration 1944*, Steven Zaloga (1996)

CAM 74 *The Rhineland 1945*, Ken Ford (2000)

CAM 80 *Tobruk 1941*, Jon Latimer (2001)

CAM 100 *D-Day 1944 (1)*, Steven Zaloga (2003)

CAM 107 *Poland 1939*, Steven Zaloga (2002)

CAM 112 *D-Day 1944 (4)*, Ken Ford (2002)

CAM 115 *Battle of the Bulge (1)*, Steven Zaloga (2003)

CAM 129 *Operation Barbarossa 1941 (1)*, Robert Kirchubel (2003)

CAM 134 *Cassino 1944*, Ken Ford (2004)

CAM 143 *Caen 1944*, Ken Ford (2004)

CAM 145 *Battle of the Bulge (2)*, Steven Zaloga (2004)

CAM 147 *Crete 1941*, Peter Antill (2005)

CAM 152 *Kasserine Pass 1943*, Steven Zaloga (2005)

CAM 158 *El Alamein 1942*, Ken Ford (2005)

CAM 159 *Berlin 1945*, Peter Antill (2005)

CAM 183 *Denmark and Norway 1940*, Doug Dildy (2007)

CAM 184 *Stalingrad 1942*, Peter Antill (2007)

CAM 186 *Operation Barbarossa 1941 (3)*, Robert Kirchubel (2007)

CAM 215 *Leningrad 1941–44*, Robert Forczyk (2009)

ELITE SERIES

ELI 34 *Afrika Korps 1941–43*, Gordon Williamson (1991)

ELI 63 *German Mountain and Ski Troops 1942–45*, Gordon Williamson (1996)

ELI 100 *Axis Booby Traps and Sabotage Devices*, Gordon Rottman (2009)

ELI 105 *World War II Infantry Tactics: Squad and Platoon*, Stephen Bull (2004)

ELI 106 *Wehrmacht Combat Helmets 1933–45*, Brian C. Bell (2004)

ELI 114 *Knight's Cross and Oak-Leaves Recipients 1939–40*, Gordon Williamson (2004)

ELI 123 *Knight's Cross and Oak-Leaves Recipients 1941–45*, Gordon Williamson (2005)

ELI 124 *World War II Anti-Tank Tactics*, Gordon Rottman (2005)

ELI 133 *Knight's Cross, Oak-Leaves and Swords Recipients 1941–45*, Gordon Williamson (2005)

ELI 139 *Knight's Cross with Diamond Recipients 1941–45*, Gordon Williamson (2006)

ELI 156 *World War II Combat Reconnaissance Tactics*, Gordon Rottman (2007)

ELI 157 *The German Home Front*, Brian L. Davis (2007)

ELI 177 *German Special Forces of World War II*, Gordon Williamson (2009)

ESSENTIAL HISTORIES SERIES

ESP 3 *The Second World War: A World in Flames*, Max Hastings, Geoffrey Jukes, Russell Hart and Stephen A. Hart (2004)

FORTRESS SERIES

FOR 23 *German Field Fortifications 1939–45*, Gordon Rottman (2004)

MEN-AT-ARMS SERIES

MAA 22 *The Luftwaffe Airborne and Field Units*, Martin Windrow (1972)

MAA 24 *The Panzer Divisions*, Martin Windrow (1982)

MAA 34 *The Waffen-SS*, Martin Windrow (1982)

MAA 53 *Rommel's Desert Army*, Martin Windrow (1976)

MAA 124 *German Commanders of World War II*, Anthony Kemp (1982)

MAA 139 *German Airborne Troops 1939–45*, Bruce Quarrie (1983)

MAA 147 *Foreign Volunteers of the Wehrmacht 1941–45*, Carlos Cabellero Jurado (1983)

MAA 213 *German Military Police Units*, Gordon Williamson (1989)

MAA 220 *The SA 1921–45: Hitler's Stormtroopers*, David Littlejohn (1990)

MAA 229 *The Luftwaffe Field Divisions 1941–45*, Kevin Conley Ruffner (1990)

MAA 234 *German Combat Equipments 1939–45*, Gordon Rottman (1991)

MAA 254 *Wehrmacht Auxiliary Forces*, Nigel Thomas (1992)

MAA 266 *The Allgemeine-SS*, Robin Lumsden (1993)

MAA 274 *Flags of the Third Reich (2)*, Brian L. Davis (1994)

MAA 311 *The German Army 1939–45 (1) Blitzkrieg*, Nigel Thomas (1997)

MAA 316 *The German Army 1939–45 (2) North Africa and the Balkans*, Nigel Thomas (1998)

MAA 326 *The German Army 1939–45 (3) Eastern Front 1941–43*, Nigel Thomas (1999)

MAA 330 *The German Army 1939–45 (4) Eastern Front 1943–45*, Nigel Thomas (1999)

MAA 336 *The German Army 1939–45 (5) Western Front 1943–45*, Nigel Thomas (2000)

MAA 363 *Germany's Eastern Front Allies (2) Baltic Forces*, Nigel Thomas and Carlos Cabellero Jurado (2002)

MAA 365 *World War II German Battle Insignia*, Gordon Williamson (2002)

MAA 380 *Germany Army Elite Units 1939–45*, Gordon Williamson (2002)

MAA 385 *The Herman Göring Division*, Gordon Williamson (2003)

MAA 401 *The Waffen-SS (1)*, Gordon Williamson (2003)

MAA 404 *The Waffen-SS (2)*, Gordon Williamson (2004)

MAA 415 *The Waffen-SS (3)*, Gordon Williamson (2004)

MAA 420 *The Waffen-SS (4)*, Gordon Williamson (2004)

MAA 434 *World War II German Police Units*, Gordon Williamson (2006)

NEW VANGUARD SERIES

NVG 1 *Kingtiger Heavy Tank 1942–45*, Tom Jentz and Hilary Doyle (1993)

NVG 22 *Panther Variants 1942–45*, Tom Jentz and Hilary Doyle (1987)

WARRIOR SERIES

WAR 2 *Waffen-SS Soldier 1940–45*, Bruce Quarrie (1993)

WAR 38 *Fallschirmjäger: German Paratrooper 1939–45*, Bruce Quarrie (2001)

WAR 46 *Panzer Crewman 1939–45*, Gordon Williamson (2002)

WAR 59 *German Infantryman (1) 1933–45*, David Westwood (2002)

WAR 61 *German Security and Police Soldier 1939–45*, Gordon Williamson (2002)

WAR 74 *Gebirgsjäger: German Mountain Trooper 1939–45*, Gordon Williamson (2003)

WAR 76 *German Infantryman (2) Eastern Front 1941–43*, David Westwood (2003)

WAR 93 *German Infantryman (3) Eastern Front 1943–45*, David Westwood (2005)

WAR 102 *The Hitler Youth 1933–45*, Alan Dearn (2006)

WAR 110 *Hitler's Home Guard*, David Yelton (2006)

WAR 146 *German Pionier 1939–45*, Gordon Rottman (2010)

WAR 149 *Afrika Korps*, Pier Paolo Battistelli (2010)

INDEX